To dear Earl Miller.

This is now an old book.
May it be a token of appreciation
for an old ! valued friendship.

Paul Périgord

THE INTERNATIONAL
LABOR ORGANIZATION

THE INTERNATIONAL LABOR ORGANIZATION

A STUDY OF LABOR AND CAPITAL IN COÖPERATION

BY

PAUL PÉRIGORD, Ph.D.

FORMERLY OF THE FRENCH HIGH COMMISSION TO THE UNITED STATES;
PROFESSOR OF FRENCH CIVILIZATION IN THE UNIVERSITY OF
CALIFORNIA, SOUTHERN BRANCH

WITH AN INTRODUCTION BY

HENRY M. ROBINSON, LL.D.

OF THE SUPREME ECONOMIC COUNCIL AT THE PEACE CONFERENCE OF
1919; OF THE DAWES COMMISSION IN 1925; PRESIDENT OF THE
FIRST NATIONAL BANK OF LOS ANGELES

D. APPLETON AND COMPANY

NEW YORK   LONDON

1926

PREFACE

If further evidence was really needed, the experience of the last decade must have convinced thoughtful men throughout the world that war should be definitely outlawed. But, as repeatedly stated by one of the keenest minds of our age, Elihu Root, war cannot be outlawed and peace cannot be preserved except through the establishment of international institutions. These institutions, if planned and directed by statesmen animated with a genuine international spirit, will foster the growth of an international morality which should facilitate the settlement of international conflicts on the basis of justice and fair play.

One of the social groups most vitally interested in the preservation of peace is labor. Hence labor has recently followed the example of capital and no longer confines its concern to national problems. They are now both extending their activities to fields far beyond.

We have grown accustomed to the idea of capital as an international force. Since the War more than ever we have realized the power of American capital in international relations. The growth of labor as an international force has not perhaps been so apparent but it is no less real. Labor is now claiming a voice in international councils and formulates policies of world import. It has discovered that its security and the maintenance of high standards of living depend upon universal peace. Labor, therefore, seeks to use its growing influence in national politics and in foreign affairs in the attainment of that end.

vii

On the other hand, the men who after the World War endeavored to erect the edifice of peace saw the close connection existing between an economic peace and a political one and formally declared that "universal peace can be established only if it is based upon social justice." That social justice, however, did not seem attainable without a measure of state intervention in industrial relations.

Moreover, as war was to be averted by a method of plain discussion and honest investigation, so social justice was to be promoted and industrial conflicts were to be avoided through a policy of coöperation between labor, capital and governments, periodically defining or restating their respective rights and duties in our ever-evolving economic system.

Finally, the development of international competition and of world markets demanded that that coöperation should be international and should preferably be expressed in terms of international legislation.

These, briefly outlined, are the various currents which have given rise to the International Labor Organization.

The International Labor Organization seeks to promote the international adjustment of labor conditions and to do generally in the field of economics what the League of Nations is doing in the field of international politics. It has brought together for the first time, in a spirit of friendly coöperation, representatives of the capitalists, the working men and the statesmen of nearly sixty countries. The Organization has stood the test of time and has already built for itself a background of solid achievement. Its importance and influence are steadily increasing.

Abroad, the International Labor Organization has received widespread attention but in this country it has remained little known and appreciated. This is not as it should be, for American vision and genius played as great a part in founding the International Labor Organization as in the formation of the League of Nations. According to Mr. Gompers the American delegation to the Peace Conference wrote the heart and soul of its constitution.

Moreover, the Organization represents one of the most significant steps in the history of industrial relations and cannot be overlooked by a nation such as ours. When in 1919 Mr. Gompers was attacked regarding the Labor Charter incorporated in the Versailles Treaty he said that he defended that instrument, not because it was perfect, but because it constituted the fairest statement of labor principles that had ever been incorporated in an international treaty.

President Wilson called it a most admirable document and second in importance only to the Covenant itself.

One of the most highly respected statesmen in Europe, Doctor Benés, premier of Czechoslovakia, has referred to the International Labor Organization as follows:

"One feels that the International Labor Conference is a permanent organ, that it has become a firmly established institution and that it has definitely taken its place as part of the machinery of international life.

"A second impression is that the Labor Conferences have incontestably become a school for the propagation of a wise, moderate and at the same time profound international spirit. The workers' organization has for long pursued the task of international organization; the employers are now doing the same, but they are doing it in a spirit totally different from that which guides them when it is merely a question of organization for the exploitation of economic undertakings. It is the spirit of international solidarity which, in spite of everything, is necessarily spread through this organization and from it to the world outside!"

In view of its origin and of its importance it is hard to understand the comparative neglect of the Organization in the United States. No doubt it is attributable chiefly to the overshadowing controversy surrounding its sister organizations, the League of Nations and the World Court, but it may be due in some measure to the fact that no complete and comprehensive treatment of its history and operations has been published for American readers. The aim of this present volume is to fill this need, without becoming too technical or ponderous.

It is our purpose to call the attention of the American public to the International Labor Organization of the League of Nations, by which labor has officially entered upon its international stage, to show its sociological and political background, to describe its genesis, structure and achievements, and to study the problem of American participation in this first attempt at world-wide coöperation between labor and capital.

The author has been especially fortunate in having had throughout the writing of the book the advice and assistance of Henry M. Robinson who, as a member of the American delegation to the Peace Conference, had much to do with the creation of the International Labor Organization.

I take place in expressing my thanks for valuable help and encouragement in the preparation of this work to numerous officials of the International Labor Organization, particularly to M. Albert Thomas, the Director, to Dr. Royal Meeker, formerly chief of the Research Division, to Mr. E. J. Phelan, chief of the Diplomatic Division, to Messrs. Devinat, Grimshaw and Guerreau, and to Mr. Magnusson, the American "correspondent" of the International Labor Office in Washington.

For many courtesies I am also indebted to the Faculty of the Law School of the University of Paris and for valuable suggestions and criticisms to the Department of Political Science, Economics, and Sociology of the University of Minnesota.

I also owe my thanks to M. Georges Scelle, Professor
of International Law at the University of Dijon, and to
Doctor James H. McBride of Pasadena, who were kind
enough to read and criticize the manuscript.

I wish gratefully to acknowledge likewise the liberalism
and generosity of the Trustees and of the Executive Council of the California Institute of Technology who, while
I was Professor of Economics and History in that institution, graciously granted me a year's leave of absence to
undertake this investigation.

PAUL PÉRIGORD

CONTENTS

CHAPTER VII

RESULTS

CHAPTER VIII

CRITICISM AND DEFENSE

CONTENTS

CHAPTER IX

THE UNITED STATES AND THE INTERNATIONAL LABOR OFFICE

APPENDIX I

THE CONSTITUTION OF THE INTERNATIONAL LABOR ORGANIZATION

APPENDIX II

APPENDIX III

APPENDIX IV

APPENDIX V

APPENDIX VI

INTRODUCTION

Dr. Périgord has asked me, because I was one of the delegates to the International Conference for Legislation for Labor, to write an introduction to his book on the International Labor Organization of the League of Nations.

This book, the fruit of a year's intensive study of the work of the Conference, is the only summary of the history of that Organization and of its background written in English for American readers. It lights up a field which is growing in importance but which is relatively disregarded in America. Dr. Périgord has worked earnestly to awaken a greater interest here in international questions. He does well to do so. Whatever individual opinions may be regarding the wisdom and the efficiency of the International Labor Organization, we in America should be as accurately informed as possible concerning the three organizations of world import that have grown out of the war: the Permanent Court of International Justice, the International Labor Organization, and the League of Nations.

Probably the best introduction to the book I can give the reader will be to describe the background of the Labor Conference as I saw it. Although I do not attempt to stand in agreement with all of Dr. Perigord's economic and political theories or with his conclusions, I am anxious that they be considered with an adequate knowledge of the events on which they are based. Moreover, since Mr. Gompers' death, I am the only American who can give such an outline.

My experience in employment problems began early in

my business life. For many years, in the capacity of director, in many instances as a more or less active officer, in many instances as an attorney, and always as an employer or his representative, and in many lines of industry, including iron and steel, coal and coke, lumber, traction lines and other public utilities, I had met with representatives of organized labor and had also dealt with labor unorganized. Always it had been my task to uphold an employer's definite policy, to effect a special compromise or to make peace between the parties. Like other men of my training and my generation, I have always been, and am now, a confirmed individualist, opposed to all forms of paternalism. I do not mean that I was not eager to introduce more humane conceptions into the conduct of business, but that by nature and training I have been on the side of conservative action in all such matters and, with most employers, very desirous that the workers should be self-respecting, self-supporting, and that they should cultivate the fundamental virtues of industry, foresight, thrift, and fair play.

Mr. Edward N. Hurley was in Paris at the time of the signing of the Armistice and was then appointed by President Wilson a member of the Supreme Economic Council of the Allies and also the employer member of the International Conference for Legislation for Labor. As he was forced to return to this country, I was asked to substitute for him in the various services he had been called to by the President. Of all of the tasks and enterprises that have fallen to my lot in the last thirty-five years, this was certainly the most unexpected. I had never been an especially deep student of such problems, but of course had unconsciously through the years built up a philosophy which, in its fundamentals, I found did not differ as widely from that of Mr. Gompers as I had always thought.

During the war the labor people of the various nations

had obtained agreements from their respective governments that when peace came, they, the labor people, should be allowed to participate in its making, especially with reference to labor problems. This agreement on the part of governments was met by the setting up of the International Conference for Legislation for Labor. Theoretically the membership was to be composed of two delegates from each country, one representing the employer class and one the employees. As a matter of fact, in no case except in that of the United States were the delegates chosen on this specification.

Great Britain sent Hon. George Barnes, Minister of Labor without portfolio, and Sir Malcolm Delavigne, who had been in the Labor Office in England for twenty years. The Italian representative, Baron des Planches, who had been Ambassador to the United States but had certain socialistic philosophy, could hardly be said to represent the employer class, and M. Cabrini was a leader of what is generally known as the socialistic group. Belgium sent M. Vandervelde, who was a Socialist Minister of Labor, and Mr. Maheim, an academic with socialistic leanings but with the highest aims. I might describe the other members, but none of them falls quite within the class of either employers or employees.

As Mr. Gompers, in his position as Chairman, did not feel that he wanted to participate with entire freedom in the discussion, it devolved upon me largely to present the position of the American delegation. We had many discussions of the questions involved, and except for some disagreement with Fureseth there was very little difference between my own attitude on the one side and that of these representatives of American organized labor on the other, in so far as the international phases of the labor problem were concerned.

There were in Paris with Mr. Gompers several of the

Vice-Presidents of the American Federation of Labor, such as Alpine of the Plumbers; Duncan of the Stone Masons; Berry of the Pressmen's Union; and William Green, then Secretary of the United Mine Workers and now President of the American Federation of Labor; as well as Andrew Fureseth of the Seamen's Union, who came on his own motion.

As I have said, my economic and labor philosophy was not a very complete equipment to meet in discussion the type of representatives of the other countries who were present, because they were generally the advocates to us of new social, political, and economic doctrines which, from my point of view, were academic and not likely to succeed under the existing economic conditions in the world. Fortunately, I felt that my viewpoint was shared by the majority of my countrymen present in Paris, and particularly did I feel that there was unanimity at home regarding the safeguarding of our sovereignty in every particular and in every way that was at all consistent with the general and inescapable duty of working out peace and maintaining justice, so far as possible, in international relations.

To those familiar with the history of labor movements in Europe, and particularly with the history of labor's international organizations, and to those who know he character of the several members of our Conference, it is evident that the aim of the representatives from the Continental European countries was to make the most of the opportunity given them by the disorganization of the world and by the prestige and power acquired by labor during the war.

The American delegates had no plan to submit. This was true of all the other national delegations except that of Great Britain. The representatives of many of the countries were given to forensic efforts reminiscent of some of our own political leaders, bewailing the situation of the working people and attacking capital but without offering any construcive method of reform. It was natural that following the war the labor groups should hope for an extraordinary control of governmental matters. Some thought the example of Russia might prove contagious, and as a matter of fact there were periods during the Peace Conference when it looked as though it would. Yet the Allied Nations represented at the Peace Conference were relatively free from the contamination of the Bolshevist philosophy. Generally the leaders hoped for the setting up of an International Labor Organization of a superparliamentary character which would legislate in the interests of the labor of the world.

As an example of how universally labor hoped to take advantage of the opportunity offered by the war, we might quote from Mr. Gompers' memoirs: ''When the Convention of the Federation met in Philadelphia in November, 1914, I prepared a resolution in which I presented a series of preambles deploring the waste of war and proposing that the Executive Council should hold itself in readiness to summon an international Labor Conference to meet at the same time and place that the Peace Congress should be assembled, to determine the treaty ending the war. In my first draft I included the suggestion that labor work for some form of international agency that could deal constructively and continuously with international problems and thereby minimize the probabilities of war.''[1]

From the beginning, and continuously, the differences between the old world and the new were very marked, and generally quite definite. Our political, social, and economic philosophy and methods are in sharp contrast with those of the older nations, as they have grown out of different

---

[1] *Seventy Years of Life and Labor,* page 390.

environment and racial characteristics. Our individualism and initiative, different from those of any of the nations of Europe, have shaped our thinking and our activities. The old world has been accustomed to dealing with the labor problem by legislation, and it was natural for the old world representatives to think of international labor problems and their ajustment and correction only in terms of legislation—preferably international legislation. They had in mind the development of a superlegislature and a supergovernment which should bring about improved standards for workers everywhere. In our opposition to the attempt to set up a supergovernment there was no disagreement between the American delegates.

In the atmosphere of the Peace Conference the European peoples were looking upon President Wilson as their saviour. They thought that his idealism would succeed in restoring to the world peaceful international relations which, built upon a basis of justice, would make war a remote possibility and bring about ideal conditions for all peoples.

One thing that was demanded by the whole world was that a peace be concluded promptly so that the people could get back to work under the new rules that would result from the peace treaty. It was natural that all peoples should have as a primary consideration a desire to help in the great task of establishing as permanent a peace as possible.

The entire peace program needed the support of labor. Labor was entitled to a hearing. In Europe the labor forces had been promised this by their governments, and they were demanding and expecting the organization of a new institution that would, in an international way, promote their welfare. Some wanted to destroy the present economic system and establish a new one, doing away with private ownership. Others sought to advance their interests through legislation, believing that it should be international because, if limited to domestic levels, there would always arise the capitalistic necessity of meeting foreign competition where the hours, standards, and wages were not in any sense parallel.

Even a conservative thinker felt that one of the best ways of holding back Bolshevism and various forms of socialism would be to set up an organization where the labor problem could be discussed and recommendations made for legislation that would tend to meet all proper demands. If an agency could be devised that would give a hearing to the claims of labor and harmonize them with the rights of employers, at least in so far as it is possible to do this at any one time, a valuable contribution would be made to the industrial future of the world. At the same time, it was necessary to take into consideration not only the possible but also the probable dangers in the setting up of any organization that endeavored to treat such a problem internationally. It was evident that under our political, social, and economic system and under our conditions and laws, it would be impossible, even if it had been desirable, for us to participate in a superlegislature. As this was the desire of practically every representative in the Conference, it will be understood that *our difficulties in preventing the incorporation of such a provision in the Peace Treaty proved onerous.*

Quite conscious of our responsibility and conscious also that we were alone in our stand, we undertook to maintain our position and to protect what we believed to be the attitude and belief of the American people. The whole discussion was based on a Draft Convention submitted by the British delegation,[2] which contemplated the setting up of a superlegislature as described. This was largely the work

---

[2] See Appendix I.

of Sir Malcolm Delevingne, long attached to the Home Office of the British Government, who stated that he had worked on the problem for twenty years and that the draft presented was the result of such work. The Honorable George Barnes presented the draft and argued for its passage.

I was compelled to resist the creation of a superlegislature, and as this was the most important provision of the Draft Convention, the discussion carried through most of the meetings of the Conference. The other members were nearly all in favor and believed that the position I was taking was obstructive, and while I hoped and trusted that they thought it was in good faith, they believed that it was narrow and unjust. Even some other Americans in Paris, not leaders of organized labor, took the view that the position we were taking, as presented by me, was definitely and purposely obstructive. It was, but it was maintained only to protect our people, employees and employers, from *a superlegislature with all the possibilities of control by people whose philosophy, social, economic and political, varied so widely from our own.*

Many spirited speeches and acrimonious discussions followed. I recall that there were three different speches by M. Jouhaux, who was substituting at certain meetings for M. Loucheur, in which we were promised immediate action on the part of labor if we did not promptly provide for such a superlegislature. On the other hand, Mr. Maheim of Belgium was deeply hurt by the resistant attitude of the American delegation. The Italian delegation and Minister Vandervelde talked as though they were convinced that we had some ulterior motive. However, we were finally able to reduce the proposed superlegislature to a body where labor problems could be discussed, and whence, if proposals relating to such problems were adopted by a two-thirds vote, they would go as recommendations to the legislatures of the various countries, with the obligation on the part of such countries as became signatories to the convention to submit the proposals for ratification by their respective legislatures.

Among other things that labor demanded was the setting up of principles that should govern in labor problems, what the labor leaders called a "Bill of Rights." These finally were reduced to a series of statements, nine in number, known as the "Nine Principles." [3]

When the Nine Principles were originally considered, the Peace Conference adopted the Draft Convention which provided for the setting up of the International Labor Office but returned the Principles for further consideration. Shortly after, Mr. Barnes, as Vice-President, asked for a plenary session of the Peace Conference. As Mr. Gompers and the other labor members had left, I feared that there might be something more than appeared on the surface and protested against any modification of the Draft Convention. This matter was taken up by the Big Four, and I was compelled to present my views that any such reconstruction would be illegal and unfair and might be harmful because the American labor leaders had left. At the following plenary session the Draft Commission was given pretty broad authority and there was a good deal of rather sharp discussion about it, but it finally resulted in no marked change in anything except the Nine Principles. By some agency the wording of the Nine Principles was changed, and when the word reached Mr. Gompers of the changes, he was particularly disturbed by the insertion of the word "merely" in the First Principle, which made it read "that the labor of a human being could not be regarded *merely* as a commodity or article of commerce." Mr. Gompers protested very sharply by cable-

_____
[3] See Appendix I.

gram, both to me and to President Wilson, but it was allowed finally to stand.

It might be interesting to know that the eighth of the Nine Principles came from the hand of President Wilson. All of the members of the Commission, together with their associates in their respective Peace Conference delegations and those of greatest experience in the phrasing of such subjects, had been working for at least three weeks without finding phraseology for the Eighth Principle to which all could agree. I feared that we would not be able to find a proper formula for Eight, and in writing a note to President Wilson among other things I stated my fear in this respect. The next morning early I received a note from the President in which he asked, "Would this phraseology do?" and then followed Section Eight as it now appears. I presented it to the Commission without giving them the information that President Wilson was the author—this because it was difficult at that time to know what the effect on them would have been had they known he was the draftsman. This phraseology was immediately and unanimously accepted.[4]

It would not be becoming in me to endeavor to make an appraisement of Samuel Gompers, but I feel I must say that in my contacts with him I found him fully alive to the value of American institutions and always on guard to

---

[4] The note sent by President Wilson read as follows:
Paris, 23 April, 1919.
My dear Mr. Robinson:
How do you think a clause of this sort would do as a substitute for clause number eight in the Labor Resolution:
"The standards set by law in each country with respect to the conditions of labor shall have due regard to the equitable and humane treatment of all foreign workers lawfully resident therein."
Cordially and sincerely yours,
(Signed) WOODROW WILSON.
Hon. Henry M. Robinson,
Hotel Crillon, Paris.

protect them. I believe that his work on behalf of labor was honest, sincere and whole-hearted, indefatigable and courageous, as he said himself, "What we are doing may be crude but it is better than a legislative course and no one has yet shown me a better philosophy."

I might add that the attitude of the other labor leaders, in so far as they related to belief in and protection of American Institutions, ran parallel with that of Mr. Gompers.

I wonder if it would be presuming for me to add that wherever President Wilson touched any of the work with which I had to do, whether with this Labor Conference or elsewhere, *his attitude was constructive, sincere, and broad.* I cannot but feel that the work of this Conference, while we of the United States have not officially participated, brought about a situation that in some degree at least helped to prevent the spread of Bolshevist tendencies in Western Europe, and that it will probably prove to be a means of discussion, recommendation, and at times legislative action that may be helpful to the employee class of the world, and, as I believe, improvement in their standards means improvement in the lives of all.

It is very easy to criticize the provisions of the Peace Treaty and the labor provisions of the Peace Treaty. It is better to study them and find out whether, after all, they do not contain elements that may prove to be of great constructive benefit. It would seem to one who has had something to do with the reconstruction period since 1919 that the International Labor Organization was one of the elements that has helped to bring about readjustment. Whether it will finally prove of great value remains to be proven, but it certainly contains definite favorable possibilities.

HENRY M. ROBINSON

THE INTERNATIONAL
LABOR ORGANIZATION

This that they call the organising of labour is, if well understood, the problem of the whole future for all who in future pretend to govern men.

CARLYLE.

The world has been made safe for democracy. . . . But democracy has not yet made the world safe against irrational revolution.   That supreme task, which is nothing less than the salvation of civilization, . . . the United States, as the greatest of democracies, must undertake it.

WOODROW WILSON, in his last article, *Atlantic Monthly,* August, 1923.

THE INTERNATIONAL LABOR ORGANIZATION

CHAPTER I

INTERNATIONAL STATESMANSHIP

PERHAPS the most lasting and significant result of the World War will prove to be the vivid realization it violently brought to us of the constructive power of men in friendly coöperation and of their destructive force in hateful conflict. That experience, both comforting and dreadful, hastened, more than any other factor in the last century, the development of an international spirit.

The living spirit of unity, which sprang, so to speak, out of the chaos of the battlefields, immediately sought a permanent embodiment so that men could focus their attention upon it, foster its growth, and give it ample opportunity for service. Thus were born the League of Nations, the International Organization of Labor, and the Permanent Court of International Justice.

Elaborately to conceive international institutions is not, however, the most trying of our tasks. The real difficulty consists in assuring their efficient and continued operation. It would be futile, therefore, to enter upon a discussion of the latest international institutions without making clear the indispensable conditions of their success. Institutions such as the Permanent Court of International Justice, the League of Nations, the International Organization of Labor cannot endure and bring forth the expected fruit unless we

1

create for them a propitious environment and adopt political methods suited to their character and their purpose. The indispensable condition for the success of an institution like the League of Nations, the International Organization of Labor, or the World Court is an appropriate political philosophy and practice. To meet the needed requirements of success the political philosophy and practice of modern governments must be submitted to considerable revision. Many of our traditional political principles need restating and rethinking. We must realize that we have entered into a new period in the life of nations.

There was a time when we could concentrate upon domestic issues, solve our problems in perfect independence, maintain our general well-being in relative isolation, occasionally casting a glance of passing curiosity or interest over our frontiers. We can do so no longer. We have learned, at no small cost, that the emphasis has to be placed alike upon the interdependence and the independence of nations, even perhaps that the latter cannot be long preserved except through a generous and timely recognition of the former.

Heretofore we have gone through a strictly political phase; we are now clearly in the midst of an economic one. The center of our political life has been for many years man the citizen; our main concern the conquest or the defense of political rights against the oppression of governments or majorities: now the center of our political life tends to be man the producer, and our first care has become the organization of society upon a basis of economic liberty, equality, and justice. Moreover, the experience of the last decade has fully convinced us that the organization of society upon a basis of economic liberty, equality, and justice to be really efficient will have to be planned upon an international scale.

The resultant of these late developments is a delicate

intermingling of political and economic problems which renders the task of governments more difficult than ever and demands of our representatives new qualifications in intelligence, in training, and in character.[1]

In presence of such crying need for new and higher forms of statesmanship, it is not particularly comforting to have to confess that, no matter how far we may have advanced in many spheres of human endeavor, the art of government has not kept pace with the other activities of the age. The post-War condition of the world—its huge debts, its armaments, its depreciated currency, its unemployment, its hatreds and distrusts, its dread of new conflicts—is a sad commentary upon our political wisdom. We grant that, after nearly five years of ruthless destruction, the nations could not instantly recover. It is far easier to tear down than it is to build up. It will be decades before the devastation of the War is no longer felt. But, due allowances being made for the complexity of reconstruction problems, it remains evident that things have not progressed even normally.

We have all said very loudly we wanted peace and justice. But if the nations of the world had wanted them supremely and consistently, we would have them in satisfactory measure. Had you entered the various parliaments of the world during these last six years, listened to the addresses delivered, or read the official press, could you have said, in all honesty, that governments want peace and justice?

The initial and most glaring guilt was certainly incurred by the rulers of Germany. No amount of sophistry can

---

[1] Addressing the luncheon of the Anglo-American Press Association of Paris at the Hotel Petrograd, March 2, 1923, M. Loucheur, who is one of the leading industrialists of France, said: "We are suffering, at the present time, from a great error committed by statesmen. That error lies in the fact that economists do not want to be politicians and politicians do not want to be economists. Yet, in making the peace of Europe, the two are inseparable."

ever convince clear and impartial thinkers of their inno-
cence, but who could doubt that, on this seventh year of
official peace, the other Powers must bear not a little blame
for the present distress and turmoil? Surely, no matter
how proud and how fond we may be of our respective countries, we cannot say in all sincerity that either the governments of Europe or of America have taken the best means
to promote peace and make justice prevail. The Allied
Powers are guilty in the sense that they failed to
apply new methods to new conditions. After a war which
fundamentally altered the terms of individual and national
relations they reverted to ways of acting and ways of
thinking of an outgrown character instead of developing
policies in harmony with changed conditions. The great
mistake of the American Senate, for example, when not
purely actuated by party considerations, was that they
failed to see that a new age had arrived.

Undoubtedly the Covenant and the International Organization of Labor seemed to them a dangerous departure
from tradition. It would disturb their habits of thought
and action; it would introduce confusion in the constitutional prerogatives of the branches of the government; it
might condition the full exercise of our sovereignty, and
so forth. But, so reads the history of man. In every
epoch, contemporaries have an impression of disorder caused
by innovations and reforms. This disorder, however, is not
pure confusion. Later, with adequate perspective, we discover in it elements of wisdom and harmony. We may
even find in it evidences of a law of constant progression
towards better forms of human associations, of political
and economic solidarity. What we call disorder may be
ideas in motion trying to find their level. Experience
proves that we may claim a certain right of selection among
these new ideas, even the power to influence their evolution,
but not the power entirely to arrest their motion, for that

would be stagnation and with stagnation comes decay. Not a few Senators stubbornly ignored these elementary principles. Similarly, the European parliaments betrayed an incapacity to rise to that new level of political understanding which alone can establish peace and prosperity upon a secure foundation. The parliamentary history of Great Britain, France, and Italy, during the last seven years, affords abundant illustration of this weakness, which is common to them all.

It is then true to say that the art of government has not kept pace with the general progress of society. We have wished for and devised international institutions but have not acquired the spirit required for their successful operation. The most optimistic observer is forced to register a failure in world statesmanship. What may be the cause of such a failure?

The most evident reason for the general failure in international statesmanship seems to be that the whole problem of international relations was not approached in a dispassionate and objective way. We have not as yet developed a political mentality abreast of the grave obligations of a new age. It is of the greatest importance, therefore, that those who ask the people to intrust them with the administration of their home and foreign affairs should be open to the reception and understanding of these new ideas. The statesman we need must not simply voice mob impulses or class interests. It must be he who, perhaps in a measure by instinct, through a keen moral sense, through the influence of a sound environment, by persevering and disinterested study of political and social problems, has a broad view of the permanent and real interests of his country and of the world at large. The life of the representative of the people must no longer be the life of a political equilibrist but the life of an untiring and honest thinker. A wise and fruitful political

activity is impossible to-day without a corresponding
amount of thought and study.

The most crying need, therefore, in political life is a
change of attitude. In the sphere of government, a revolution must take place similar to the one by which astron-
omy succeeded to astrology and which replaced the medi-
cine man by the physician and the surgeon, so that we
may have in politics less intellectual anarchy and more of
the scientific and positive spirit. The part of emotion,
impulse, prejudice, self-interest inseparable from politics
will ever interfere with the serenity that characterizes
purely scientific pursuits, but there is no doubt that a
true scientific spirit, infused in the public activities of
man, is the great desideratum of the political life of the
world.

The writer of this book has had the privilege of teach-
ing for the last five years, in a school of high scientific
ideals which takes pride in the permanent or temporary
possession of men of international fame, as, George E.
Hale, Robert A. Millikan, Arthur A. Noyes, Charles G.
Darwin, Paul Epstein, Richard Tolman, Albert Michel-
son, Hendrick Lorentz. Through his association with both
men and students, he has been impressed with the manner
in which minds scientifically trained, bent to rigorous
methods of investigation, accustomed to render judgments
after careful weighing of evidence, would approach economic and political problems. Their conclusions might
not be exceptionally wise or correct, as neither politics nor
economics is their specialty, but there was enough of a
difference in the results to lead one to believe that a
greater regard for the scientific method, and a confident
and permanent application of it, would give us surprisingly valuable returns.

We should endeavor to extend the spirit of our labora-
tories into the political field. If we were to foster in

government these habits of careful investigation, we would soon cause our political debates to lose a vagueness of thought suggestive of sewing circles and a bitterness which savors more of religious fanaticism than of the scientific method.

Above all things, let us not resign ourselves to present evils by saying that such a reform is impossible and visionary. Before yielding to skepticism, attend a few meetings of various groups of men engaged in different avocations, and you will soon detect that their deliberations reflect the intellectual or moral discipline that their studies or occupations impose. Their way of thinking or speaking will bear the impress of their professional training. Similarly, there is a sane, accurate, conscientious political type attainable; it can be developed and must be. It is inadmissible that the wonderful scientific method that the human mind has evolved and has applied with so much success to the natural and physical sciences should not be applied, with all the reserves that the nature of the subject demands, to that most important of all the sciences, the science of life and society.

How can we more specifically define this new political orientation which promises us a greater measure of success in the solution of the trying problems of the day and has become indispensable in the management of international institutions?

We would not presume to offer here an extensive program of political and economic action; we shall merely, for the sake of illustration, suggest two or three of the more outstanding directive principles.

The eighteenth century had evolved a technique of government which, because of its moral superiority over the medieval forms, has been too readily thought absolute and final. We can understand the enthusiasm of our forefathers for that new system. To them it was at last reason and liberty. We may share unreservedly that enthusiasm provided, however, we keep alive the spirit out of which this modern age was born: the spirit of adaptation and progress. The duty, then, of those who have at heart the public good is not simply to hold fast that which they have received but ever to vivify tradition by a constant, even though prudent, adjustment to new conditions. This policy must be pursued with vision, measure, courage, and firmness. Does that progressive spirit preside over our domestic and international relations?

After a willingness to go forward, a most vital requisite is an intelligent organization of political and economic thought. A few sound principles, honest and experienced officials, high-minded executives, and clever representatives are not enough; all these scattered qualities are not effective unless they be at the service of some comprehensive policy, some well connected theory of government based upon the best findings of the social sciences. Politics should rest more and more upon political science, scientific economics and sociology as these sciences develop and win, gradually, by the sincerity of their research and the reliability of their method, the confidence of men. The lack of agreement in the various schools of thought should not be a deterrent. Their important differences could be reduced to very few if influences, foreign to scientific standards, ceased to act. There is, moreover, a political pragmatism upon which almost complete unanimity would be secured on most of the questions which press for solution. Again, how much of that scientific preparation enters into the education of our representatives?

This new political doctrine should likewise put to profit the best experience of our large business enterprises. Much of the talent of the world in organization, management, and technical ability has been drawn within the sphere of business. If we cannot attract it to public service, as would be eminently desirable, we must gain by such wisdom as they do place at our disposal. To rule any modern state, we must be versed in practical economics; the War has demonstrated that truth beyond cavil. How much of that business experience have we brought into the study of international problems?

Thus, because principles such as these are ignored or overlooked, our modern international policy has been, on the whole, bad sociology, bad political science, bad economics, and bad business.

Undoubtedly, the best place to inaugurate this experimental method in politics would be the League of Nations, the International Labor Organization, and the Permanent Court of International Justice, as many of the aforesaid requisites are there already provided for by the presence of scholars, experts, statesmen, and business men. Henceforth, the nations should send to Geneva or The Hague some of the best minds they possess. Their financial contributions are meager enough. The most valuable gift they could make is an intellectual one by sending the type of officials and delegates that would guarantee the application and development of the most perfect political method. It is to be hoped that men of remarkable achievements will allow themselves to be tempted to represent their countries. If the League of Nations, the International Labor Organization, and the World Court could become a school and laboratory for the best type of political, economic, and legal thought, they would be entitled to the gratitude of mankind.

Besides a proper method of approach, there is, in our modern democracies, another indispensable requisite to a progressive national and international life: the creation of a national and international conscience. In the past, under autocratic forms of government, the welfare, the stability of the group at home, and its prestige abroad, were primarily, almost exclusively, the concern of the ruler. Now, things have changed. That which binds the people together in an efficient organization, and gives them a place of honor in the world, is the conscience of the members. To-day, the tribunal of last resort is the people, and no government can succeed, no matter how lofty its ideals, unless it is intelligently supported by the masses. The great problem confronting us, therefore, is to marshal the most efficient means to create in each individual citizen and in every community, large or small, this light and power, more than ever indispensable, which we call a national conscience and which is the mainspring of political conduct. This is by no means an impossible task. We have seen a high-minded and powerful man like Theodore Roosevelt, single-handed, electrify the conscience of his generation, impart to a whole nation an entirely new conception of their moral and political responsibilities, and save them from a blindness and an apathy which were threatening the foundations of the Republic. During the War, we have seen how public opinion can be influenced, almost controlled. We dispose of well-nigh irresistible pressure to act upon the minds of men; the press, the school, the church, the stage, and the screen are molders of public opinion, and if we can win a respectable fraction of these forces to the support of a measure or of a policy which we deem vital to the public good, its success is assured.

The national conscience through these agencies should be made to react intelligently and dispassionately regarding international relations instead of being daily inoculated with the poison of blind prejudices, distorted facts and biased interpretations.

Not only can we thus act within our national boundaries but we can exercise a similar influence abroad and set out deliberately for the creation of an international public mind. For instance, it should be possible to determine in every nation that particular trait, policy, or practice which interferes with the peace of the world, that something which perpetuates unrest, which is not vital to the nation concerned, and which it ought to renounce or avoid to become a safe, beneficent member of the family of nations. That something should be so branded that the thinking men of the world would unremittingly denounce it and condemn it. It might be autocracy and bad faith in Germany, political tyranny in Russia, economic imperialism in England, oversensitive nationalism in France, self-sufficiency in the United States of America; the world might then arrive, through such a gradual selection and elimination, at the formation of a sound international public opinion and of an international conscience as well. And the herald of that conscience could be the League of Nations.

These—a new political method, more under the control of science and reason and less under the influence of passion and private interest, plus the creation of a high, alert, well informed national and international conscience—are what we call the indispensable requisites to a successful growth and development of our international institutions. Without that political and moral minimum, we shall proceed slowly, if at all, along the road of world peace and coöperation. And as we hope to demonstrate, in the course of this study, only in the measure in which we develop such a political method, have we a chance to bring order out of the present world-wide economic chaos and particularly a chance to bring Labor into working harmony with the other forces of our civilization in the international sphere in which it has but lately made its appearance.

CHAPTER II

LABOR AN INTERNATIONAL FACTOR

EVERY epoch finds itself confronted with the task of bringing into working harmony currents of thought which seem at first to run counter to each other: authority and democracy, state sovereignty and federation, Capitalism and economic justice, individualism and solidarity. The most recent problem proposed to our generation is the reconciliation of Nationalism and Internationalism.

Nationalism is a most precious concept, one which it does not seem possible to dispense with at this stage of civilization. It is one of the most enduring sentiments of the human heart and, at times, it seems as though it were the only vital factor that can be invariably relied upon in ever changing political situations. Many crimes have been committed in its name but it is one of the conspicuous failings of men to abuse the best and holiest institutions.

A proper balance of independent states, directed by well defined rules of intercourse but each one preserving a maximum of individuality, seems to be the best means of supplying stimulus to progress, of protecting the rights of individuals, and of giving us variety in unity.

Men are, therefore, justified in jealously protecting Nationalism against inconsiderate attacks. Especially, when a young nation like the United States, having earned her independence by sheer will power and at a great cost, has succeeded in organizing, under the protection of an admirable constitution of liberty and justice, a polity of one hundred and ten million people, and in solving, with an unusual amount of success, the intricate problems involved

12

in the assimilation and blending of so many heterogeneous elements and has finally brought them to a high degree of education and well-being, such a nation may justly fear contagion, entanglements, and encroachments upon a sovereignty which she has, on the whole, wisely exercised.

There are, however, forms of Nationalism which are very dangerous to the individual countries which harbor them and to the world at large. A well-known type, which most great nations have experienced and which frequently appears after brilliant military victories, is that Nationalism which believes itself invested with a special mission to regenerate mankind and wishes to impose its conception of civilization on other nations, presumed decadent or inferior. Germany was the latest one to be afflicted with this fatal illusion.

Another dangerous form is the self-centered Nationalism, a Nationalism of selfishness and isolation. It often follows great waves of industrial and commercial prosperity which are falsely assumed to be permanent and independent of world conditions. It carries with it a perilous disregard of the complex interdependence of the material and moral interests of all nations.

That Nationalism alone is progressive and helpful which, though primarily concerned with the welfare of its own people, stands ready to coöperate, to mingle with sympathy and generosity with the life of the world.

If we were to analyze the patriotism of these two types of Nationalists, who always bar the road to the forward march of ideas of brotherhood and fellowship, we would discover that their boasted patriotism is an insult to the real virtue. It is really the corruption of patriotism, its very denial, for in either case it is the kind that will grow priggish, imperialistic, antidemocratic, antiliberal, and ultimately undermine the foundations of the state and endanger its security.

In spite of the present feverish agitation of short-sighted Nationalists the world over, the idea of Internationalism is here to stay. It was anticipated and predicted by daring thinkers and prophets centuries ago, but now it is imposed upon us by circumstances beyond the control of any one nation, and we must be open-minded enough to consider it dispassionately. We must stop being frightened by it. It must be critically analyzed. It contains nothing mysterious. There are sane elements in it which must be put to good service, and extreme implications which must be resolutely guarded against.

Internationalism is the clear recognition of the natural independence of all the races of men, of their equal rights to "life, liberty, and the pursuit of happiness." It is really the extension to the whole world of the principles which bind together and protect the citizens of our civilized countries. It is based on the noblest instincts and truest interests of the human race. It tends to create a science of right relations among nations. For Internationalism, properly understood, is founded upon the nations themselves and not upon their suppression. It is, therefore, opposed to Cosmopolitism which, essentially unitary, looks upon the whole of humanity as one single social group. In political organization, Internationalism favors federation and opposes centralization.[1] Far from being destructive of patriotism, it ennobles it and makes it a constructive force. No man will love his country less because of his appreciation of other nations and of his sympathies for their vital needs and legitimate aspirations.

Internationalism is the resultant of a great many forces which have been at work to bring about, wittingly or unwittingly, a closer coöperation between the peoples of the earth. The way was prepared, first intellectually, by these

[1] Christian Lous Lange, *Histoire de l'internationalisme*, Christiania, 1919, Intro., p. 14.

philosophies and religions which emphasized the brotherhood of men, and, later physically, by the inventions which,
through improved methods of transportation and communication, brought the nations into permanent and close
contact.[2] These contacts in turn brought inevitably with
them institutions of an international character.[3]

All the great economic factors, such as production and
exchange, are now organized on an international plan and
with a view to a world market.[4] Capital has long ago
become international. It is not entirely invested in the
country which owns it, even though at times it might be
desirable for the national good, but seeks abroad for lands
and enterprises, not infrequently under the control of
potential enemies, which promise the larger returns. Labor
migrates also from country to country in search of better
opportunities and gives rise thereby to a multitude of social
and economic problems reacting upon international relations. Science is perhaps the most international of our

---

[2] The railway, the steamship, and the telegraph made of man
a citizen of the world. Successive steps which have given the world
a whole system of perfected and standardized communication are:
agreements establishing uniformity of maritime signals (1857);
the right of way at sea (1863); the Telegraph Union (1865); the
Postal Union (1874); the protection of submarine cables (1884);
the technical unification of railways (1886); the transport of
goods by rail (1893); the radio; Telegraphic Union (1906); auto-
mobile traffic (1909); aërial navigation (1919). These imply naturally the creation or adaptation of ports, rivers, canals, transcon-
tinental routes, aërodromes, land beacons, lighthouses, etc.

[3] Since 1843, from decade to decade, the number of International
Conferences has regularly doubled: 9; 20; 77; 169; 309; 510;
1,020. For the first four years of the decade beginning with 1910
it reached a total of 494. The War and the international compli-
cations resulting from it have interfered with these Conferences.
It is interesting to note, however, that the *Annuaire de la vie internationale*, which has investigated 400 international organizations,
says that almost all International Associations have survived the
War.

[4] Lord Burnham, in his speech of acceptance when elected president of the Fourth International Labor Conference, Geneva, 1922,
said: "In the real sense of the word, practical men of business are
all internationalists now. The balance of modern trade depends
upon international agreements."

activities. Many discoveries have become so international, are the results of so much international coöperation, that it becomes difficult, at any one time, to say which country has had the most prominent part in their development.

Our entire civilization is such a collective and composite product that no one nation can claim it as its own. It is essentially an international heritage.

And all that philosophy, religion, science, interest, have moved or enabled men to do to bridge the distance that separated the nations from one another was tremendously intensified during the last war. More than ever before, we were forced during those trying days into close international partnership. It is true that a reaction has since taken place and that Nationalism has reasserted itself with renewed vigor, but this is only a temporary phenomenon. The lesson has been learned and in due time it will bear its fruit.

This much at least seems definitely gained, that everywhere men and women have become accustomed to look at problems from an international standpoint. No question seems to-day thoroughly treated or satisfactorily handled unless it be considered in its international bearings. The number of books and publications devoted to international topics, the university courses, the conferences and lectures, the newspapers, the platforms of political parties, all testify to an increased interest in the study of international problems.

In this field of Internationalism, whose character and growth we have briefly outlined, there has appeared lately a new factor which asserts itself with a growing insistence. That factor is Labor.

For some time, the world-wide uniformity of industrialism had tended to create in the workers a kind of international mind or psychology. At the time of the Industrial Revolution, it was the concentration of the great means of production and the consequent concentration of laborers, their life in common, their grouping in large cities, which developed in them a class spirit; they became conscious of their solidarity. Thus also, they gradually acquired a national spirit. The textile operative from Leeds, the docker from London were no longer strangers, they became comrades.

Now, in a measure, in spite of the bitterness of sectional conflicts, in spite of racial antagonisms, something similar is taking place. The workers become class conscious internationally and realize their universal solidarity;[5] the more so because they have substantially the same problems to solve regarding wages, housing, unemployment, insurance, and organization.

Moreover, as they live in an environment which by the very nature of the industries that employ them has much in common the world over, they are similarly influenced, and again a common psychology is the result. It is a fact that everywhere the worker is subjected more and more to the same discipline. As the technique of production becomes standardized, the workman of France, of America and of England goes through very much the same motions, begins to look at things in the same way, and, as there is nothing which molds the mind better than the occupation, the workers of modern nations find their ideals similarly determined by like conditions of labor.

As the workers were developing an international outlook, they were becoming more and more conscious of their power.[6] This awakening of Labor to the realization of

[5] More than thirty different international trade federations exist, among which those of the miners, sailors, dockers, metal workers, diamond cutters, glove makers, compositors, and railway workers are the best known. *Cf. International Labor Directory*, 1925.

[6] "As civilization is now organized on a world basis, so the Labor movement now has international relations and international interests. Its activity and its purposes are as universal as the cause of human welfare and as instinctively associated and interdependent

its power is not of yesterday. Like the growth of other social forces it has been progressive. It began in England in the middle of the eighteenth century, continued with the spread of industrialism to the neighboring countries, was hastened by the French Revolutions of 1793, 1830, and 1848, and seemed to grow apace with the development of democracy.

But it was during the last war, more than ever, that Labor became aware of its importance. The workers saw that it was in their power to paralyze national defense, that without their hearty coöperation victory could not be obtained, and therefore they made up their minds quite early that, if victory there was, it would be a victory for Labor as well as for the ruling classes.

There was a time when international problems were the reserved domain of specialized, astute diplomats. They could juggle freely with the interests of nations, their territories, even with the peoples themselves. Now, not only the people as the great democratic electorate, but the people as workers and, particularly, as organized workers, were determined to make their influence felt in the deliberations of peace. Consequently, they held several conferences in various countries to decide upon, draw up, and set forth the principles which they wished to see embodied in the Treaty.

The recognition they demanded was granted to them and so it happened that, for the first time in a treaty of peace, a long chapter was consecrated to Labor. Instead of the classical articles on the prerogatives of royal dynasties, or princely alliances, we find provisions relating to the needs of the people.

as the welfare of human beings. The workers, through their economic organizations, have secured for themselves recognition as a factor in national and international life that must be recognized, considered and dealt with." *American Federationist*, January, 1916, p. 19.

Why this change? Why bring an economic problem into a treaty intended to settle questions of frontiers, indemnities, territories, liberation of oppressed peoples? It was because the Treaty of Versailles was ending a very unusual war. It had been in reality a war of peoples. It was the people who did the fighting, in the largest measure, and not only professional soldiers, and the people who won the War. At the close of the struggle they demanded not applause but justice.

Now, as then, to the working classes, justice means predominantly industrial and social justice. That justice, they have recently learned, can no longer be attained except through international action, and is incompatible with war or even the fear of it. Hence they have a double international labor program: economic and political.[7]

In the economic field, Labor realizes that the workers of the world are solidary, that the standard of life of the workers of one country is not secure, and that further betterment of working conditions may be barred, unless the standard of life of workers of competing industrial nations is proportionately high. There are two enemies of the improvement of labor conditions: the foreign manufacturer underselling the home producer, because of labor's lower cost, thereby bringing about unemployment or reduction of wages; and the imported foreign worker underbidding native labor, through inferior standards of life. These two enemies, Labor knows, cannot be conquered except with the help of international legislation. To that end, therefore, Labor plans to use its new international influence.

In order to safeguard that same economic justice, Labor believes it must also enter the field of international

---

[7] *Cf.* "The Third International Trade-Union Congress, Rome, April, 1922," *International Labor Review,* June, 1922, which gives such a program.

politics.[8] In a world constantly threatened by wars, terribly destructive of life and wealth, a scientific or efficient organization of economic life is impossible. In such a world, it is most difficult for workmen to go ahead with their program of improvement and reform. They maintain, moreover, that in the last war the masses of the people have borne the heaviest share of the burden of sacrifice, of physical suffering, of injury, and they are more interested than any other class in its suppression. And thus they are forced into politics.

"War against war" seems the most vital point of their political program. Go and interview them, as we have, in the factory and the mine, in the labor exchanges, in their meetings throughout Europe, and they will invariably tell you that it is shocking that men be led into war by the folly or ambition of a king, that it is not right that a prosperity which is the fruit of years of toil should be destroyed in a moment, not right that a nation enriched by patient work should be forced to surrender her wealth to the victor, not right that a world, in which man's first duty is to produce, to build, and to coöperate, should deliberately consecrate itself to destruction. They feel more and more that to drive this specter of war from the world we cannot rely on kings, philosophers, jurists, diplomats, capitalists, and therefore Labor must at last assume that responsibility.

And immediately they argue that one of the firmest guaranties of peace is the end of economic privilege among nations, as the best guaranty of national concord is the

---

8 Professor Shotwell (*Labor as an International Problem*, p. 45) pertinently remarks that, when one examines the pronouncements of the Socialist and Trade-Union International before the Peace Conference, "one is struck with the fact that a large part of the program they laid down had nothing to do with economic matters at all, but concerned things so remote from the factory and workshop as the Balkan boundaries or colonial adjustments. This in itself is a significant and withal an inspiring fact."

end of economic privilege among individuals. Their new power in international politics they wish to use to bring about that international economic justice—fundamentally, a fair access to the raw materials and to the markets of the world—which would eliminate the principal causes of conflict.[9] Hence there is a very prevalent belief among the working classes that the reign of Labor will be the reign of peace.

Thus they repeatedly condemned the occupation of the Ruhr by France, not that they wished to condone Germany's guilt or bad faith, but because they saw in that policy a seed of future wars.[10] They have likewise criticized French military operations in Syria and Morocco. The trade-union organizations of Great Britain[11] and Switzerland[12] made constructive proposals for the economic recovery of Europe. The International Federation of Trade-Unions, representing over twenty million workers, submitted an elaborate program to the Genoa Conference of the Powers.[13] The International Federation of Christian Trade-Unions prepared a likewise program for its Innsbruck Congress.[14] The French Confédération Générale du Travail has never ceased to advocate a settlement of the entire reparation problem by submitting it to the League of Nations.[15] It has consistently supported the Geneva Protocol and the Treaty of Locarno.

This, then, is the fact we are confronted with: Labor,

---

[9] *Cf.* Léon Jouhaux, *The International Federation of Trade-Unions and Economic Reconstruction,* International Federation of Trade-Unions, Amsterdam, 1922.

[10] *Cf. Le Peuple,* January and February, 1923, daily organ of the Confédération Générale du Travail.

[11] "Unemployment: a Labor Policy," Trade-Union Congress and Labor Party, London, 1921.

[12] *International Labor Review,* Vol. V, No. 6, June, 1922, pp. 929-930.

[13] *Ibid.,* pp. 917-920.

[14] *Ibid.,* Vol. VI, No. 2, August, 1922, pp. 209-210.

[15] *Cf. Le Peuple,* January to June, 1923.

conscious of its power, conscious of a great mission to fulfill, and determined to overcome all obstacles that may bar the way to a recognition of its rights.

How are we then to meet these new claims of Labor? For many it is difficult to approach a discussion of the problem with anything like equanimity of spirit. They have little faith in Labor. They hold numberless grievances against it, such as the breaking of contracts, excessive demands in wages and hours of leisure, unnecessary strikes, the use of violence, sabotage, restriction of output, disregard of the public welfare. But they forget that, under every one of these heads, we find parallel offenses by the employers, that, in the course of ages, Labor has been more sinned against than sinning.

People so minded have lately taken comfort in the fact that Labor in many countries, particularly Organized Labor, is under a cloud. It is evidently not wise to trust to that temporary depression in the popularity of labor policies or in the strength of the Labor movement. Labor is a factor that will ever be with us. It will require a few years before it fully recovers from the effects of the War and the disastrous results of the Bolshevistic folly, but prudent thinkers and statesmen will deal with it as potentially the most powerful factor in human society, for its strength is the ineluctable consequence of democracy.

As for those who would continue to advocate a policy of stern repression, they should remember that after the Bolshevistic experiment in Russia a social upheaval can no longer be looked upon as an idle dream. The practical failure of Bolshevism is no guaranty that similar attempts will not be made in the future. No matter how good at heart the masses of the people may be, they are not always capable of judicious discrimination between fact and fiction, between reason and fancy, between the possible and the visionary, and they may be terribly misled by fanatics

before a cruel and costly awakening. Even unorganized
they are a respectable force; organized they would be overwhelming. It is a grave error to judge of the influence of
the unions by their number. They are often simply the
vanguard of the great army of workers which may act as
the shock troops to be followed by the masses which may
be expected to rally to them as soon as they feel unjustly
treated. But even if all are not likely to become unionized
and syndicated, Organized Labor could be the nucleus
which, in a moment of crisis, might temporarily solidarize
all their interests, and thus, for the time being, give them
control for good or evil.

A revolution destructive of the work of several genera-
tions, inaugurating a system of social, political, and economic tyranny, is not to be scoffed at, but to be guarded
against in the interest of all, rich and poor, because through
it the poor are not made rich, but all, rich and poor, are
made equally wretched and destitute.

To forestall revolutions, there is only one way, as history
testifies. It is not the use of violence and oppression, nor
is it the blind and obdurate opposition to all social reforms,
but the release in due time of the forces that will bring
about an orderly evolution. This evolution, under the
intelligent control of farseeing statesmen, takes place
gradually, almost imperceptibly, by the modification of the
juridical principles upon which society is founded, and
although it may hardly be noticed by the many, it quietly
prepares a day of safer and fairer human relations.

We, in America, should be the most receptive of all the
nations to an international program of improvement of
the conditions of labor. First, we have a high estimate
of the intrinsic worth of every human being. We also
have a clear sense of the dignity of labor. We believe
in fair standards of life for all our citizens. We wish for
social justice as a source of domestic peace. "Truly,"

retorts the capitalist, ''but we are also discriminating and essentially practical, we are reluctant to surrender plain facts for vague theories.'' To this we can confidently reply that we need not leave the domain of facts to substantiate our contention. Even in that experimental field for which we have shown special aptness, have we not perhaps reached these two most significant conclusions, first, that, in the measure in which we improve the lot of the workingman, we make him more individualistic, less socialistic, and second, that the intervention of the state will go on decreasing as the individualism of man unfolds. If these deductions, which would elsewhere call for ample developments, are correct we should be prepared heartily to support an international labor policy which aims at a progressive improvement of labor conditions.

In approaching the whole problem from an international point of view, however, a new objection may arise. It will be argued that this economic question complicates itself with a grave political question, the question of national sovereignty, and that America's safety requires the preserving of a state of things which has cost so much to elaborate. We cannot intrust to others the shaping of that greatest of domestic policies—the labor policy.

But in an improvement of conditions of labor through international action we have less to fear than any other nation, for our standards are the highest. Therefore, it is mostly a question of bringing to other peoples the benefit of our civilization and, aside from the moral satisfaction that contribution can give to the idealistic section of our people, there is also the advantage of considerably reducing the competition of other industrial nations and of lessening the menace of inferior peoples which may become more dangerous to us in proportion as they remain steeped in degrading ignorance, in inveterate prejudice, in political and economic serfdom. This, however, cannot be done with any degree of effectiveness without us, because of the weight of our opinion and of our economic preeminence.

To us, then, conscious as we are of the dangers of ultra-reactionary methods, two attitudes only seem acceptable.[16] We may either heartily welcome Labor both upon the national and international stage and cheerfully give it an increasingly larger share of responsibility in domestic and foreign questions, knowing that there is room and need for their coöperation, and hoping that experience will teach them, at not too great a cost, prudence, moderation, and reserve; or we may bow before the inevitable, grudgingly accepting the facts, realizing that when a great force like Labor can neither be ignored nor destroyed, it is elementary wisdom to utilize it in ways that substantially will assure our well-being and safeguard our civilization, lest it become destructive of general prosperity.

In any case, we are in the presence of a new fact which we cannot lightly set aside. It is as important to follow to-day the trend of the thought of Labor as it was to know the mind of the Third Estate before the French Revolution. The failure to do so might meet with like punishment.

Labor, then, has lately entered upon a new phase: the international phase. This will add immeasurably to its power for good or evil. It depends on us that it be for the greater good. Those of us who have the opportunity should help in the arduous realization of that hope. Labor can no longer be enslaved, it cannot be silenced, it cannot

---

[16] The reactionary spirit "represents a menace to the stability of our established institutions vastly more serious than that of socialists, communists or bolshevists or any other group of labor agitators. The fulminations of the agitator will carry little weight provided the legislation of the country is permitted to develop along progressive lines." Henry R. Seager, "Apropos of the Minimum Wage of the District of Columbia," *The Survey*, May 15, 1923.

be subdued; but it can be educated, it can be given a sense of dignity and of responsibility, it can be as great a constructive force in the intellectual, moral, and political order as it is in the material order, provided in due time these things come to it: unselfish and intelligent guidance, honest and competent leadership, just and sympathetic treatment. We believe that this task can be facilitated by an enlightened international labor policy expressing itself in progressive international legislation.

CHAPTER III

THE PHILOSOPHY OF LABOR LEGISLATION

LET it be assumed that we approach the problem of labor with an entirely unbiased mind, that we really desire the promotion of the general welfare. We wish to do what is right provided we can be convinced.

A man bred according to the pure American tradition begins the consideration of the problem of labor legislation with a definite stock of ideas and feelings. His political education is generally more thorough than his economic education. His enthusiasm in regard to certain political facts and theories amounts to an almost sacred tradition. In some cases, it recalls the enthusiasm of Revolutionary days.

He is for liberty, his fathers fought for it, it has made America what it is. He must remain loyal to it. His political rights are guaranteed by the Constitution. And in economic matters he looks upon the freedom of contract as the best means of securing just relations between the parties concerned.[1] Strongly individualistic, moved by the magic of the word freedom, he is naturally inclined towards economic "liberalism" or laissez faire.

This psychological attitude is interesting as it is a reminder and a survival of a parallel historical situation.

---

[1] In the United States "the presumption is always in favor of the freedom of contract and so strong are these presumptions that American Labor Legislation is easiest explained and best understood as a collection of exceptions to these general rules." Adams and Sumner, *Labor Problems*, New York, 1920, p. 464.

The writings of Locke, Rousseau, and Voltaire initiated a movement for political liberty which culminated in the Declaration of Independence and the Declaration of the Rights of Man. Hence there was created an atmosphere favorable to the development of similar ideas in other fields of action. And when Adam Smith began to advocate economic freedom, he found a ready response because men had already heard a similar political gospel. Wherever political liberalism grew, there was a chance for economic liberalism.[2]

But in both these cases, the personal and the historical, the unqualified indorsement of Liberalism[3] will not resist searching criticism.

These expressions—liberty, equality, and fraternity—which constitute "thrilling" slogans for holiday occasions, must be analyzed with care when we begin to apply them to our daily existence. They are useful only in the manner in which they are properly understood, and become weapons capable of incalculable harm in the hands of the un-

---

[2] "In the United States, the new philosophy of laissez faire exercised a profound and even more lasting influence than in France or England. Coinciding so opportunely with the political demands and movement of the Revolutionary Period, it was not only welcomed with eagerness by the American people but it was incorporated in the organic law of the state and federal governments, from which vantage ground it has conditioned and, in a negative sense, controlled all the labor legislation of the United States from that time to this." *Ibid.*, p. 462.

[3] This use of the term liberalism may be confusing on account of the new meaning the term has taken in the last fifty years. Liberalism must be taken here in the sense which the word had during the first half of the nineteenth century. It meant then a very definite body of political and economic doctrine built around the principals of individualism and laissez faire. Liberalism to-day has a different connotation. While it cannot divorce itself entirely from certain individualistic implications, the principles of liberalism, both economic and political, are now identified with various socialistic activities of the government. The theory is no longer thoroughgoing individualistic but is the theory of the general good. One feels, however, that modern liberalism tends to be an attitude toward problems rather than an agreement with any particular set of conclusions.

thinking. They need rigorous definition and must be nicely adjusted to the complexity of human relations, otherwise we are left with but empty phrases and may lose the very reality we pursue.

It is difficult to define political liberty. In the abstract, liberty means the right to do what one pleases. But in the concrete, as soon as we mingle with our fellows, we discover that limitations are immediately placed upon personal rights, for others will assume, as we do, that they also have the right to do as they please and their right will so run counter to ours that, on the whole, we will enjoy a greater sum of liberty by accepting a compromise and substituting for a theoretical absolute liberty a practical relative liberty to do certain things and abstain from others.

In politics, then, the concept of liberty is necessarily relative. It is so with all types of liberty. The liberty of the automobilist materially reduces the liberty of the man on foot.

One sees, therefore, why anarchy, the absence of government, would not be, at least as practiced by such human beings as we know, a régime of liberty, but an odious form of oppression. It is as great an illusion to believe that the government which refrains from any interference necessarily favors freedom; noninterference may become an accomplice of tyranny. If we enjoy some individual freedom, it is because a vast system of legal restrictions holds back the pack of opposing wills.

The average American realizes the truth of this contention in the political order, but he is likely to part company with us when we enter the economic field. He is willing enough to concede the practical impossibility of unlimited political liberty, for the consequences of such a policy would strike him instantly and directly; but the consequences of unrestricted economic freedom are not as immediate and he may personally escape them.[4] Therefore, he is for a vague economic freedom and fails to see that this freedom is a very one-sided affair. Indeed, it is decidedly to the advantage of the rich. It is not freedom for the poor, as freedom is not simply the theoretical right to be free but as well the power to be free. That power, however, frequently is lost by the worker because he cannot truly choose between two alternatives when one of the two is misery and starvation.

Notwithstanding the shocking industrial abuses still existing, not a few of our fellow citizens continue to look upon the freedom of contract as the best possible agency for securing efficiency and justice. The National Association of Manufacturers at their convention in May, 1924, in New York City, in their Statement of Principles declared: "We cannot surrender our interest in working out these problems [labor and industrial] by the exercise of the largest of individual freedom of contract and employment necessary to achieve the best welfare of both the individual and the nation." Now, that freedom of contract is not any more to be relied upon to secure social justice than a number of individual agreements freely entered into could safely guarantee the political rights of the community.

As unconditioned political liberty would mean the destruction of the state, so would complete economic freedom be the destruction of the economic system. In reality, complete economic freedom never existed long enough to

---

[4] Here is one of the clearest illustrations of that attitude. Apropos of the decision of the Supreme Court declaring the District of Columbia Minimum Wage Act unconstitutional, Charles Cheney, although a progressive New England manufacturer, says with an accent of profound conviction (*The Survey*, May, 1923): "Unquestionably the enactment of minimum wage laws is an abridgment of the freedom of contract and a very direct interference with personal liberty. . . . There is almost no price too big to pay for the maintenance of this principle of liberty and freedom of action." Thousands of his fellow employers hold fast to the same philosophy.

bring forth its logical results, for soon after coming into operation it had already caused so much misery that it had to be limited.

There are, therefore, few informed men who to-day oppose all forms of labor legislation. The history of the nineteenth century has taught us what evils may flow from unrestricted economic freedom.[5] In every industrial country, the state has found it necessary to interfere.[6] The illusions of our ancestors of the eighteenth century are no longer permitted. Our experience has been particularly conclusive in regard to the employment of children. Hence, the majority of capitalists declare that they no longer object, in principle, to laws regulating child labor.

Thereupon some have thought that the case of labor legislation was won for good. But the conversion of many employers is only apparent. First of all, even in relation to child labor, they oppose all kinds of hindrances to the honest enforcement of the law. They will hold fast to their theory, that it is wrong for the state to interfere because thereby force is substituted for private initiative and because the state has demonstrated its inability to regulate wisely industrial relations.[7] They tolerate child-labor legislation but only as an exception because the child is really incompetent to enter into an intelligent agreement and to protect his interests through bargaining. They firmly deny, however, the validity of that principle in relation to adult workers, men and women, on the ground that here legislation would be an undue interference with the freedom of contract.[8]

---

[5] Engels, *Condition of the Working Class in England in 1844;* Toynbee, *Condition of English Wage Earners in 1760;* Taylor, *The Modern Factory System;* Webb, *The Case for the Factory Acts.*

[6] B. G. de Montgomery, *British and Continental Labor Policy,* London, 1922, pp. 147-148 and *passim.*

[7] Special Report No. 12 of National Industrial Conference Board, "Should the State Interfere in the Determination of Wage Rates?"

[8] *Cf.* "The Minimum Wage Law," *The Survey,* May, 1923.

We have already shown the fallacy involved in that supposed freedom of contract. We should like, at this juncture, briefly to point out that the protection of labor through legislation rests upon a principle which holds good equally in the case of men, women, and children.[9]

Every man has the right to live, but to live does not mean simply physical existence. It means to live a truly human life. It so happens, however, that the conditions which the worker must at times accept are such that he cannot live that human life. He becomes thereby unable, although theoretically endowed with all the rights that a progressive democracy affords, to discharge his obligations either toward himself or toward his family. Is it not evident that in such cases wisdom and justice demand the intervention of the state, whatever be the hostility of the employer or the indifference of the worker? To think otherwise would be to prepare the subversion of our entire social organization, for these wage earners would gradually be reduced to a condition little short of slavery.

It must not be forgotten, moreover, that the general interests of the nation are just as truly threatened as the rights of workers by the abuses which arise under a régime of laissez faire. The strength and wealth of a nation is made of the vigor of its composing units, individuals and families, for, in the words of Ruskin, "the only wealth is life." It is, therefore, nothing less than suicide for a nation to tolerate industrial conditions which undermine the health, morality, and efficiency of its members.

Again, no one ignores the disastrous social results flowing from the unrestricted and uncontrolled employment of children.[10] We would be ashamed to oppose openly child-labor legislation, but employers and capitalists fail to fol-

[9] Paul Pic, *Législation Industrielle*, Paris, 1922, pp. 471*ff*.
[10] Hannah R. Sewall, "Child Labor in the United States," *Bulletin* No. 52, United States Bureau of Labor.

low this principle to its logical conclusion. There is a flagrant inconsistency in protecting children and abandoning men and women to their fate. To assume to protect the child without protecting the mother is an offense against reason. There can be no efficient protection of the child which does not extend to the mother, to the actual mother and to the potential one, that is, practically to all women.

On the other hand, what wisdom is there in assuring the physical and intellectual education of the child at a great cost, but to allow his strength to be sapped and wasted by excessive and unsanitary labor ten years later, and to deny him the necessary leisure for the further development of his mind and heart?

There is, then, a minimum which the proper understanding of the fundamental interests of society will demand for adults as well as for children. It is that minimum which has been called a national minimum. To insure respect for that national minimum will ever be the duty of our governments. However, it is not an obligation which can be discharged once for all; as this minimum is, of its nature, necessarily variable, it must be a ceaseless adaptation of our laws to changing standards of life and conditions of general prosperity.

Even the opponents of labor legislation do not deny the existence of unfortunate industrial conditions, but they expect a greater improvement from the free play of economic forces than from state intervention. The economic history of the last hundred years forbids us to share their confidence. Why did the law interfere in the nineteenth century in England, in Prussia, in France, in Austria? Was it simply in response to the appeal of theorists? Certainly not. The governments interfered because they discovered shocking and dangerous abuses in no wise remedied but daily aggravated by the play of blind economic forces. And where the governments failed to intervene, the abuses persisted. In Belgium, during the greater part of the nineteenth century, the government refused to regulate labor. As a result, abuses continued until 1889, abuses almost as serious as those which necessitated labor legislation in England in the beginning of the century.[11]

One may acknowledge that in some cases the initiative of a farseeing and generous employer will give his labor fair and acceptable terms. But, speaking broadly, experience has demonstrated beyond all doubt that social reform cannot be left to the good will of employers. Indeed, private initiative is quite powerless. Many years ago, for instance, physicians and moralists began denouncing the evils of night work, particularly for women, and still at the beginning of the twentieth century, private initiative had failed to suppress it.

The industrial prosperity of England and of the United States has been appealed to in support of the contention that higher standards of labor, in the long run, mean also a more efficient economic system and that, therefore, employers moved by self-interest, will of themselves improve the conditions of labor. True as are the premises, the inference is not verified in practice. The more immediate result of the progressive policy of an individual employer is not always prosperity for his enterprise; it may even mean failure in periods of keen competition. And so it happens that the individual employer, no matter how kindly disposed, cannot assume the initiative in costly reforms, for, unless the law intervenes to make these reforms binding upon all, we shall see the patriotic and humane employer penalized for his idealism.

The adversary of state legislation reminds us also that whatever the employer will not freely concede, the workers through their powerful associations can wrest from Capital without the intervention of the state. Although we grant

---

[11] Raoul Jay, *La protection légale des travailleurs*, Paris, p. 31.

that much of the economic inequality which formerly rendered the freedom of contract illusory has been done away with through the organization of Labor, still this new industrial struggle is not the ideal means of securing the desired reforms. First of all, labor unions do not enroll the majority of workers; they often make unwarranted demands, adopt unwise policies. Then, their activity determines a similar organization of Capital in national and international federations. We have thus two large armies facing each other, frequently animated with a spirit of hatred and distrust, and not particularly sensitive to the moral character of their actions. The settlements resulting from such a conflict are not likely to be more equitable than the terms of peace ordinarily imposed by the victor upon the vanquished.

Labor organizations alone, in spite of their strength and influence, cannot wisely guard or efficiently protect the rights of the workers.[12] The English trade-unions and the French syndicates realized long ago that they could not successfully carry on the fight without the help of the state. The British Industrial Conference of 1919 illustrated this fact. Representatives of the employers and trade-unions of all the manufacturing industries drew up a national scheme for a forty-eight-hour week, but in order that it might be binding on all alike they demanded that it should be given legal effect by Parliament.

There remains little doubt, therefore, that to oppose labor legislation, to restrict it to the protection of minors and hinder its enforcement, is materially to retard social progress.

Before acting upon our own convictions, however, it is well briefly to consider the main solutions economic thinkers have offered for this ever actual problem and see the position we occupy in the field of economic theory.

---

[12] *Cf.* B. G. de Montgomery, *op. cit.*, Chaps. IV, XIV, XV.

Two general conceptions have dominated the interpretation of economic phenomena since the end of the eighteenth century, namely the liberal [13] and the socialistic.

The Physiocrats of the eighteenth century had considered the economic life of nations as a natural phenomenon subject to laws superior and anterior to those of the legislators. Those laws, like unto the physical laws, we should discover and respect without interfering with their action. The interests of the laborer and the employer are in harmony, not in conflict, and this harmony is more likely to be realized and to bring forth its fruit if the state allows the economic forces free play. Thus thought Adam Smith and Spencer. Let individual freedom act: it always and everywhere is the best qualified agent to give us the maximum of utility and justice. The happiness of men depends on them alone; it is through their own initiative, their perseverant efforts that they will add to and maintain their well-being. History shows that state intervention has always been inefficient, despotic, and arbitrary. On the whole, the Liberal School of economic theory, the partisans of laissez faire, espoused the same doctrine.

The Socialists would believe, on the contrary, that the social order is a human institution, deliberately brought about. The Socialist is not interested in economic freedom because for him that freedom, without equality, is deception. He looks upon the two concepts as complementary; one cannot go without the other and retain any meaning. He hopes to realize this equality through the collective ownership of the instruments of production. In a word, he would solve the conflict between Capital and Labor by removing one of the belligerents. While he awaits the economic revolution, the law should force the employers to

---

[13] "Liberal" here used again in the sense defined on page 1. What is spoken of on the Continent as the Liberal School is more generally referred to in English-speaking countries as the Manchester School.

agree to these concessions which justice should move them to make, but which the fear of competition causes them to deny.

While we recognize the partial truth contained in these warring theories, we are neither as dogmatic as our ancestors nor as confident as modern reformers about economic formulas of too absolute a character. On the one hand, we know that we can improve upon nature, that we can counteract her malignant tendencies and harness her beneficent powers; and, on the other, we have grown skeptical about the ability of the masses to reconstruct, through an emotional uprising, anything as intricate as a fair and working system of production, exchange, and distribution. We believe in evolution, in motion, in adaptation, not in stagnation, or turmoil. Laissez faire and Socialism have appeared, therefore, equally unsatisfactory, and the school which seems to have rallied the largest number of suffrages is the Interventionistic School, that of the doctrine of state intervention.

Interventionism,[14] the regulation by the state of these economic relations which Capital and Labor fail to adjust in due time, does not pretend to solve the question of economic equality, which men have tried to settle since the dawn of civilization, an apparently insoluble problem. They simply wish to substitute for the order of nature, which is the ideal of the economists of the old Liberal School, a legal order morally and practically superior.

Interventionism is a policy equally distant from the two dangerous currents of thought alluded to above: Individualism and Socialism. Its opposition to Liberalism or laissez faire is obvious enough, but it is necessary to bring out clearly the radical difference that exists between Interventionism and Socialism, for many fear Intervention-

---

[14] Paul Pic, *op. cit.*, pp. 20-45; Richard T. Ely, *Outlines of Economics*, Macmillan, 1923, Chaps. VI, XII.

ism as leading to Socialism. Socialists and Collectivists look upon all social legislation as steps towards the social-ization of the means of production; they are essentially revolutionary. Either through force or through gradual reform, they hope to bring about a radical change of the present social structure. The Interventionists, on the con-trary, are opposed to any violent overthrow of the actual régime; they are not even contemplating a substantial modification of it. They are really conservative people and believe that the only way to preserve the present eco-nomic system is by timely concessions to Labor.

The duty of the legislator placed between eminent repre-sentatives of these two schools is delicate and difficult to fulfill. The conciliation of the freedom demanded by the Liberals and of the equality advocated by Socialists, is an arduous task. But fortunately, the legislator was not permitted to spend his time working out a theoretical recon-ciliation of these conflicting doctrines. Facts stared him in the face, irrefutable facts crying aloud for a solution, and Interventionism was the only palliative in sight. For, facts are stronger than theories and the evolution of the life of the people carries with it the evolution of doctrines.

In the presence of threatening social conflicts and phys-ical and moral degradation, the state realized that the easy doctrine of nonintervention was no longer wise. The coun-tries which first saw that need and resolutely entered into a policy of labor legislation had no occasion to regret it. The proof of it is found in a comparison between the in-dustrial prosperity of states, like England and Germany, who before the War had frankly gone into the protection of labor, and those, like Spain, who had not. Although the various states have proceeded differently, some like Belgium, acting with great caution, others like Australia, fairly falling into Socialism, the theory which has influ-enced all these governments is Interventionism.

The truth of the proceeding is made manifest by the rapid growth of legislation. Born with the capitalistic system, it has grown apace with it. For as soon as the old corporative system broke down, almost immediately there appeared laws for the protection of labor.

Labor legislation originated in England right after the great Industrial Revolution of the eighteenth century, with the advent of the machine and the factory. From the day in which the régime of absolute freedom extended to labor contracts, it gave rise to evils so flagrant that the public conscience protested. The first law was this modest Act of Parliament of 1802 which forbade children, some of whom were six years old, to work more than twelve hours a day.[15] It remained a dead letter until 1833, when state inspectors independent of the local authorities were appointed.

As England had preceded the other nations in industrialism, she preceded them in legal protection. On the Continent, the first labor law, a law regulating child labor, was passed in Prussia in 1839. In France the writings of Villermé gave the alarm. The first child law was enacted in March, 1841. Then came the two decrees of 1848, one of which limited to twelve hours the working day of adults in factories. Thereafter, labor legislation extended rapidly the sphere of its competence. We might pass in review all the prominent industrial countries and show that gradually this legislative movement spread to all states, those of the Old World as well as those of the New, and to all forms of industrial activity.

In the presence of this sometimes exuberant growth, we would not leave the reader under the impression that all of the labor legislation thus far enacted is an unmixed blessing. We are not oblivious of its shortcomings. Legis-

---

[15] Hutchins and Harrison, *History of Factory Legislation*, London, 1903, p. 5.

lation also remains a product of human nature and betrays the imperfections of its origin. Labor legislation is extraordinarily rich in contents; it is not so rich in guiding principles. It seems to be frequently in doubt as to its goal, at least on two points: the share to leave respectively to the state and to free associations of workers and employers in the reform of the conditions of labor, and the nature and limitations of property rights. There is urgency for a little careful thinking along these lines.

Thus the sociological and economic basis of legislation should be carefully analyzed and our conclusions should be periodically revised as we proceed with our labor laws. We must avoid waste and duplication in our political organization and not strive to secure, at a great cost, reforms which men can bring about without the assistance of the state. For the welfare of all, we must also keep our economic organization a going concern, and therefore abstain from any political measures which tend towards a confiscation of capital and a depressing curtailment of the rights of the individual in the immediate enjoyment of the fruits of his labor. The claims of labor legislation must broadly remain within the actual limits of economic possibility.[16] Social and labor legislation are necessary, but they must not become the unlimited and indiscriminating pressure of the mass upon the individual, that is, ultimately upon the élite, these few so indispensable to progress because they initiate, discover, and dare. No intervention should be permitted which is not clearly commended by justice.

Convinced as we are of the necessity of state intervention, we should heed the warning of a distinguished French sociologist: "Will not the destiny of our children be to see the conflict between a liberal democracy and a social

---

[16] Cf. Professor I. P. de Vooys, "Labor Legislation and Economic Possibilities," *International Labor Review,* February and March, 1923.

democracy contemptuous of every personal right and which after having subdued a crude and irrational economic anarchism, will bring about for the future a new Cæsarism, more tyrannical and debilitating than the later Roman Empire?''[17] Unless, then, we remain within the limits of a well reasoned and judiciously controlled legal activity, we must witness the appearance of an economic system incompatible with all political and moral autonomy, the enemy of self-government and of true democracy.

While giving the philosophical and sociological basis for labor legislation, showing its growth and pointing to some of its dangerous tendencies, we have not distinguished between national and international legislation, for they are both substantially justified by the same arguments. As a matter of fact, international labor legislation has become an indispensable complement of the other. It may be difficult to proceed much further in national and state legislation, or it may become dangerous and ruinous to do so, without promoting international labor legislation. It is likely also that the growth of the latter will strengthen the position of the former. For instance, international agreements will eliminate the principal objection of manufacturers against labor legislation, as it will deprive them of the arguments drawn from the consequences of international competition.

Some economists, however, do not share that opinion and have taken the stand that international labor legislation is not really necessary in order to secure an improvement of labor conditions. They hold that much has already been done in that direction through purely national action and without recourse to international arrangements. They question whether the lack of factory legislation in a foreign country really acts as a justifiable hindrance to such legis-

---

[17] Gaston Richard, *La question sociale et le mouvement philosophique au XIXème siècle*, Paris, 1914, p. 346.

lation in one's own country. As a proof of their contention they point to England, who has not been prevented from developing her labor legislation by the fact that many of her competitors lag behind her in this respect.

It is no doubt possible to improve labor conditions to a certain point through national legislation. It may be possible for a country who, like England, was first in the industrial field and had built up an unquestioned industrial supremacy, to disregard labor conditions abroad. Her acquired superiority in industrial, financial, and commercial organization, her wealth in natural resources indispensable to modern production, her supply of skilled labor, may enable her to overlook certain losses because of the larger gains she can reasonably anticipate. The question reduces itself finally into a problem of comparative costs.

The law of comparative costs holds that, unless there are artificial hindrances, goods tend to be produced within the countries in which there is a comparative advantage over other countries in regard to the same goods. Now, these comparative advantages may be of many kinds. Agriculturally, for instance, climate and soil conditions confer advantages in the growing of such commodities as wheat or oranges. Greece cannot compete with Roumania in wheat growing, and France cannot compete with Spain in producing the citrous fruits. Again, although Great Britain has both a soil and a climate favorable to the growth of cereals, it has too great an advantage in regard to the development of industry, owing to the contiguity of coal and iron, to make it worth while to attempt competition with Canada and the Dakotas in the production of wheat.

In the raising or manufacture of these things in which a country enjoys a decided advantage, she can well afford to improve the conditions of the labor engaged in these occupations until the cost of that improvement offsets the natural advantage she possesses. But when that level is

reached, then, it would seem that she could no
afford to disregard the standards of labor of the actua
potential competitive countries.

At this point, however, another factor intervenes.
we assume that labor is constant in regard to quality, the
of course, a difference in labor conditions will cause a
corresponding difference in advantage or disadvantage so
far as production is concerned. For the country with the
more expensive labor conditions will naturally suffer from
competition with the country whose labor is cheaper. This,
however, is not always the case. For the productive capacity of the cheaper labor is seldom equal to that of the
dearer. Labor cost is a resultant of the combination of
labor rates with labor productivity and the true comparison, therefore, is not that of either labor rates or conditions
of labor, but of labor cost.

Can we then grant that improved labor conditions increasing the productivity of labor will make up the difference between the cost of production in high-standard countries and low-standard countries? We can to a certain
degree, but a point may be reached at which the low-
standard country may undersell the high-standard country. In that case the high-standard country may be stimu-
lated to greater efforts toward a more perfect technique
of production, a better organization, and more economical
management, but, if these fail wholly or in part, *there is
for her no other policy than either to reduce her labor
standards or through some form of international action
to bring about a raising of labor standards in the competing countries.*

It may appear, therefore, that international labor legislation is the device on the part of advanced industrial
countries virtually to force upon backward countries higher
labor standards in order to safeguard themselves against
low-cost competition in these backward countries. In a

way that is true, but thus stated it may be misleading. The primary purpose of international labor legislation is not to eliminate some countries as competitors, but to eliminate them as unfair competitors, as competitors dangerous to the welfare not only of rival nations but as equally destructive of their own well-being. It is not commercial ruin of the backward countries that the more advanced nations seek, but the protection of their own artisans and of the human race as a whole. There is in this attempt an intermingling of economic and sociological motives, but all quite praiseworthy.

Upon this entire controversy additional light will be thrown by the history of the movement for international labor legislation as it will reveal the causes which prompted international action in the regulation of labor conditions.

Against international legislation, there is another objection which in the minds of many retains considerable force. It is that such legislation is an unwarranted attack upon the sovereignty of the state, that the state is the sole judge of what is necessary or useful or expedient within its frontiers, and that no authority superior to it must be recognized which either directly, through laws, or indirectly through moral pressure, should force it into adopting policies which are not the result of the free deliberation of the official representatives of the nation.

This is an objection we have partly met elsewhere [18] and which will invariably arise in dealing with most cases of international relations. It will then behoove us to find a satisfactory formula which, while not infringing upon the essential prerogatives of national sovereignty, will open up the widest range of international coöperation and permit the enactment of international laws which may some day, strange as it may seem now, prove the strongest support and safeguard of that very nationality and sovereignty

---

[18] *Cf*. Chap. II, pp. 24, 25.

we so jealously protect. For, a Socialistic or Bolshevistic régime would be more disastrous to our traditional conception of nationality and sovereignty than any program of international legislation.

But a generation ago, the expression "international labor law" was hardly in use. To-day it is heard in the courts and the universities. To judges and professors there seemed at first to be some impropriety in associating interternational law, the consecrated reserve of higher diplomacy, with the commonplace grievances of the miner and factory operative. Now they recognize that the labor question has its place in international law. "Behold the emigrant workman, the crippled of the factory, the injured and poisoned by dangerous industrial processes, the woman and the child, which enter the gilded conference rooms of diplomats and demand a hearing as they have demanded it of all governments, of all political parties, of all statesmen at home." [19]

Labor issues have penetrated already all the divisions of national law and procedure; how could they be ignored by international law? It is true that strictly speaking there is as yet no international labor legislation. No legal enactments for the protection of labor have ever been so generally accepted as to be invested with the authority of international laws. There are already, however, treaties and conventions which bid fair to fulfill very soon the conditions of international obligations.

A codification of international labor laws now in the making would not be as difficult as it may seem at first, for there is a growing similarity between the labor laws of the various countries. There is a much greater resemblance than we find, for instance, in civil legislation. This is principally due to the fact that labor legislation is of much

---

[19] Ernest Mahaim, *Le droit international ouvrier*, Paris, 1913, p. 2.

more recent date and that it was conceived under influences which are very much alike in the various countries.

What is the attitude of the representatives of the various economic schools, referred to above, toward international labor legislation? The Socialists will evidently support it, but it is obvious that they cannot look upon it as the end of their activities. According to their own utterances, in the Berne Conference, for example, "the degradation of the laboring classes pursued by Capitalism cannot be stopped completely except by the abolition of capitalistic production itself. But, meanwhile, it can be mitigated by the opposition of Labor and by State intervention."

Be that as it may, there is no reason why it should prevent those who reject Socialism from giving their support to international labor legislation, for, we are convinced that one of the most efficient ways to ward off Socialism and Communism is constantly to improve the lot of the workers.

The followers of the Liberal School, or laissez faire, on the other hand, think it an undue interference not only with individual liberty but with national sovereignty as well. We have already attempted to allay their fears.

In the case of the United States, there is another aspect of the problem well worth considering. We, in America, are very proud of the civilization we have developed. We wish to guard against any servile imitation of other nations. We have confidence in our national genius which has already accomplished so much along paths not traveled by others heretofore, and we must continue. The United States may be said to have its own industrial philosophy.[20] Generally, Americans believe in the open shop, in direct negotiations between the employer and his employees, and not in collective bargaining through trade-union representatives; they believe in a minimum of state interference

---

[20] For fuller development of this idea *cf.* Chap. IX.

and of state ownership, and attribute to this industrial philosophy the unprecedented growth of their nation.

Whatever we think of the truth of that claim, it cannot be denied that new conditions have arisen, for which solutions must be found and old conditions must be met in new ways. Those solutions, however, must not be imposed from without but adapted to the particular character of our people. We must, indeed, draw inspiration from the past, learn also from the present, but we must preserve our own personality and devote to the unfolding of it our highest energies. America has certain well defined ideals of individual and social well-being; those we must cultivate, and the pride and joy of an increasingly larger number must be to enrich the lives of our people, through the actual possession and appreciation of all that American standards imply.

But we can see no hindrance to the pursuance of such a policy arising from international labor legislation, because we are leading the world in standards of general well-being,[21] and, far from being controlled by other countries, it is we who are likely to influence them. It will be replied that cases may arise which would be attempts to impose on us practices contrary to our own traditions. As far as we know, the best way to prevent such an occurrence is to take part in the deliberations of such bodies as the International Labor Organization. The case, at any rate, is very unlikely, and there are ways of meeting that difficulty, should it ever arise.

Many, therefore, have lately been won to a policy of international labor legislation because they have reached the

---

[21] This statement is not inconsistent with the fact that the United States is relatively backward in labor legislation for the benefit of the working classes. The general well-being attended to is not the result of a more progressive industrial policy than that of Europe but a consequence of the general prosperity of the entire country due to the abundance of natural resources, the application of science to industry and agriculture and other causes.

conviction that it is in no way a fad, a legal luxury, but a growing necessity. They deem it necessary to make national legislation efficient and less dangerous to business. It is necessary to avoid further turmoil the world over. According to them, the value of such legislation is to prevent renewed revolutionary outbursts in Europe, to spare even Asia the terrible and wasteful struggle between Capital and Labor, which Europe has already witnessed, and which has so fundamentally disturbed our economic prosperity, perhaps to save western civilization, for, if Asia were to run amuck in the spirit of Russia, what would become of all our boasted culture and prosperity? If, in due time, some social justice had been brought to the Russian masses the appalling waste in the empire of the czars might have been avoided.

It is folly to think that if violence is advocated as the means of overcoming the indifference of the ruling classes to the welfare of Labor, it will never be resorted to. Those who maintain that the Russian Revolution can be explained by the temperament of the Russians and their inferior stage of development, are not entirely right if they deduce from it that similar upheavals are not to be feared elsewhere. Beware of the wiles of the politicians, the exaltation of reformers, and the credulity of the crowds. Such violence may occur anywhere and under frightful forms. It is not deliberately wanted and pursued at first, but once started, it may be impossible to direct its evolution. It was beyond imagining in Soviet Russia; it could be more terrible still in countries with a more advanced economic organization.

The advocates of international labor legislation do not mean to put the entire burden of social reform upon the state or the employer. The working classes cannot be happy and prosperous unless they practice the fundamental virtues of honest labor, thrift, and temperance, but the duty of society is to supply them with that indispensable minimum which will make these virtues easier in the long run.

It would be an evidence of simplicity to attach an excessive importance to legislation. "Legislation in itself will never solve the industrial problem. Its solution can be brought about only by the introduction of a new spirit in industry, the spirit of coöperation and brotherhood." [22] True, legislation is not a cure-all, but it is a valuable help, it is a great moral support to the weak and the oppressed. We are aware of the dictum, "The more education, the less legislation," but we also know that it is through legislation that education is made possible and productive.

---

[22] John D. Rockefeller, Jr., *International Labor Review*, Vol. XI, No. 1.

CHAPTER IV

HISTORY OF INTERNATIONAL LABOR LEGISLATION

LABOR legislation was the result of the anxiety caused by the disastrous consequences of a policy of laissez faire. In order to protect the worker, however, without injuring the employer it was imperative to have the labor laws honestly enforced within the confines of a whole nation, otherwise one set of producers, and perhaps the least deserving, would be favored to the other's detriment. Labor legislation tends to become national as soon as producers begin to sell to a nation-wide market.

Likewise, as soon as that market extends to the world, we begin, for the same reasons, to realize the need of international legislation. Buying and selling do not assume international proportions, however, until adequate means of transportation and communication have been developed. This development, we know, took place during the second half of the nineteenth century. It is during that period, therefore, that we shall witness the growth of the movement for international labor legislation.

PIONEERS IN INTERNATIONAL LEGISLATION

The first statesman who seemed to have understood that the protection of labor is an international question, was Necker, the French statesman and financier of Louis XVI. In his book called, *The Importance of Religious Opinions,* published in 1788, Necker states, speaking of Sunday rest, that this institution cannot be successfully maintained unless it be universally observed. "If one nation gives up Sunday rest, competition will force the other countries to do likewise." The fact that Sunday rest disappeared in all industrial countries at the time when industrialism was triumphant, shows that Necker had reasoned rightly.[1]

The first to uphold consistently and openly that the protection of labor, if it wishes to be free from the depressing influence of competition, must become international, was Robert Owen (1771-1858). He rightly deserves the title of pioneer of international labor legislation. It is not surprising that Robert Owen should have been among the very first to understand the importance of that movement. He was a manufacturer, a Christian, and a philosopher. As a manufacturer, he had the opportunity to witness the evils caused by industrialism; as a Christian, he was inspired by motives of sympathy for the poor; and as a philosopher, he could readily see the necessity of extending such measures to the whole world, if they were to be really effective.

The main features of his social program were good housing, the education of the young, insurance against illness and old age, and the fostering of habits of order, cleanliness, thrift, and temperance. He ceaselessly emphasized the importance of environment, much though he may have exaggerated it, and he realized that the leisure of the working people and the intelligent use of it was as vital a problem as work itself, for it affects directly quality and quantity of work. At least until the year 1817, when he developed Socialistic and Communistic theories, we cannot but admire the value of his contributions. "Crude as was his social philosophy, he was a pathfinder who had a vision for the realities of modern industrial life when they were dim, strange and unknown to his contemporaries."[2] For

---

[1] *Cf.* André de Maday, *La charte internationale du travail*, Paris, 1921, p. 16.
[2] B. L. Hutchins, *Robert Owen, Social Reformer*, p. 24.

Americans, he is of special interest because of his attempts to work out his social theories in the United States, and because his four sons became very creditable citizens of our country.

A firm believer in education, he organized a model school at New Lanark for the children of his factory. In the course of his opening address, he said: "I like to forget these imaginary divisions and differences that frontiers draw between peoples. Could a reasonable person tell us why one section of humanity should be destined to hate and destroy the other?"[3] According to him, the advantages of protective legislation must by no means be limited to one country.

About 1815, Owen began to turn his attention to measures of a public character which would improve the condition of the operatives employed in the rapidly growing textile industry. In 1818, the Bill on the Employment of Children in Factories had been read twice in the House of Commons and was to be read a third time. Owen wrote an open letter to Lord Liverpool, then Prime Minister, in support of the measure: "Security," he said, "can now be found only in that system of policy which regards the proper training, education and advantageous employment of the working classes, as the primary objects of government."[4]

In 1818, we find him in Lausanne, Fribourg, and the Swiss cities. In September, 1828, he went to Frankfort and there wrote to all the governments his "Memorial on Behalf of the Working Classes." He held that "the dominion of wealth and the evils arising from the desire to acquire and

---

[3] An address delivered to the inhabitants of New Lanark on January, 1, 1816, at the opening of the institutions established for the formation of character. *The Life of Robert Owen*, written by himself, Vol. V, p. 333.

[4] Robert Owen, *Observations on the Effect of the Manufacturing System*, London, 1818, p. 25.

accumulate riches are on the point of terminating. In consequence, the dominion of Ignorance, of Fraud and Violence is also on the point of terminating.''[5] These results, he believed, could be better secured through an understanding between governments.

In October, 1818, he sent his well-known "Memorial" to the delegates of the Holy Alliance at Aix-la-Chapelle. Therein, he described the consequences of the Industrial Revolution for the working classes and the gratifying results obtained at New Lanark. He was "most desirous of cordially uniting the Governments and the People in those measures which he is ready to prove ought now to be put in practice for the interests of both.''[6]

It is said that Frederick William III of Prussia expressed his satisfaction to Owen. But the soul of the Holy Alliance, Friedrich von Geutz, would have replied: ''We have no wish to see the masses become prosperous and independent of us, how could we then control them?''[7] Was it this cynical remark which cooled Owen's enthusiasm? At any rate, during the remaining forty years of his life he never again approached foreign powers. The strong political reaction which followed the fall of Napoleon must have discouraged many similar efforts.

Moreover, Owen's message was no doubt premature. Before international protection could become a reality, it was necessary that every country develop a measure of national legislation. His pleas remained entirely unheeded and were soon forgotten. It has taken the work of scholars to bring them to light again.

Owen's appeal completely failed to convince his fellow citizens. Somehow his oft repeated pleas fell on deaf ears.

---

[5] Robert Owen, *Two Memorials on Behalf of the Working Classes*, London, 1818, p. 7.

[6] *Ibid.*, p. 25.

[7] Stephan Bauer, *Geschichtliche Motive des Internationalen Arbeiterschutzes*, p. 183.

England was indeed interested in labor legislation, but she had taken the lead in manufacture and had little to fear from foreign competition. Hence the principal stimulus to the creation of an international outlook in labor legislation was wanting. For, in accepting international agreements a nation inevitably sacrifices a measure of sovereignty; she accepts a certain degree of inspection, supervision, and control, and no nation could be willing to make that sacrifice unless there were offered her corresponding compensations. These compensations, in the form of protection against foreign competition, did not appeal to England at that time as she had no competition to fear.

It is not surprising, therefore, that the next demand for international legislation came from France. France in her endeavor to compete with England was forced into tolerating conditions of labor which were shocking in the extreme. In 1835, Louis Villermé (1782-1863) had undertaken, upon the request of the Academy of Moral and Political Science, an investigation in the conditions of the textile industry. His report,[8] now famous, is a heartbreaking tale of misery and oppression. The abuses of that industrial period are too well known to detain us here, but the contribution of Villermé, which is of particular interest to us, is the conclusion he arrives at that no permanent improvement of labor conditions is possible without international coöperation.

Villermé says in substance: "The individual proprietor of a mill is powerless whenever he has to meet competition. All the manufacturers, not only of his own locality, but also of the countries which trade in the same markets, should combine with him to stop the evil which alarms us, instead of exploiting it. Naturally, we could not well expect that

[8] Villermé, *Tableau de l'état physique et moral des ouvriers employés dans les manufactures de coton, de laine et de soie,* Paris, 1840.

degree of disinterestedness; no class of men heretofore has given such an example." [9]

Robert Owen and Villermé, although earnestly endeavoring to awaken the interest of European rulers and employers in the international protection of labor, had not arrived at a conviction of the necessity of doing so through international treaties. The first one to originate that idea was the French economist, Adolphe Blanqui.[10]

In his lectures on "Industrial Economy," given at the Sorbonne in 1838, referring to labor legislation, Blanqui declared:

This reform so just, so necessary, is not as easy to bring about as it seems to those who see merely the present plight of the working class for its first fruit may be a deadly one; it may bring about, through foreign competition the enforced idleness and therefore the starvation of those who so far have been able to survive. There is but one way of bringing it about: it is to secure its adoption by all the industrial countries which compete with each other. Heretofore, the Powers have signed treaties binding them to kill men, why could they not draw up modern agreements to preserve and enrich human life? [11]

The efforts of Robert Owen and the suggestions of Blanqui proved fruitless. Their theories were upheld with greater success by an Alsatian manufacturer, Daniel Legrand.[12] Convinced of the necessity of state intervention in labor problems, Legrand proposed to the French govern-

9 Cited by Stephan Bauer, *op. cit.*, p. 95; *Vierteljahrschrift für Sozial und Wirtschaftsgeschichte*, 1903.

10 Jérôme Adolphe Blanqui, the brother of the famous Socialist Louis Blanqui, but by no means a Socialist, professor of political economy at the Conservatoire des Arts et Métiers in Paris.

11 Adolphe Blanqui, *Cours d'économie industrielle*, 2d. ed., 1839, pp. 119-120.

12 Nicolas Krautchenko, "Un précurseur du droit international ouvrier," *Revue générale de droit international public*, February and March, 1910. For a complete account of Legrand's influence see S. Bauer, *Geschichtliche Motive des internationalen Arbeiterschutzes*, pp. 79-104; also L. Mahaim, *Le droit international ouvrier*, Paris, 1913, pp. 190-196.

ment the adoption of a law similar to the English law of 1838, protecting children and young people employed in the textile industry. It was in trying to win public opinion to the support of that measure that he arrived at the conclusion of the inevitableness of an international protection of labor. In his request, directed to Germany and Switzerland in 1840, he said that national protection of labor could not be sufficiently effective, and that a collective understanding between industrial nations was a necessity. In 1841, Legrand appeals, in the name of the manufacturers of Mulhouse, to the French government to request that an international congress take up the question of the protection of labor. But this petition to the French government and to foreign powers remained unanswered.

Thereafter, he welcomes every opportunity to spread the idea of international protection. The child-labor law of 1841 had not been enforced for want of efficient penalties. Legrand writes to Guizot, Prime Minister, requesting him to take the initiative of international regulation.

The following year, in 1845, France had signed a treaty with England for the abolition of slave traffic. Legrand appealed to Guizot, again begging him to abolish as well the slavery of the whites. If France and England could coöperate to build the Suez Canal, they could coöperate to reduce the length of the working day. No results were obtained. Then Legrand turned toward Great Britain and sent his project of international legislation to Lord Ashley, Sir Robert Peel, and Lord John Russell. But England was going ahead alone in her labor legislation and in 1847 she enacted the ten-hour law regarding women in textile industries.

The economic crisis of 1847 and the awakening of Socialism seemed to Legrand favorable opportunities to resume his propaganda. He wrote a new memorandum entitled, "Respectful appeal to the Governments of France, England, Prussia, the States of Germany and Switzerland to request them to enact particular laws and international agreements intended to protect the laborer against premature and excessive labor, principal cause of his physical deterioration, of his moral breakdown and of the debasement of his family life.'' But the Revolution of February, 1848, blasted the hopes of Legrand.

He then appealed, in 1853, on two different occasions to Prussia, but was told that the government's first duty was to safeguard the interests of the fatherland.

Two years later, during the World's Fair at Paris, Legrand approached again the principal industrial countries, proposing a program of labor legislation containing among other measures the following: a twelve-hour working day, Sunday rest, no night work for young men under eighteen nor for women and girls of all ages, no employment of boys under ten, nor of girls under twelve years of age, compulsory primary education, an eight-hour day for miners, regulation of unhealthy or dangerous industrial processes.[13]

This was the last attempt of Legrand, who died in 1859. He was undoubtedly a pioneer in international legislation. His philosophy was broad and human, his vision right. Realizing the value of independent national legislation, he saw clearly that labor legislation would not be fully successful until it became international.

The appeals of the Alsatian manufacturer, like those of the Scottish Utopian were forgotten for many years, but the idea they had so tenaciously defended, lived on. It reappeared over and over again with increasing insistence until the day when the Swiss federal government made it the object of the first official act.

---

[13] "Appel respectueux adressé aux gouvernements des pays industriels dans le but de provoquer une loi internationale sur le travail industriel dont les dispositions seraient à arrêter par leurs délégués réunis en un Congrès à Paris." *Archives diplomatiques*, 2ème série, tome XXXVI, p. 37.

DEVELOPMENTS, 1855-1889

It might prove wearisome if we were to record every public or written reference to the necessity of such legislation during the thirty years following.[14] Of the many we shall recall only the more significant, simply to trace the development of the idea.

One of the most noteworthy efforts in that direction is the report addressed, in 1855, to the Cantonal Council of Zurich by the Canton of Glaris. It suggested an international agreement to regulate the length of the workday, child labor, and like problems, pointing out that the competition between spinners could not be controlled without the creation, by an international understanding, of greater uniformity in conditions of production.[15] Nothing came of the proposal. It is natural enough that Switzerland should have been the first country to promote officially international labor legislation. Being a federal state, in which the cantons enjoy great independence, she felt early the need for intercantonal agreements which, very logically, came to suggest international understandings.

The year following, for the first time, an international body, the Congress of Mutual Benefit Societies, held in Brussels, adopted a resolution in favor of the enactment of international laws for the regulation of labor. The same resolution was adopted a year later at the Congress of Frankfort.

The International Workingmen's Association, founded in London in 1864, and known as the First International, embodied the idea of international labor legislation in its program at its first congress in Geneva, in 1866. Although primarily interested in a violent overturn of the existing

---

[14] For fuller account in English see Frederick Ayusawa, *International Labor Legislation*, Chaps. I, II, and III, New York, 1920.

[15] *Actes de la conférence diplomatique pour la protection ouvrière*, Berne, 1906, p. 9.

economic structure, many were eager to improve the present lot of workers by international agreement.   Therefore, in Geneva, and at all their subsequent meetings, they made the same plea for the recognition of the general principle of international legislation and proposed a list of regulations to be enacted into laws.[16]

In 1868, we even find a well-known representative of the Liberal School, Louis Wolonski, a Polish social economist, professor of law at the University of Paris, accepting the validity of the principle of international regulation, although as yet denying its utility.   "If it were true," he said, "that the nations, in order to maintain a necessary balance of industrial power, were forced to the exploitation of children, women and men in industry, it would be necessary to have recourse to an international understanding to put a stop to such traffic as we put an end to the shocking scandal of slave traffic.   But it does not appear that foreign competition will necessitate such a measure." [17]   It was he, nevertheless, who five years later (1873) entered a resolution before the National Assembly, for the international regulation of labor.

In 1871, Bismarck himself betrayed a certain interest in the problem, although he appeared later on, as a resolute opponent of international protection.   He arranged a conference with Austria to settle social problems; the meeting took place in Berlin, November, 1872, but was without result.[18]

In 1877, the Socialistic Congress of Lyons and, in 1879, the Congress of Christian Manufacturers of Lille, passed similar resolutions.[19]

---

[16] Cf. Morris Hillquit, *History of Socialism in the United States, passim;* Jean Longuet, *Le mouvement socialiste international.*

[17] L. Wolonski, *Le travail des enfants dans les manufactures,* 1868, p. 31.

[18] Ernest Mahaim, *op. cit.,* p. 199.

[19] Chatelain, *La protection internationale ouvrière,* p. 15.

In June, 1876, opening the session of the Swiss Federal Council, the President, Colonel Frey, once minister to the United States, wondered whether it would not be opportune to consider the feasibility of inviting the industrial nations to sign international treaties to regulate labor questions in a uniform manner, and, in 1880, he made a formal motion to that effect. The invitation was sent to the governments of Germany, Austria, Belgium, France, Great Britain, and Italy; the answers were anything but enthusiastic, and because of this coldness the contemplated meeting did not take place.

Thereafter, Socialistic and Labor congresses never cease to agitate for such legislation.

In scientific circles, particularly in Germany, the same question was warmly debated. Well-known professors, like Schoenberg, A. Wagner, Adler, and Brentano, advocated international protection of labor. The Verein für Sozialpolitik took up its discussion but, under the leadership of Professor G. Cohen, professor at the Polytechnikum of Zurich, the majority seemed to oppose the idea. Lorens von Stein spoke favorably, insisting on the point that any labor legislation, which materially increased the cost of production, in order to be fair should be uniform in all countries.

In the French parliament, the eloquent Catholic leader, De Mun, brought it to the Chamber of Deputies in 1884. He urged the government to prepare the adoption of international legislation which would allow every country to protect the worker, his wife and children, without penalizing national industry. Having recalled that formerly the Church was a mediating power respected by all, the official tutor of the young and the weak, he adds, "To-day, the world has turned away from her, who shall then take her place, if not an association of civilized states? We have international conventions to regulate warfare, we have laws for the postal service, why not for the regulation of labor?" [20]

The Paris Municipal Council, March, 1885, passed a similar resolution. And a few months later, the German Catholic Social Party did likewise. In January, 1885, a debate takes place in the Reichstag on the protection of labor and Bismarck opposed any international action as unpractical. The French Chamber of Deputies, in December, 1885, passed favorably upon a proposition containing an elaborate program of international legislation. A little later, the same legislative body supported a motion to the effect that a commission of twenty-two members be appointed to study the question of the protection of labor with a view to concluding international agreements.

The workers, on the other hand, were showing a growing interest in the furtherance of international labor legislation. In 1883, the Swiss Labor Association, the "Grütli," demanded international regulation. In 1884, an International Labor Congress at Roubaix adopted a large program of international labor legislation, containing among other claims an international minimum wage and an eight-hour day. In 1885, the Socialist deputies proposed a bill in the French Chamber to the effect that the French government, after consultation with the Swiss government, urge the foreign powers to discuss at the earliest opportunity the question of international labor legislation. Their program included the following questions: child labor, labor of women and minors, measures for the protection of the life and health of the workers, accident insurance, inspection of mines and factories, maximum workday, weekly rest. It was also proposed for the first time to create an international office in order to collect statistics and study the best

[20] *Discours du Comte de Mun*, III, pp. 123 *ff.;* Max Turmann, "Les origines et les étapes de la législation internationale du travail jusqu'à la Conférence de la Paix," *Le Correspondant*, March, 1919.

means to extend and codify international labor legislation.[21]

In 1886, the German Social-Democratic party enacted a similar proposition. In 1889, the International Socialistic Congress in Paris made the eight-hour day one of their most vital and emphatic claims. After that date, it may be said that every workers' congress included in their resolutions the eight-hour day for women and young people.

The Berlin Conference, 1889

The Swiss Federal Council took the initiative of a preliminary conference to be held in September, 1890, in order to study the possibility of an international agreement upon the following questions: interdiction of Sunday work; minimum age of children employed in industry; maximum of working hours for young people; interdiction of the work of women and children in dangerous occupations; restriction of night work for women and young people; ways of enforcing agreements.

This time, the governments showed themselves more favorably disposed than in 1881; Austria, Hungary, Belgium, France, Luxemburg, the Netherlands, and Portugal signified their willingness to attend the Conference. Russia entered a formal declination. Germany, Denmark, Sweden, and Norway did not reply. The Conference was to meet in Berne on May 5, 1890.

Suddenly, the young Emperor of Germany burst upon the scene. He ordered his ambassadors in France, England, Switzerland, and Belgium to ask these governments whether they were ready to enter into negotiations with him for the study of social questions. He had rightly sensed the situation, for in his rescript to Bismarck he

---

[21] "Débats parlementaires," *Journal officiel de la République Française*, December 7, 1885, p. 177.

said: ". . . The difficulties which oppose themselves to the betterment of the condition of our workers and which result from international competition can be, if not surmounted, at least lessened, in no other way than by the international agreement of the countries which dominate the international market." [22]

Thereupon Switzerland, looking primarily to the success of the undertaking, graciously consented to give up her plans for the Conference. All the European states were invited with the exception of Russia. The Conference was held in Berlin on the 15th of March. Twelve countries were represented. The delegations comprised diplomats, statesmen, manufacturers, engineers, and one workingman.

The debates lasted a fortnight. The following recommendations were agreed upon almost unanimously:

I. *Regulation of work in the mines.* It is desirable that no woman shall be employed and no child under fourteen. In southern countries the limit may be lowered to twelve years. Measures shall be taken for the protection of the health and life of the miners. Arbitration shall be resorted to in order to avoid strikes.

II. *Day of rest.* It is desirable that all workers be given a day of rest every week, and as far as circumstances permit that day should fall on Sunday. Exceptions may be allowed, but should be the result of international agreements.

III. *Child labor.* It is desirable that no child under twelve and in southern countries under ten years of age be employed in industry and that any child shall have previously satisfied the requirements of elementary instruction. Children under fourteen should not be allowed to work either at night or on Sunday, and their actual work should not exceed six hours per day.

IV. *Work of young persons.* It is desirable that young workers between the age of fourteen and sixteen shall not work either at night or on Sundays, that their actual work shall not exceed ten hours per day, that special restrictions shall be provided for operations particularly unhealthful or dangerous.

---

[22] *Archives diplomatiques*, 1890, tome XXXIII, pp. 325-326.

The work of young men between sixteen and eighteen shall be
regulated in the same spirit.

V. *Regulation of women's work.* It is desirable that girls
and women shall not work at night, that their actual work shall
not exceed eleven hours, that lying-in women shall not be admitted to work within four weeks after their delivery.

VI. *Enforcement of the provisions adopted by the Conference.*
It is recommended that the enforcement of the measures undertaken in each State shall be supervised by government inspectors,
that the annual reports of these officials shall be communicated
to the other governments. It is desirable that similar conferences take place in the future to pool the common experience
and further the progress of labor legislation.[23]

The results of the Conference were rather disappointing.
It resolved itself into a formulation of pious wishes. It
was evident from the outset that the fruits would be meager
because the governments had manifested no intention of
binding themselves, and therefore invested their delegates
with very limited powers. Only a greater sincerity of purpose, a better organization of the Conference and a wiser
selection of competent delegates could guarantee a reasonable measure of achievements in similar undertakings.

The Liberal School, or partisans of laissez faire, looked
upon the Conference as a solemn vindication of their
theories. Rolin Jacquemyns wrote in a French review:

This confirms in their views those who believe that the regulation of labor is exclusively the right of the individual, that such
regulation is entirely foreign to international law and that the
establishment of an international legislation of labor would be
ineffective or dangerous for the autonomy and sovereignty of
industrial nations.[24]

The Conference, however, was not entirely in vain. Regardless of the motives which may have moved William II
to call the meeting, his very intervention drew the attention

---

[23] *Actes de la Conférence de Berlin,* official ed., pp. 195*ff.*
[24] "Le socialisme dans le droit international," *Revue du droit
international,* 1890, tome XXII, p. 21. Cited by Mahaim, *op. cit.*

of the world to this vital problem. Moreover, this particular failure could not invalidate the fundamental principle; it rather demonstrated that, properly introduced and carefully studied, international agreements were possible. The program of reforms suggested was sound and was to be the basis of later developments.

THE INTERNATIONAL ASSOCIATION FOR LABOR LEGISLATION, 1900

In 1897, the Swiss Workingmen's Society called an International Labor Congress to be held at Zurich. It was the first congress at which the United States of America was represented. The program resembled that of the Congress of Berlin. It insisted, moreover, upon the importance of creating an international labor office and demonstrated by the spirit of tolerance and good will which presided at the discussions between Catholics and Radical Socialists that coöperation of all parties in some such organization was possible.

A month later there was convened at Brussels the Congress for International Labor Legislation.[25] It was attended by such celebrated economists as Yves Guyot, Raffalovitch, Paul Pic, Schmoller, Brentano, and Herkner. The debates, although very learned and thorough, did not lead to any practical conclusion. Its most valuable result seems to have been to concentrate the attention of economists of all schools upon the international aspect of the labor problem. After the session, the delegates favorable to international intervention appointed a committee of three to study the practical means of bringing it about. Evidently there was but one way, and that was the organization of an international association of the supporters of labor legislation.

---

[25] *Bulletin of the International Labor Office*, Vol. I, pp. 1-3. United States Department of Labor, *Bulletin* No. 9, pp. 1080-1086.

The problem was further studied for another year, and at the Congress for Labor Legislation, held in Paris in 1900,[26] there was founded the International Association for the Legal Protection of Labor. The hour seemed propitious. Paris had never seen so many international societies within its gates. In the year previous, sixteen nations invited by the Czar Nicholas of Russia had assembled at The Hague to study the problem of international peace. It was opportune, therefore, to devise international methods for the promotion of industrial peace. The Association made known its purpose in the following program:

1. To serve as a bond of union to all who believe in the necessity for labor legislation.
2. To organize an international labor office.
3. To facilitate the study of labor legislation in all countries and to provide information on the subject.
4. To promote international agreements on questions relating to conditions of labor.
5. To organize international congresses on labor legislation.

The destinies of the organization were intrusted to six men of international standing: Mr. Scherrer, former President of the Congress of Zurich; Cawés, Dean of the Law School of the University of Paris; Philippovitch, of the University of Vienna; Tonolio, of the University of Pisa; Mahaim, of the University of Liége; and Baron Barlepsch, from Berlin, former Minister of Labor.

The Association established its headquarters in Switzerland and grew rapidly in influence and in membership. In 1912, it claimed fifteen national sections. Each section had its own official title; thus, the American section called itself "The American Association for Labor Legislation." Its most valuable contribution was the creation of an International Labor Office which began to function in 1901. It

---

[26] See *American Journal of International Law*, Vol. I, pp. 818-819.

published in three languages a periodical containing the texts of laws and regulations affecting labor adopted in the different countries, called the *Bulletin of the International Labor Office.* In 1919, the Office and the *Bulletin* were practically absorbed by the International Labor Organization of the League of Nations which publishes the *Bulletin* under the title of *Legislative Series.* The Association itself lived on until 1925 under the direction of its same competent Secretary, Stephan Bauer,[27] meeting yearly in Geneva in close coöperation with the international Labor Organization.

The Association found a strong support in the labor unions and in the International Secretariat of the National Federations of Labor Unions, representing about ten million workers. Other organizations coöperated with the Association. Amongst them the Permanent International Committee of Social Insurances, founded in 1889, and the International Association against Unemployment. The latter assembled valuable information in its *Quarterly Bulletin* and strove to prepare public opinion for international understandings to remedy the great evil of unemployment. It is primarily the migrations of laborers which make unemployment an international problem. It is well-nigh impossible to harmonize in this case the interest of the densely populated nations and of the new countries, such as the United States, unless it be through international agreements.

INTERNATIONAL LABOR TREATIES, 1904-1914

Thanks to the activity of the Association, international conventions for the protection of labor are agreed upon by

---

[27] Austrian professor of political economy, once a lecturer at the University of Chicago, with a very wide experience in Austrian, French, Swiss, and American factories.

the various powers since 1904.[28] France and Italy began
the movement by the convention of April, 1904, covering
workingmen's insurance, protection of young men in industry, factory inspection, and free transfer from one country
to another of the savings of working people.

Critics in their attacks upon these agreements initiated
the charge which is made more vigorously to-day than ever,
that such legislation gives the contracting parties a right of
supervision, of control, upon the legislation of the other
and thereby infringes upon its sovereignty.

In the third assembly held at Basel, in 1904, M. Mille-
rand, later President of the French Republic, said in reply:
"Why should it be a humiliation for my nation not to have
imposed upon, but to impose upon herself freely the obligation to foster social progress through legislation?" He believes that to introduce a higher degree of justice in human
relations will not simply serve an ideal, but promote with
absolute certainty our material interests because it thereby
eliminates causes of hatred and conflict which inevitably
result in heavy financial losses. Such international conventions as the Franco-Italian open an era of justice and peace
among the nations.

Besides these general commendations, they have other
advantages: they are better adapted to the special conditions of the contracting nations; they are more carefully
observed as their nonobservance calls for definite penalties;
and they are more easily entered into because of their
clearly defined contents.

The Franco-Italian Agreement of April 15, 1904, is a
typical example of a treaty containing features which char-
acterize international labor legislation. Italy wished to secure for her nationals working in France certain advantages,

---

28 *Cf.* E. Mahaim, *op. cit.*, pp. 219-243; Albert Metin, *Traités
ouvriers*, Paris, 1908; Justin Godart, *Les clauses du travail dans le
traité de Versailles*, 1920, pp. 33-40; Chatelain, *op. cit.*, p. 193.

such as equitable treatment in case of industrial accidents, old-age pensions, special protection for juvenile workers. As the number of Italians working in France far exceeds the number of Frenchmen working in Italy neither reciprocal measures nor commercial concessions could provide adequate compensation for France. It was decided therefore that Italy would enact progressive labor laws more in harmony with those regulating French labor, thereby doing away with the competition quite detrimental to French industry. Thus the Franco-Italian treaty is a good example of international legislation regulating the general conditions of labor and benefiting alike Frenchmen and Italians.

The Franco-Italian treaty is the type of bilateral agreement. Nearly a dozen states [29] soon followed the example of Italy and France, and inserted in their commercial treaties terms for the protection of labor. These treaties were the following:

France—Italy, 1904
Switzerland—Italy, 1904
Germany—Italy, 1904
Germany—Austria, 1905
Luxemburg—Belgium, 1905
Germany—Luxemburg, 1905
France—Italy, 1906
France—Luxemburg, 1906
France—Italy, 1906
Germany—Netherlands, 1907
Great Britain—Sweden, 1907

France—Great Britain, 1909
Hungary—Italy, 1909
France—Italy, 1910
Germany—Sweden, 1911
France—Denmark, 1911
Germany—Belgium, 1912
Germany—Spain, 1912
Germany—Italy, 1912
United States—Italy, 1913
France—Switzerland, 1913 [30]

All these treaties between two nations imply mutual obligations. Belgium protects her subjects in France, France

---

[29] A very useful collection of international treaties, of labor laws internationally adopted and of labor resolutions internationally subscribed, is given in English by Low in *The International Protection of Labor*, New York, 1921, pp. 171-329.

[30] Post-War treaties: France—Poland, 1919; France—Italy, 1919; Italy—Argentine, 1920; Luxemburg—Italy, 1920; Belgium—Netherlands, 1921; Italy—Czechoslovakia, 1921; Austria—Poland, 1921; Brazil—Italy, 1921.

protects hers in Belgium. When circumstances do not permit identical concessions of approximately equal importance to be made, concessions of another nature, legislative or commercial, are offered as a compensation.

THE BERNE CONFERENCES OF 1905, 1906, AND 1913

The outstanding achievement of the Association, however, was the Berne Conferences of 1905, 1906, and 1913, which adopted several international conventions.

To the preliminary conference of 1905, fifteen nations sent official representatives in order to consider two resolutions proposed by the Association. The United States of America was not represented. Three methods of procedure were open to the gathering: (1) to conclude definite treaties or conventions to be later ratified by the respective governments; (2) to draft tentative agreements, reserving the authority to the governments to transform them into conventions; (3) to pass resolutions embodying suggestions for the terms of future agreements.[31] The second course was pursued and agreements were drafted for the prohibition of the importation into the respective countries of white and yellow phosphorus for the manufacture of matches, and forbidding the night work of women in industry.

In order to secure the ratification of these tentative agreements, the Swiss Federal Council proposed another conference for the following year. Representatives of fourteen states came again to Berne and the conventions were signed, final ratification being reserved to the respective governments. All the fourteen states signed the convention regarding women's work and only seven the convention on phosphorus. Other countries, like Great Britain, complied

---

[31] Cf. "Historical Survey of International Action Affecting Labor," United States Department of Labor, *Bulletin* No. 268, p. 15.

with the terms of the agreement later and the United States passed a special act in April, 1912, to bring about the same results.

Again, in 1913, the Swiss government took the initiative of calling another conference to consider a new program submitted by the International Association of Labor Legislation, embodying the complete prohibition of night work by young persons and limiting to ten hours a day the work of women and young people. Fifteen nations responded. Again tentative agreements were drafted to be accepted at a later diplomatic conference. Such a conference was called for September, 1914, but the following September the nations were at war.

The thirteenth assembly of the International Association for Labor Legislation was held in Berne on September 23, 24, and 25, 1925. The assembly decided in favor of the fusion in agreement with the organizations concerned, of the International Association for Labor Legislation, the International Association of Unemployment, and the International Social Insurance Committee, into a single association to be called the International Association for Social Progress.

While giving due credit to the International Association for Labor Legislation, to its founders and its supporters, it must be confessed that in a century of efforts by high-minded employers, statesmen, economists, and Labor leaders, after more than twenty years of debate, negotiations, and congresses, little had been as yet accomplished. A few treaties between two contracting parties, two treaties signed by more than two governments, and two international conventions cannot constitute a brilliant record of achievement. It is evident that an organization endowed with greater authority was necessary to develop labor legislation and such an institution could not but appear at the first opportunity, for indeed the time was ripe for it.

CHAPTER V

BIRTH OF THE INTERNATIONAL LABOR ORGANIZATION

IT is an evident truth that we cannot claim to understand
an institution unless we consider it in its historical setting,
unless we know the successive waves of thought and feeling
which, with increasing momentum, have impinged upon individuals, parliaments, and conventions, awakening their
interest and whipping them into action. Thus, much of the
prejudice which certain classes entertain regarding the International Labor Organization would be removed if its
genesis were better known. Not a few, for example, have
opposed it because they think of it as a visionary scheme devised by astute politicians to occupy the attention of the
public and divert the thought of Labor from the real issues
involved in the Peace settlement. Surely, no such political
Machiavellianism entered the minds of the eminent delegates to the Peace Conference. But if that interpretation
is too cynical to be probable, neither would it be correct to
say that this Charter of Labor was a gracious grant due to
the foresight and generosity of governments. A short historical survey will reveal that, after all, but little was initiated at the Peace Conference. One might say with greater
truth that propositions, previously worked out by men of
varied shades of opinion, were here sanctioned and officially
registered and that the Organization was the result of a
well-nigh irresistible evolution. More than any other
group, the workers were instrumental in hastening it. During the War, and particularly in the period immediately

preceding the Treaty, representatives of Labor throughout the world had been very active.

Even as far as America, and in spite of our official neutrality, perhaps because of it, Labor began to take a deep interest in this great struggle and its possible reaction upon the rights and well-being of wage earners. Labor immediately realized that this was a war of unprecedented significance and magnitude. "This conflict has demonstrated," they said, "the dependence of the governments upon the coöperation of the masses of the people. Since the masses perform indispensable service, it follows that they should have a voice in determining the conditions upon which they give service." [1]

At the annual meeting of the American Federation of Labor, held in Philadelphia in 1914, a resolution was adopted favoring the holding of a labor conference at the same time and place that a general congress should be held at the close of the War in order to determine conditions and terms of peace and safeguard the rights of Labor. The resolutions instructed the Executive Council to hold itself in readiness to call together representatives of the Organized Labor movements of the various nations. The Executive Council of the American Federation of Labor was further authorized to transmit copies of this resolution to the International Federation of Trade-Unions, to all trade-union centers throughout the world. [2]

At the San Francisco Convention, held in November, 1915, the question of a Labor Peace Congress was raised

---

[1] Samuel Gompers, *American Labor and the War*, p. 291. For a proper understanding of the problems dealt with in this chapter see Samuel Gompers, autobiography, *Seventy Years of Life and Labor*, New York, Dutton, 1925, Book V, pp. 303-523.

[2] It was, then, from the United States that first came the demand for a Charter of Labor connected with the Treaty of Peace. No writer seems to have as yet given due credit to the American Federation of Labor for this initiative which was to prove of such significance.

again. The report of the Executive Council contains a re-markable expression of the new Labor spirit regarding in-ternational relations:

During the previous history of the world, international rela-tions have been left as the field of professional diplomats and politicians. As a result, this field has not been organized and there are few permanent agencies for dealing justly, compre-hensively and humanely with international questions and rights. There exists, however, what may constitute a nucleus for develop-ing permanent institutions. This nucleus consists of The Hague Tribunal and that indefinite mass of international cus-toms known as international law.

There has been no effort made to democratize these institu-tions and to make them directly responsible to the peoples of the various nations concerned.

The demand for democratic control and democratic organiza-tion of international agencies and international methods must come from the people, for it is hardly probable that diplomats and statesmen will voluntarily propose to share their power and authority with the masses of the people who suffer most grievously from wars and who must bear the brunt of war both during the time of fighting and in the period of readjust-ment that follows cessation of warfare.

Since the welfare of the wage-earners of all nations is largely affected by international regulations, in all justice it should be given primary consideration in the deliberations of a World Peace Congress.[3]

At the convention held in Baltimore in November, 1916, the Executive Council reported that the proposal to hold an International Labor Conference had not been approved by the Organized Labor of Great Britain. Moreover, President Legien of the Federation of Trade-Unions of Germany had stated that such a move would be of doubt-ful practicability and had decided to abandon the cherished project. It was recommended therefore that Organized Labor of both belligerent and neutral countries participate

---

[3] Samuel Gompers, *American Labor and the War*, New York, 1919, p. 309.

in the Peace negotiations through official representatives
from their respective organizations. "In this way, the
ideals and needs of wage-earners would be presented and
considered by the general official body." [4]

At the convention of the American Federation of Labor
held in Buffalo in November, 1917, international relations
were again discussed. The Executive Council, in its report,
insisted that "the Government of the United States provide
adequate and direct representatives of wage-earners among
the plenipotentiaries sent to the Peace Congress and urge
upon the labor movements of other countries to take like
action." [5]

American Labor indorsed the policy of President Wilson,
and recognized that "the war had become world-wide in
scope and involved issues of such a nature that our Republic could not much longer remain neutral." It therefore pledged its hearty support to the successful prosecution of war.

Henceforth, the President of the American Federation of
Labor, Samuel Gompers, devoted his energies unreservedly
and directed those of the entire organization to the successful prosecution of the War with the view of assuring the
triumph of his ideals of world democracy. His attitude is
perhaps best expressed in one of his sentences: "This is no
longer a war, it is a crusade for human freedom."

It was not only American Labor that felt that the victory
should be used to put the world upon a new basis, political
and economic, but also President Wilson who was the
spokesman of a large section of the American people.
Abundant evidence of it is found in the remarkable addresses of the President, as well as in Article 23 of the
Covenant, which, though perhaps not formulated by him,
embodies nevertheless his spirit. It reads as follows:

---

[4] *Ibid.*, p. 317.
[5] *American Federationist,* December, 1917.

Subject to and in accordance with the provisions of international conventions existing or hereafter to be agreed upon, the Members of the League will endeavor to secure and maintain fair and human conditions of labor for men, women and children, both in their own countries and in all countries to which their commercial and industrial organizations extend and for that purpose will establish and maintain the *necessary international organizations.*

In Europe, likewise, and with greater reason, while the War was in progress and no one could as yet predict its outcome, the laboring classes began to agitate for a recognition of their rights. Many of the labor laws had been suspended and the rights of combination and to strike much curtailed. The workers soon demanded to be heard in order to protect themselves against the employers. They appointed delegates in France, shop stewards in England, committees in Germany, workingmen's councils in Russia. This was the beginning of the participation of Labor in the management of factories. The governments, conscious of the importance of Labor in the carrying on of the War, supported their claims. In France, the Minister of Armament, in April, 1916, appointed a commission for the organization of Labor in factories engaged in the production of war materials. Labor was represented on that commission. In July, 1917, the same Minister of Armament requested manufacturers to recognize in the management of their plants representatives of the workers. In Germany, the law of December 5, 1916, ordered workingmen's committees to be appointed in all establishments employing at least fifty men. In Great Britain, with the coöperation of the government, Whitley Industrial Councils came into existence. These Councils, made up of representatives of Labor and employers, were organized by factory, by district, and for the entire country.

But their interest was not limited to the correction of

present evils; they too were looking forward, eager to know what benefits they would derive from this turmoil. They had heard repeatedly that this was a war for greater freedom, greater justice, and, if it were so, they wished to have a part in it. Their hopes were eloquently expressed by Lloyd George in an address to the English people in 1919, in the following terms:

Millions of brave young men have fought for a new world, hundreds of thousands have died to insure its triumph. If we fail to redeem our pledges to them, we shall be everlastingly dishonored. It should be a sublime duty for every one without any thought of personal or party interests to help in the building of a new world in which Labor will receive its just reward and culpable idleness alone will be exposed to want.

Those same expectations took a concrete form in the various congresses held during the War which gradually elaborated the substance of the plan later to be embodied in the Peace Treaty. The steps which more directly prepared the organization of Labor were the Congress of Leeds, in July, 1916, the Congress of the Christian Professional Unions of Belgium, held at Le Havre, in June, 1918, and the reports presented to the French Chamber of Deputies by the Labor Commission.

After the Armistice, besides the resolutions of many federations, two important documents appeared, one by the International Congress of Trade-Unions of Berne, February 5-9, 1919, the other by the Christian Syndicates gathered in an International Congress at Paris, March 16-19, 1919.

The Leeds Conference, the first international conference on the War, examined the proposition of the American Federation of Labor to call a world-wide Congress at the same time and place as the Peace Congress, a plan which had already been accepted by the French Confédération Générale du Travail, in 1914. The English declined at first as they objected to meeting representatives of the Central Empires before the liberation of Belgium and France. Finally, the principle was accepted, but action upon the invitation was held in abeyance.

The Congress adopted the following resolutions:

The Conference declares that the treaty of peace which will end the present war and which will give to peoples freedom, political and economic independence, must also place beyond the reach of capitalistic international competition and secure for the workers of all countries a minimum of moral and material guarantees regarding the right to work, the right to organize, regulation of imported labor, social insurances, hours of work, the health and safety of the workers.[6]

The various countries were also expected to create or perfect a labor inspection department to control the enforcement of labor laws, particularly those of an international character. An international commission was to be appointed to watch over the execution of the terms of the agreements. An International Labor Office should be organized to gather all that related to the development and enforcement of labor legislation. The Bureau of the International Association for Labor Legislation already in existence might be intrusted with this new mission.

In October, 1918, took place in Berne the International Conference of Labor Unions of the neutral states, Denmark, Holland, Norway, Sweden, Switzerland, and of the central European states, Germany, Austria, Hungary, Bulgaria. The Conference unanimously adopted a resolution embodying practically the demands of the Leeds Conference.

The Conference of Interallied Socialists held in London in September, 1919, made similar declarations.

---

[6] "Questions ouvrières," Confédération Générale du Travail, Paris, 1916; *Monthly Labor Review*, February, 1917, pp. 202-206, June, 1917, pp. 912-913; *Bulletin* No. 254, United States Bureau of Labor, p. 123.

The Congress of the Christian Professional Unions of
Belgium met at Le Havre, in June, 1918.   It adopted the
following resolutions:

WHEREAS, Christians cannot conceive of an economic progress
without a corresponding social progress,

WHEREAS, The intensity of modern industrial life renders
indispensable the legal protection of the workers in order to
safeguard their dignity, the development of their physical,
intellectual and moral faculties,

WHEREAS, Competition, in view of the rapidity of commercial
relations, reacts upon world conditions which demand an international labor legislation,

The Congress resolves that the Peace Conference, mindful of
several international conventions and particularly of the Berne
Conference, embody in the Treaty the essentials of a protective
labor legislation or at least accept the principle of it.

That the representatives of the various unions be invited to
participate in the drawing up of the treaty.

That the resulting convention be in harmony with Christian
morality and requirements of humanity as they have been emphasized in the Encyclical of Pope Leo XIII, *Rerum Novarum,*
of the 16th of May, 1891.[7]

On October 3, 1918, Justin Godart, Assistant Secretary
of War, brought before the Chamber of Deputies a resolution proposing to direct the Committee of Labor to prepare a report on international labor legislation.   He said
in part:

After the war, competition will reappear.   It is very important to see under what circumstances, without violating the
rights of labor, the nations will return to their normal economic
life.   There may be a tendency to demand of labor, in the
name of national exigency, long hours of work, the employment
of women and children.   The common good, on the contrary,
will require that we facilitate the regeneration and conserva-
tion of the race.   Hence will break out a conflict which we
should meet with a definite policy.   But if we legislate to

[7] Justin Godart, *Les clauses du travail dans le traité de Versailles,* 1920, pp. 64-65.

repress all forms of exploitation and promote the reconstruction of the nation, we must take guarantees against the competition of other countries. Therefore, after the war *labor legislation should be international.*[8]

Therefore, the Chamber agreed that the Committee on Labor should, without delay, work out a report upon principles of international legislation to be incorporated in the Treaty of Peace. This report was ready on the 26th of November. It contained draft resolutions concerning the length of the working day, fair wages, the age of admission of children in industry, social insurances. It proposed periodical international conferences and the creation of an International Bureau of Labor.[9]

This program was accepted by the French section of the Association for Labor Legislation and also by the French Association for the Society of Nations.

Soon after, on January 25, 1919, the Peace Conference appointed its commission for international labor legislation. While this commission was in session, in February, 1919, there were held in Berne an international conference of Socialists and an international conference of labor unions [10] in which neutral and belligerent countries were represented. Both conferences adopted the same resolution entitled, ''Program for the International Charter of Labor at the Peace Conference in Paris.'' In it, we read in part:

. . . so that may be coördinated the differences which exist in the labor legislation of the various countries, it has become indispensable to build up a system of international labor legislation. The need of this reform is still more crying now after the upheaval and devastation which have primarily affected the

---

[8] Appendix to the Minutes of the Session of the Chamber of Deputies, October 3, 1918, No. 5038.

[9] See Report and Minutes of the Commission on International Labor Legislation, pp. 395-397.

[10] Report of the Nineteenth Annual Conference of the (British) Labour Party, 1919, pp. 218-236.

working people. We see a possibility of getting this reform through the Society of Nations, the creation of which appears imminent.

The two conferences demanded, therefore, that the Society of Nations consider as one of its paramount duties the creation of international legislation for the protection of labor, and the adoption of adequate measures to secure its honest enforcement.

Jansen, one of the German delegates to the Conference, declared that the "slowness with which labor legislation has been elaborated must yield to a more rapid development." Henderson, the British delegate, remarked:

The workers of the world had to-day, at the drafting of the Treaty of Peace, the unique opportunity through an international convention, of removing the obstacle which heretofore had prevented the betterment of their condition, *i.e.*, the scarecrow of international competition.[11]

The Congress of American and Interallied Suffragists which opened in Paris in February, 1919, elaborated also an international Charter of Labor. They adopted as the basis of their program the platform of the International Congress of Syndicates of Berne, giving special emphasis, however to the rights of women workers.[12]

Finally, a Congress of Christian Syndicates met in Paris in March, 1919. There were present delegates from Belgium, Spain, France, Holland, Lithuania, Poland, and Switzerland. Recalling the traditional Christian principles of justice and charity, they made a plea for international labor legislation and declared in favor of the creation of an international organization of labor.[13]

One may easily see, therefore, that the Peace Conference cannot be given the entire credit or blame for the creation of the International Organization of Labor. It

[11] *Ibid.*   [12] Justin Godart, *op. cit.*, pp. 80-92.   [13] *Ibid.*, pp. 92-96.

was almost imposed upon them by a great wave of popular sentiment, and the principles embodied in the Treaty of Peace had long been considered as a necessary minimum by various conventions the world over.

It is no doubt this persistent agitation, the desire of many employers for economic peace and recovery, the newly acquired political influence of Labor, the very real fear, then, of the spread of Bolshevism to restless and disorganized sections of Europe, coupled with the prestige of President Wilson, clearly in sympathy with the masses, which brought about the immediate and unexpected appointment of a commission to report on the question of international labor legislation.

The Conference on the Preliminaries of Peace, in its plenary session of January 25, 1919, resolved:

That a Commission, composed of two representatives apiece from the five Great Powers, and five representatives to be elected by the other Powers represented at the Peace Conference, be appointed to inquire into the conditions of employment from the international aspect, and to consider the international means necessary to secure common action on matters affecting conditions of employment, and to recommend the form of a permanent agency to continue such inquiry and consideration in coöperation with and under the direction of the League of Nations.

At a meeting of the other states on January 27, 1919, it was agreed that Belgium should nominate two representatives on the Commission, and Cuba, Poland, and the Czechoslovak Republic one each.

The Commission was definitely appointed on January 31, 1919. The United States of America was represented by:

Samuel Gompers ....President of the American Federation of Labor

Hon. A. N. Hurley...... President of the American Shipping Board

Hon. H. M. Robinson....President, First National Bank of Los Angeles

Mr. H. M. Robinson was to act as substitute. Mr. Hurley was called back to America almost immediately, and thereafter Mr. Robinson took a leading part in the proceedings. Subsequently Mr. Robinson requested Professor Shotwell to assist the American delegation. The following were appointed officers of the Commission:

Samuel Gompers (United States)..President
Hon. G. N. Barnes (British Em-
    pire) ....Vice President
M. Colliard (France)............Vice President
Arthur Fontaine (France)........General Secretary
H. B. Butler (British Empire)....Assistant General Secretary
Baron Capelle (substitute: Count
    de Grunne) (Belgium).........Secretary
Di Palma Castiglione (Italy).....Secretary
Mr. Oyster (United States).......Secretary
Mr. Yoshisaka (Japan)..........Secretary

Other prominent members, acting either as representatives or substitutes, were M. Loucheur, French Minister of Industrial Reconstruction; Léon Jouhaux, General Secretary of the Confédération Générale du Travail; M. Vandervelde, leader of the Belgian Socialist Party; M. Mahaim, professor at Liége University; M. Benès, Minister of Foreign Affairs for Czechoslovakia. Labor was given a generous representation upon the Commission through such able leaders as Messrs. Gompers, Jouhaux, Vandervelde, Barnes, Caprini. Moreover, Professor Mahaim and Major des Planches had always been favorable to the working class.

The Commission held thirty-five meetings from February 1 to March 24, 1919, and drew up its conclusions in two parts. The first is a draft convention containing provisions for the establishment of a permanent organization for international labor legislation. The second part is in the form of clauses containing declarations of principle in

regard to a number of matters which are of vital importance to the labor world.[14]

The purpose which the Commission set out to realize is
remarkably well expressed in the preamble of the report:

PREAMBLE

WHEREAS, The League of Nations has for its object the establishment of universal peace, and such a peace can be established
only if it is based upon social justice;

AND WHEREAS, Conditions of labour exist involving such injustice, hardship and privations to large numbers of people as to
produce unrest so great that the peace and harmony of the
world are imperilled and an improvement of those conditions
is urgently required; as, for example, by the regulation of the
hours of work, including the establishment of a maximum working day and week, the regulation of the labour supply, the prevention of unemployment, the provision of an adequate living
wage, the protection of the worker against sickness, disease
and injury arising out of his employment, the protection of
children, young persons and women, provision for old age and
injury, protection of the interests of workers when employed
in countries other than their own, recognition of the principle
of freedom of association, the organization of technical and
vocational education and other measures;

WHEREAS, Also the failure of any nation to adopt humane
conditions of labour is an obstacle in the way of other nations
which desire to improve the conditions in their own countries;

The High-Contracting Parties, moved by sentiments of justice
and humanity, as well as by the desire to secure the permanent
peace of the world, agree to the following Convention.

The draft convention, given in the Appendix and Chapter VI, dealing with the outstanding features of the
Organization, will describe in fuller detail the mechanism
set up by the Commission.[15]   It is our purpose to recall

---

[14] *Cf.* Appendix I.

[15] For a perfect comprehension of the debates it would be necessary to read the draft convention as given in the Appendix.   It
may suffice, however, to state that the Organization consists of a

here the genesis of some of the most disputed and vital provisions. There was little controversy about the general scheme of organization, as it had been felt long ago that it should comprise three elements: periodical conferences, of delegates of member states, a permanent office, and a fairly representative governing body. Agreement could also be easily reached concerning the definite and concrete propositions to be inserted as a preliminary illustration of the working out of the above abstract principles, for there were a number of regulations concerning the employment of children and women, hours of work, insurance, right of association, which were fairly universally admitted.

There are, however, several points which were of vital importance as upon them depended the success and the vitality of the entire Organization. These were the question of the proportional representation of governments, employers, and workers at the Conferences; the legislative power of the Labor Conferences and their relation with the law-making bodies of the member states; and the measures to be taken for the enforcement of international agreements.

The difficulty, however, which dominated all the debate, and toward the solution of which Messrs. Gompers and Robinson made such able contributions, was the reconciliation between state sovereignty and the powers of this new world Labor parliament. Americans can read with pride the minutes of the sessions of the Commission, for there they will see an earnest attempt on the part of their repre-

General Conference and of a Labor Office controlled by a composite Governing Body representing the governments, the employers, and Labor. To the Conference, held at least once a year, each member sends four delegates, two being government nominees and the others representing employers and work people respectively. The Conference has no legislative power, but it elaborates draft international conventions which, when adopted by a two-thirds majority, are to be submitted by each member state to its competent authority for ratification. In case of a default after ratification, sanctions may be applied.

sentatives to conciliate the dictates of social justice with the economic and political traditions of their country and establish a practical and harmonious relationship.

At the first session, held February 1, 1919, at the Ministry of Labor in Paris, the Secretary of Labor of the French government proposed Mr. Gompers as chairman of the Commission. Mr. Gompers, in just recognition of the services he had rendered to the cause, was unanimously elected. The earnestness with which he assumed the heavy responsibilities of this position is confirmed by his speech of acceptance, wherein we read:

The world is in process of reconstruction and the work which the Commission is undertaking is of the first importance. It is a privilege to have lived in those days and to have contributed to the defeat of militarism and autocracy. If the Commission can make a substantial contribution to the welfare of humanity, the whole world will hold it in grateful remembrance.[16]

A draft convention, creating a permanent organization for the promotion of the international regulation of labor conditions, was submitted by the delegates of the British Empire at the second session.[17]   Similar draft conventions prepared by other nations had not yet been translated into English, so Mr. Barnes moved that the English document be adopted as a basis for discussion. Henry Robinson seconded the motion, and thus it was that the constitution of this international body was of English origin, but English mostly in its wording, for we have already seen that its contents, not only regarding the rights of Labor but also the essential elements of organization, had been in process of elaboration for over a decade. It is incorrectly, there-

---

[16] Report and Minutes of the Commission on International Labor Legislation, published by the Italian government, Rome, 1921, p. 48.

[17] See in Appendix I, draft convention as proposed by British delegation and draft convention as finally amended.

fore, that some writers have given the British entire credit
for this new Charter of Labor.[18]

Mr. Gompers, however, lost no time in making his contribution and at the third session read and distributed the
"Declaration of the American Federation of Labor Embodying Its Peace Platform." The declaration follows:

We declare that the following fundamental principles should
underlie and be incorporated in the Peace Treaty:

A league of the free peoples of the world in common covenant
for genuine and practical coöperation to secure justice and
therefore peace in relations between nations. The entrance
of any free nation into the League of free peoples of the world
shall be inherent.

No indemnities or reprisals based upon vindictive purposes
or deliberate desire to injure, but to right manifest wrongs.

Recognition of the rights of small nations and of the principle: No people must be forced under a sovereignty under
which it does not wish to live.

No territorial changes or adjustment of power except in furtherance of the welfare of the peoples affected and in furtherance
of world peace.

Recognition in law and practice of the principle that the
labor of a human being is not a commodity nor an article of
commerce.

Involuntary servitude shall not exist except as a punishment
for crime whereof the party shall have been duly convicted.

Establishment of trial by jury.

The right of free association, free assemblage, free speech
and free press shall not be abridged.

---

[18] "The political genius of the Anglo-Saxon mind secured the great
charter of parliaments seven centuries ago and now it is again
the British that gave to the world this potent means of developing internationalism." I. F. Asuyawa, *International Labor Legislation*, p. 109. *Cf.* Samuel Gompers, *American Federationist*, March,
1921, address delivered in the Academy of Music, Philadelphia, February 11, 1921: "The American Labor movement carried the fore-
most banner of freedom and human progress at a position far more
advanced than it seemed possible at the outset. . . . It stands to
the everlasting credit of America that the thought of American
Labor is the guiding thought expressed throughout the whole Labor
section of the Treaty. American Labor . . . wrote into the Labor
section the heart and soul of that section."

The seamen of the Merchant Marine shall be guaranteed the right of leaving their vessels when the same are in safe harbor.

No article or commodity shall be shipped or delivered in international commerce in the production of which children under the age of sixteen have been employed or permitted to work.

It shall be declared that the basis work day in industry and commerce shall not exceed eight hours.

The commercial sale or use of articles made or manufactured in the home shall be prohibited.

Fair wages will be paid, wages based upon the average cost of living in accordance with the standards of the day.

Equal wages shall be paid irrespectively to men and women for equal work.

Incorporation of the fourteen points defined by President Wilson.[19]

One of the first questions to come up for consideration was the number of votes to be given to the delegates of the various groups, governments, employers, and workers. The British proposed that a government delegate be entitled to two votes and a nongovernment delegate to one vote. Mr. Gompers vigorously opposed this provision throughout the sessions of the Commission. His argument was that the workers would not trust the Organization if they were not granted a representation at least equal to that of the state and of the employers. He confessed himself unable to understand how representatives of British Labor and Socialists could agree to anything else. Mr. Barnes reminded him that the question had two sides and that there was no reason to assume that the government delegates would invariably support the employers.

It is difficult here to agree with Mr. Gompers, for what is it after all that he feared? He dreaded, no doubt, that the governments might frequently make common cause with the employers and generally outvote Labor. But if

[19] Report and Minutes of the Commission on International Labor Legislation, Appendix, p. 378.

the governments were really unfriendly to Labor, no matter what their voting power at the Conference, they could
always interfere with labor legislation, as the final and
indispensable ratification was to be in their hands. It was
better, therefore, to gain the confidence of the governments
by conceding them a double vote, and thus secure their
hearty coöperation. The innovation was daring enough
for, as Professor Shotwell says, "For the first time in the
history of international law, it was proposed to permit
unofficial delegates, mere citizens of different countries representing home interests in labor and capital, to vote with
similar representative citizens of other countries, independently of the action of the representatives of their governments and so to help actually to bind those governments
towards certain international policies and treaties." [20]

Mr. Gompers' proposition, although tenaciously upheld
by its author, was finally defeated by a vote of 6 to 8, at
the twenty-ninth sitting.[21] It is only fair to the Commission to say that the fears of Mr. Gompers have not
materialized. An analysis of the votes cast at the Washington Conference reveals that the double government vote
was on the whole more favorable to the workers than otherwise. The government delegates sided also with the
workers frequently at the other conferences.[22] Under the influence of a fairly general reaction, their trend might be,
now, in the other direction. for the political complexion of
governments is essentially variable.

By far the most important and the most critical problem

---

[20] J. Solano, ed., *Labor as an International Problem,* p. 50.

[21] Minutes of the Labor Commission, p. 325.

[22] Of 25 votes taken on major problems at the first six conferences, government, worker, and employer delegates have voted together in 15 instances and the government delegates have supported
the workers in 10 instances. Taking all record votes, the three
groups have voted together in 41 out of 79 votes, while the government delegates have supported the workers in 23 votes. See, for
an example, the analysis of the votes of the Geneva Conference,
Appendix III.

was the nature of the power with which this new institution was to be invested. Heretofore all conferences had been merely technical and advisory. The governments had never surrendered one iota of their sovereignty over labor matters. The question arose at the tenth session as soon as the Commission took up the discussion of Article 18. In the British draft, as still unamended, it read:

1. When the conference has approved any proposals as to an item on the agenda, these proposals shall be embodied in the form of an international convention.

2. This convention shall then forthwith be laid for final consideration and decision before the conference.

3. If the convention receives the support of two-thirds of the votes cast it shall be held to be adopted by the conference [23] and a copy of the Convention, authenticated by the signatures of the President of the Conference and of the Director shall be deposited with the Chancellor of the League of Nations.

4. Each of the High Contracting Parties undertakes that it will, within the period of one year from the end of the meeting of the Conference, communicate its formal ratification of the Convention to the Director and will forthwith take all the steps necessary to put the Convention into operation unless such Convention is disapproved by its legislature.

Paragraphs 1, 2, and 3 were adopted without difficulty, but the closing paragraph met with immediate opposition on the part of the American delegation as it ran counter to the constitutional law of the United States. Therefore, it was moved that the discussion be postponed until legal authorities could be consulted.

In the course of the discussion, the Italian delegation proposed to give the Conference powers still larger than those conferred by the British draft. The decisions of the assembled delegates would automatically have force of law after one year. The American delegation instantly retorted

---

[23] This provision is a rather important innovation in international assemblies and a procedure different from the one adopted for the League of Nations where unanimity is required.

that the provisions of the United States Constitution could not possibly be reconciled with the Italian proposition.[24]

At the following session, the French delegate, M. Colliard, confessed that for the present the only resolution that seemed acceptable to the governments was the one embodied in the British draft. Nevertheless, the Commission could agree upon an additional resolution in harmony with the Italian proposition for future consideration by the governments. The hope would be expressed that, at the earliest date, an International Congress would be called with powers to enact labor legislation binding upon the members. Mr. Robinson, realizing clearly that all these propositions were tending towards the creation of a super-parliament, opposed the resolution; he reminded the Commission how jealous the states and their legislative bodies are of their independence. Resolutions such as these would not fail to strengthen the opposition to international organizations and endanger the success of the work of the Commission.[25] Before the final adjournment of the Commission, however, the majority moved to accept the Colliard resolution.[26]

On that same day, the last paragraph of Article 18 came up again for discussion. Mr. Robinson remarked that after consultation with Professor James Brown Scott, President of the American Institute of International Law, he was convinced that the paragraph, as drafted, could not be signed by the President of the United States. By the Federal Constitution, Congress alone is invested with legislative

---

[24] Minutes of the Labor Commission, p. 127.
[25] *Ibid.*, p. 132.
[26] Colliard resolution: "The Commission expresses the hope that as soon as it may be possible an agreement will be arrived at between the High Contracting Parties with a view to endowing the International Labor Conference, under the auspices of the League of Nations, with power to take, under conditions to be determined, resolutions possessing the force of International Law." *Ibid.*, p. 42.

powers. This power cannot be delegated to the Executive, even with Congress reserving the right of veto.

Mr. Robinson accordingly proposed the addition of the following words at the end of paragraph 4:

. . . and except where this undertaking is inconsistent with the Constitution or Organic Law of any of the High Contracting Parties and in such case it shall be obligatory on such High Contracting Party to use its utmost efforts to bring about such legislation as shall give full effect to any conventions so approved.[27]

He was supported by Mr. Gompers, who pointed out that the Federal Constitution was a written constitution, that the forty-eight states retained all the rights that were not expressly conferred on the Federal government and finally that any change in the Constitution was extremely difficult to effect since it required the separate ratification of three-quarters of the states of the Union. Mr. Gompers suggested, therefore, that it might be said, for instance, that the Federal government undertakes to do all it can to obtain from the states the power to legislate regarding labor, or also that it will earnestly endeavor to bring about the ratification of the convention by the respective state legislatures.[28] In view of the importance of the matter, the American delegation moved that further discussions be adjourned.

In the course of the seventeenth session, Mr. Robinson made an extended declaration giving in full the reasons why the American delegation desired the alteration of Article 18 of the British draft. He said in part:

The objections to the third paragraph of Article 18 are four in number:

1. The Senate has the constitutional power and duty to advise and consent to treaties. To allow a foreign body to make a treaty to bind the United States would be, in effect,

---

[27] *Ibid.*, p. 134.   [28] *Ibid.*, p. 134.

a delegation of the treaty-making power to the extent of the provisions of the Treaty.

2. The Congress of the United States is the Legislative Body of the United States in such matters as have been delegated to it by the States of the Union. And it is generally understood that the Police Power, as such, is not among the powers granted to the Union, but among those reserved to the States. Legislation required to give effect to a treaty would need to be passed by Congress as a whole and it is for Congress to determine, notwithstanding the terms of the treaty, whether it will or will not pass such legislation. Furthermore, the Congress of the United States cannot be bound in advance to pass such legislation, either affirmatively or negatively.

3. In regard to the reserved powers including therein the so-called Police Powers, the States retain the right of legislating for their citizens. Neither the Executive nor the legislative branch of the Federal Government can give any assurance that any legislative action will be taken in any of the States.

4. In ultimate resort the constitutionality of a treaty or of an act of Congress may be tested in the Supreme Court of the United States. The legislation passed by a State legislature may be tested in the State Courts and in the Supreme Court of the United States. The Legislation of Congress may be declared unconstitutional by the federal judiciary, and that of the States by the State Judiciary or the federal judiciary.

. . . Our internal organization does not permit us to accept this article in the form in which it is written, so that although we admit the principle, in order to fit our Constitution we offer an additional paragraph. This would read as follows:

"In derogation of the foregoing, and because of the fact that certain of the High Contracting Parties, by reason of their internal organization, may be unable to make a valid binding agreement in accordance with the terms of this convention it is understood, in that event, it shall be obligatory on such High Contracting Powers to use their best endeavor to obtain a substantial compliance with the provisions of this article. However, if, for any reason, any such Power shall fail for the period of . . . months (after the submission of any convention adopted hereinunder) to bring about legislatively or otherwise a substantial compliance with such convention, then, and in that event, the other High Contracting Parties who may be bound under this provision, shall, if they so elect, be released from the operation of this provision of the said convention."

That would be certainly as strong a provision in its practical results as the one submitted by the British, as we view it from the point of view of operation in our country.[29]

Thereupon, M. Mahaim, the Belgian delegate, remarked that the Commission was in presence of a trying dilemma: either to vote for the British text and risk losing the adherence of the United States, or to accept the Robinson amendment and thereby materially weaken the obligations assumed by a certain type of federated states.

In view of the critical character of the situation, a decision was postponed.

In the course of the eighteenth session, Mr. Gompers raised again the question concerning ratification of conventions by federated states. The amendment proposed by Mr. Robinson at a previous sitting was put to a vote and defeated. The British amendment was adopted and the whole of Article 18 stood approved.[30]

During the nineteenth session, the various delegates reported as to the state of opinion in their respective countries. Generally speaking, their governments had appeared satisfied with the main provisions of the draft convention. Mr. Gompers warned the Commission regarding the delicate situation which had arisen in the United States in view of the agreement entered into by thirty-seven members of the Senate not to ratify the Covenant. Great prudence must be exercised not to endanger the entire work of the Peace Conference. The question of free trade should be avoided and the constitutional rights of America should be scrupulously respected.[31]

At the twentieth sitting, Mr. Robinson declared that in spite of all the efforts of the American delegation, assisted by legal authorities, it had been found impossible to ac-

---

[29] *Ibid.*, pp. 175-179.   [30] *Ibid.*, p. 185.   [31] *Ibid.*, p. 224.

cept the English text. They had, therefore, undertaken to
bring out a counter-proposal which would contain the substance of the British draft and which could be accepted by
all countries, even by federal states like the United States
of America.

Mr. Barnes, in a heated reply, firmly opposed the proposition of Mr. Robinson, declaring that it would be impossible to reopen the entire question at that time. The British
delegate said he was not opposed to amendments that would
make Article 18 acceptable to all countries, but he felt that
an amendment which would make of the Conference a mere
deliberating assembly, merely to register the state of opinion
of various economic groups, vent in mere threats and in-
dulge in platonic declarations, would prove a great disappointment to the laboring classes and have deplorable consequences.[32] Thereupon further discussion was postponed.

In the twenty-sixth session, a subcommittee was appointed to work out a text apt to reconcile the British and
the American point of view. It was made up of Sir Malcolm Delevingne and Messrs. Robinson and Mahaim.[33]
They agreed upon a new Article 19, presented at the
twenty-eighth session, and which reads as follows:

When the Conference has decided on the adoption of proposals
with regard to an item in the Agenda, it will rest with the Conference to determine whether these proposals should take the
form (a) of a recommendation to be submitted to the High
Contracting Parties for consideration with a view to its being
given effect by national legislation or otherwise, or (b) of a
draft International Convention for ratification by the High
Contracting Parties.

In either case a majority of two-thirds of the votes cast by
the Delegates present shall be necessary on the final vote for
the adoption of the Recommendation or draft Convention, as the
case may be, by the Conference.

A copy of the Recommendation or draft Convention shall
be authenticated by the signature of the President of the Con-

[32] *Ibid.*, p. 230.   [33] *Ibid.*, pp. 282-285.

ference and of the Director, and shall be deposited with the Secretary-General of the League of Nations. The Secretary-General will communicate a certified copy of the Recommendation or draft Convention to each of the High Contracting Parties.

Each of the High Contracting Parties undertakes that it will, within the period of one year at most from the end of the meeting of the Conference, bring the Recommendation or draft Convention before the authority or authorities within whose competence the matter lies for the enactment of legislation or other action.

In the case of a Recommendation, the High Contracting Parties will inform the Secretary-General of the action taken.

In the case of a draft Convention, the High Contracting Party will, if it obtains the consent of the authority or authorities within whose competence the matter lies, communicate the formal ratification of the Convention to the Secretary-General, and will take such action as may be necessary to make effective the provisions of such Convention.

If, on a Recommendation, no legislative or other action to make such Recommendation effective is taken, or if the draft Convention fails to obtain the consent of the authority or authorities within whose competence the matter lies, no further obligation shall rest upon the High Contracting Party.

In the case of a Federal State, the power of which to enter into Conventions on labor matters is subject to limitations, it shall be in the discretion of the Government of such State to treat a draft Convention to which such limitations apply as a Recommendation only, and the provisions of this article with respect to Recommendations shall apply in this case.[34]

Mr. Gompers had already told the Commission [35] that if the proposition of the American delegation was accepted, the United States of America, although less strictly bound than other nations, would not fail to come up to the expectations of all and would not be the last in the development of labor legislation. The case of the legislation of white phosphorus stands as an example of what they will do, even free from any legal obligation. They had not taken part in the Convention of 1916, which forbade the

---

[34] *Ibid.*, pp. 315-316.   [35] *Ibid.*, p. 280.

use of that product, and the Federal government had, moreover, no right to take measures to forbid its use in the United States. But it could forbid the importation of white phosphorus; it could, on the other hand, so tax the matches thus manufactured, that their cost would be prohibitive. The Federal government resorted to both these means and it thus reached the goal desired by those who had signed the convention, but in ways proper to itself. If one leaves the United States a certain freedom of action, one may rest assured that they will walk alongside the other countries without ever lagging behind.

The Commission, influenced no doubt by these declarations, accepted the American amendment,[36] ten voting in favor and four abstaining—the two Japanese delegates because they had no instructions from their own government, and the Italian delegation because they felt that the amendment curtailed excessively the powers of the Conference.

Throughout the long and laborious discussions, three tendencies had appeared. One supported by the Italian and French delegates gave the Conference very extensive powers and endowed its decisions with binding force, with the possibility, however, of recourse to the Executive Council of the League of Nations. It was the creation of a Parliament of Labor and evident infringement upon national sovereignty. Another tendency, represented by the British delegates, invested the Conference with the power to draw up international conventions which would become binding within one year upon each one of the members, unless disapproved by its legislature. Even this contained a considerable restriction of state sovereignty in the sense that a convention adopted by two-thirds of the delegates might become binding upon a government, even though the delegates of that government had voted against it, as

[36] *Ibid.*, p. 319.

cases could very well arise when the contemplated delay
of one year would elapse without any action being taken
by that particular legislature. The third tendency was
personified by the United States delegation. According to
the principle underlying it, the Conference would formulate resolutions not to become binding until formally ratified by the legislatures of the respective members. *That
solution alone fully safeguarded the sovereignty of the
individual states.*

Finally, the solution of this vital difficulty, which several
times had threatened to wreck the entire structure, was
found in a compromise. And that compromise, to use the
words of Professor Shotwell, "enlarged instead of lessened
the scope of the proposed Labor Conference." The American amendment to the British plan was therefore an addition to it rather than a limitation.[37]

During the fourteenth and fifteenth sittings, Article 34
came under discussion. As first proposed in the British
draft, it read: "The self-governing Dominions of the
British Empire and India may become parties to this Convention and have the same rights and obligations thereunder
as if they were independent States."

This, of course, gave the British Empire a very large
representation in the Conferences. Should even the smaller
British Dominions be given as much power in the Conferences as the largest industrial state of the world with her
hundred million people, especially when the British Empire as a whole was already represented? Mr. Robinson
brought out the excessive character of that claim and
maintained that, as the component states of the American
Federation were sovereign states and particularly self-
governing in respect to labor legislation, they should be
granted rights equal to those of the British Dominions.
Thereupon, Mr. Robinson, warmly supported by Mr.

[37] J. Solano, ed., *op. cit.*, p. 62.

Gompers, offered to substitute for the British text the following:

The British Dominions and India and the several States of a Federation of States, when the States have reserved in whole or in part their autonomy in respect to labor legislation, shall have the same rights and obligations and, in such case, the representation at the Conference shall in number have reference to the population and industrial importance of the Federation of States, such representation to be fixed by the Conference.[38]

The motion, however, was defeated on the strength, it would seem, of the several objections: first, this addition would increase the number of delegates to such an extent that the Conferences would be unwieldy; second, other federated states might claim a similar privilege; and finally, it would increase the difficulty of applying sanctions and obtaining ratifications.

It might seem, however, as though fair enough justifications could be found for giving the Dominions separate representation in the Conferences, such as their large industrial importance, the diversity of their economic interests, the geographical distance from the mother country, but where British ambition revealed itself as rather excessive was when it made possible the representation of the Dominions in the Governing Body as well. When the constitution of the Governing Body came up for discussion, the British delegation proposed the following:

Of the twelve members representing the Governments, eight shall be nominated by the High Contracting Parties which are of the chief industrial importance and four shall be elected by the Government Delegates to the Conference.[39]

Mr. Gompers immediately raised the question whether this proposal eliminated the possibility of the autonomous

---

[38] Minutes of the Labor Commission, p. 161.
[39] *Ibid.*, p. 173.

Dominions of a particular state or of the individual states of a federation being represented separately on the Governing Body, in addition to the representation which might have been accorded to the mother country or to the federal power.[40]

Recognizing the importance of the point raised by the American delegation, the French delegate, M. Fontaine, moved an amendment, which, as finally embodied in the draft convention, reads:

No High Contracting Party, together with its Dominions and colonies whether self-governing or not, shall be entitled to nominate more than one member.[41]

Somehow, this amendment, although passed by the Labor Commission, did not survive the deliberations of the Peace Conference and is not found in Part XIII of the Treaty of Versailles. And now we have two of the Dominions, Canada and India, represented on the Governing Body, and out of twenty-four members which compose the Governing Body seven are British. Such a policy on the part of the British Empire is not likely to disarm the American opposition to international institutions. It is not under the control of any one nation that the League and the International Labor Organization can render the best service but by enjoying the confidence of all in an atmosphere of justly conditioned equality.

Article 35, given above, and referring to the representation of the Dominions in the annual Conferences, was also eliminated by the Peace Conference, not in order to give less recognition to the Dominions, but rather to strengthen their position by giving them a more perfect equality with other nations. It was felt, no doubt, that if they were mentioned at all, specifically, they would be considered in

---

40 *Ibid.*, p. 174.
41 Protocol to Art. 7 of draft convention.

a class by themselves, enjoying a privilege, while they wished to have equal rights with other nations. If that interpretation is correct, their claim is rather excessive for, then, the Dominions are represented twice, once by their own delegates and again by the delegates of the British Empire.

In the course of the long discussions regarding the binding force of the decision of the Conference and the status of the British Dominions frequent references were made to the respective powers of federated states such as ours, of unitary states, and of the British Dominions. It is important to keep well in mind the special political character of each group. The American delegation had two objects in view: first, to prevent the adoption of any provision in the constitution of the International Organization of Labor which would fail to recognize the very real rights of our individual states in relation to labor legislation and therefore which could not have been ratified by the United States; secondly, to endeavor to obtain as important a representation as would be given Great Britain in the deliberations of the International Organization of Labor. It is to that end that our delegates claimed for our individual states as much as Great Britain was claiming for her dominions.

While the points of our delegates were well taken, there may be in the argumentation *ad hominem* a danger of inaccurate definition of the powers of our states in matter of labor legislation and of the real status of a state and of dominions in international relations. Perhaps the tendency of foreigners to misunderstand the nature and functions of our government is due to the fact that, in the words of Madison, "our constitution is in strictness neither a national nor a federal constitution but a composition of both. In its foundation it is federal, not national; in the operation of its powers it is national, not federal; in the extent of them, it is federal, not national; and finally, in the authoritative work of introducing amendments it is neither wholly federal nor wholly national.'' [42]

In the American scheme of government the states are the original source of governmental powers. All power now possessed by the national government has been delegated by the states at some time or other. By their adoption of the national Constitution, the states parted with certain great powers, delegating them to a new national government. Among these powers were the power to make treaties, to regulate commerce with foreign nations and among the several states. It follows, therefore, that our states have now only a limited power, although in their own sphere a very real power, to deal with questions of labor legislation. For example, all legislation affecting the interests of labor in the matter of interstate and foreign commerce are within the jurisdiction of the Federal government and what is even more significant, from the standpoint of international relations, is the fact that it is the Federal government alone which can enter into agreements with foreign states for the adoption of uniform principles of labor legislation. Through the treaty-making power, the Federal government can control the activities of the states even in respect to the residuary rights which they possess in the matter of labor legislation. And still it remains true that the Federal government could not bind the states in matters of labor legislation in so far as it relates to intrastate commerce or deals strictly with production.[43]

The American delegation was right, therefore, in warning the Labor Commission that the United States government could not promise to ratify the conventions of the International Organization of Labor even when approved

---

[42] *The Federalist*, No. 39.
[43] *Cf.* Decision of the Supreme Court in Baily *v.* Drexel Furniture Co., 1922, and Harrison *v.* Dagenhart, 247 U. S. 251, 1918.

by Congress, and suggested that it might be said, for instance, that "the federal government will earnestly endeavor to bring about the ratification of the Conventions by the respective state legislatures whenever these provisions fall within the domain of the states or again that the federal government undertakes to do all it can to obtain from the states complete control of labor legislation."

As to the comparison between our states and the British Dominions whereby an attempt was made to secure similar prerogatives for our states and the Dominions or at least to prevent an excessive representation of the British Empire, it should be made clear that there are important differences between them. First, the Dominions have complete control on their labor legislation problems, and, secondly, they have an international status. In other words, a dominion can deal internationally as well as constitutionally with the subject of labor legislation. One of our states cannot. The equality of status of the Dominions with the mother country recognized within the Empire during the War, had not, up to the time of the Peace Conference, been fully admitted by other nations. The question of the status of the Dominions and their right to direct participation in the Peace Conference, while still members of the British Empire, was therefore considered by the Conference, and the right of the Dominions to participate in the deliberations of the family of nations was recognized and granted.

The view of the British government of the international status of the Dominions is clearly set forth in the statement made by the Prime Minister of Great Britain at the Conference of Prime Ministers held in London in June, 1921.

In recognition of their services and achievements in the war the British Dominions have now been accepted fully into the comity of nations by the whole world. They are signatories to the Treaty of Versailles and all other treaties of peace. They

are members of the Assembly of the League of Nations and
their representatives have already attended meetings of the
League. In other words, they have achieved full national
status. . . .[44]

Labor has been generally favorable to international regulations. The only possible objection to it could arise from
the fear of the lowering of standards. In order to meet
the varying economic conditions in drawing up general
legislation, a compromise might at times be agreed upon
which would tend to lower the labor standards of the most
advanced countries. Mr. Gompers was aware of the danger
and efficiently met the objection. Through his uncom-
promising insistence, he secured the adoption of a provision safeguarding whatever rights Labor had already
acquired.[45] The provision reads:

In no case, shall any member of the League of Nations
be asked or required, as the result of the adoption of any
recommendation, or draft convention by the Conference, to
lessen the protection afforded by its existing legislation to the
workers concerned.[46]

We should not overlook the interest taken by the women
of Europe and of America in the proceedings of the Labor
Commission. They insisted upon being heard by the Commission and an entire session was devoted to them. Six
great associations of women were represented, two of the
best known being the International Women's Council and
the Conference of Allied Women Suffragists. The American representatives were Mrs. Borden Harriman, Mrs.
Rublee, Miss Drexel, Miss Alice Riggs Hunt. All the
associations were in agreement as to the claims that should

---

[44] *Cf.* "Canada a Nation," p. 13. Address delivered by the Hon.
N. W. Rowell, American Bar Association meeting, Minneapolis,
1923.
[45] Minutes of the Labor Commission, p. 366.
[46] See Appendix I: *Cf.* Art. 19 of the draft convention or Art. 405
of the Peace Treaty.

be laid before the Conference. Although disappointed not
to have a woman on the Labor Commission, they felt that
the reception of their delegation by the Commission was a
red-letter day in the history of the feminist movement.

"Called through the force of circumstance to bear directly and personally their share of responsibility, of devotion and work, in the prolonged effort which determined
victory," they believed that until now "the intellectual,
moral and social force they represented had been too much
neglected."

In order that the rights of women should be properly
protected, the delegation asked that they be invited to
participate, on the same footing as men, in the deliberation
of all international commissions created with a view to labor
organization; also, that women's labor commissions should
be set up in every country consisting of representatives of
governments, trade-unions, scientific women, and so forth,
to whom would be submitted all exceptional legislative measures. They drew the attention of the Commission particularly to the importance of protecting children and
women through labor legislation.[47]

There is no doubt that the activity of these associations
of women exercised a noticeable influence upon the decision of the Labor Commission, which not only strove to
protect the rights of women workers but opened fairly
wide to women the doors of the new organization.

The Commission was unanimous in thinking that their
work would not be complete if it were simply confined to
setting up a permanent machinery for International Labor
Legislation. It was not within their competence to deal
with specific questions relating to industrial conditions and
to work them out with the necessary details to make them
acceptable. Impressed with the urgent need for giving
expression to some fundamental principles, they adopted

---

47 *Ibid.*, pp. 289-308.

nine resolutions, the realization of which might be contemplated in the near future. They were as follows:

1. In right and in fact, the labor of a human being should not be treated as merchandise or an article of commerce.

2. Employers and workers should be allowed the right of association for all lawful purposes.

3. No child should be permitted to be employed in industry or commerce before the age of fourteen years, in order that every child may be ensured reasonable opportunities for mental and physical education.

Between the years of fourteen and eighteen, young persons of either sex may only be employed on work which is not harmful to their physical development and on condition that the continuation of their technical and general education is ensured.

4. Every worker has a right to a wage adequate to maintain a reasonable standard of life having regard to the civilization of his time and country.

5. Equal pay should be given to women and to men for work of equal value in quantity and quality.

6. A weekly rest, including Sunday, or its equivalent for all workers.

7. Limitation of the hours of work in industry on the basis of eight hours a day or forty-eight hours a week, subject to an exception for countries in which climatic conditions, the imperfect development of industrial organization or other special circumstances render the industrial efficiency of the workers substantially different.   The International Labor Conference will recommend a basis approximately equivalent to the above for adoption in such countries.

8. In all matters concerning their status as workers and social insurance foreign workmen lawfully admitted to any country, and their families, should be ensured the same treatment as the nationals of that country.

9. All States should institute a system of inspection in which women should take part, in order to ensure the enforcement of the laws and regulations for the protection of the workers.[48]

---

[48] These principles did not represent all that Mr. Gompers wanted. *Cf. American Federationist*, March, 1921. In order to realize the influence of the United States in drawing up this charter, *cf.* these principles with the clauses proposed by the American delegation; Minutes of the Labor Commission, pp. 379-380, and this chapter, pp. 87, 88.

These declarations are looked upon as most significant in the history of Labor, and the workers consider that the foundation has now been laid for a great Charter of Labor whose elaboration and perfection it is their ambition rapidly to bring about.

In order to give the workers, whose hopes had run rather high, further proof of their earnestness in their professions of humanity and social justice, the Commission decided that a conference should be held as early as possible to begin immediately the preparation of international legislation. The place unanimously chosen was Washington and the date, October, 1919. The government of the United States was requested to convene the conference. An international organizing committee of seven members was to be appointed by the United States, Great Britain, France, Italy, Japan, Belgium. In view of the great interest Switzerland had always taken in international labor legislation she was also included, although during the War she had been a neutral.[49]

The Washington Conference was to consider the following propositions:

1. Application of the principle of the eight-hour day or of the forty-eight-hour week
2. Question of preventing or providing against unemployment
3. Women's employment
   (a) Before and after childbirth, including the question of maternity benefit.
   (b) During the night
   (c) In unhealthy processes

---

[49] The members of that committee were: For the United States, J. T. Shotwell, professor at Columbia University; for Great Britain, Sir Malcolm Delevingne, Assistant Under-Secretary of State; for France, Arthur Fontaine, Counsellor of State, Director of Labor; for Italy, Di Palma Castiglione, Inspector of Emigration; for Japan, O. Oka, former Director of Commercial and Industrial Affairs at the Ministry of Commerce; for Belgium, E. Mahaim, professor at University of Liége; for Switzerland, William Rappart, professor at the University of Geneva.

4. Employment of children
   (a) Minimum age of employment
   (b) During the night
   (c) In unhealthy processes

5. Extension and application of the international conventions adopted at Berne in 1906 on the prohibition of night work for women employed in industry and the prohibition of the use of white phosphorus in the manufacture of matches

During the discussion of the first item of the agenda, "Application of the principle of the eight-hour day and the forty-eight-hour week," Mr. Gompers declared that, speaking in the name of the American Federation of Labor, he was absolutely opposed to a day of over eight hours and offered the following amendment:

The working day in commerce and industry will not be over eight hours except in cases of extraordinary necessity, as for instance when life and property are in danger.

But the amendment was lost.

The reading of the minutes of the thirty-five sessions of the Labor Commission reveals the important part played by the American representatives. Mr. Gompers presided at every one of the thirty-five sittings with a vigor that never relaxed. Professor Shotwell attended ten sittings as the substitute for Mr. Robinson, and took a scholarly part in the proceedings. Mr. Robinson attended twenty sittings and made most constructive contributions to the discussions. He applied himself to help in setting up an organization which, while very liberal and humane in its general purpose, would be conservative enough in its attributions and legal prerogatives to prove acceptable to the governments.

The American delegates, throughout these long debates, evidenced a sincere desire of bringing the whole scheme to a successful issue. They brilliantly and vigorously upheld the American point of view and worked hard to bring about a reconciliation between the exigencies of an efficient international organization and the peculiarities of the government of the United States. Altogether, they showed a thorough grasp of legal and economic principles, a sincere devotion to the cause of social progress and an unfaltering loyalty to American rights and ideals.

The Labor Commission adjourned *sine die,* on March 24, 1919, and was heard by the representatives of the Allied and Associated Powers at the plenary session of the Peace Conference, on the 11th of April following. The Hon. G. M. Barnes submitted the report. At the closing of his speech, President Wilson rose and said:

I have admired what Mr. Barnes has said altogether and concur in the conclusion with the greatest heartiness. I rise merely to say that no detail of the document is more welcome to my ears than the suggestion that the first Conference should be held in Washington in the United States, and I can assure you that a most cordial invitation will be extended to the Conference to meet there.[50]

Appropriate remarks of commendation and some reservations were made by representatives of various nations. As Mr. Gompers had been called home, President Wilson expressed his deep regret at his absence in the following terms:

Mr. Chairman, no one could have desired a more adequate exposition of this report than that which Mr. Barnes has given. But I cannot let this occasion pass without expressing my personal regret that my fellow countryman, Mr. Samuel Gompers, is not here. Mr. Gompers, as you know, was the Chairman of this Commission. He went home only under the compulsion of imperative duties there. I know how thoroughly and truly he represents the sentiment of the working men of America. I wish very heartily that he were here to do what I am not qualified to do—express their sentiments and their entire concurrence in what I regard as an admirable document.[51]

---

[50] Preliminary Peace Conference Protocol No. 4, p. 7.
[51] *Ibid.,* p. 15.

At the close of the session, the following resolution was unanimously adopted:

The Conference approves the Draft Convention creating a permanent organization destined to bring about the international regulation of the conditions of labor, draft of which has been submitted by the Labor Commission.

With it was also accepted the amendment of Sir Robert Borden:

The Conference authorizes the Drafting Committee to make such amendments as may be necessary to have the Convention conform to the Covenant of the League of Nations in the character of its membership and in the method of adherence.

Harmless as that amendment may have then appeared, it is, very probably, through it that the status of the Dominions, as defined in the draft convention, was substantially modified through the omission of the first two paragraphs of Article 35 and an entire sentence of the protocol to Article 7.[52]

On April 11, the Peace Conference had approved the entire report with the exception of the famous nine clauses. This general statement of principles was found too specific by the Dominions concerning several points; namely, the obligation assumed by the signatory Powers regarding their universal application, the age of working children, and the treatment to be accorded foreign labor. Thereupon, Sir Robert Borden proposed several amendments [53] which were accepted at the plenary session of the Peace Confer-

---

[52] *Cf.* Chap. V, p. 100 .

[53] These amendments, whatever Sir Robert Borden may have told the Conference, weaken considerably the strength of the document. The age limit of 14 for working children was removed and a general declaration substituted for it (Art. 6). As to foreign workers, instead of guaranteeing them equal treatment with native labor, only "equitable" treatment was promised to all (Art. 8). Finally, the character of the preamble was substantially altered by making possible all sorts of exceptions to the nine clauses.

ence on April 28, 1919. The Labor Commission had successfully completed its task.

With the signing of the Covenant of the League of Nations began the principal period in the history of the protection of labor, namely, the legislative period.

Let us now understand fully the organization which is to bring it about.

CHAPTER VI

CONSTITUTION OF THE INTERNATIONAL LABOR ORGANIZATION

THE countries which in order to establish universal peace were joining together in a League of Nations, primarily on the insistence of the President of the United States, realized that such a peace could not be permanently secured unless it were based upon social justice. Hence, moved as well by "sentiments of justice and of humanity," they agreed to found an institution which could do, within the sphere of economic relations, what the League of Nations was hoping to accomplish in the political field.

Indeed, such an institution, competent to preside over the shaping of international labor legislation, had been in the making for well-nigh a century. During the last twenty years, the essential features it should embody in order to insure its efficiency had become more and more definite. It was evident that one of the first requisites in the progressive elaboration of an international labor code was that the nations take counsel among themselves in periodical assemblies and that a permanent organism be devised in order to carry out the decisions collectively arrived at. This scheme of organization was so clearly suggested by the nature of things that the plan proposed by the Labor Commission of the Peace Conference was readily adopted. And thus came into existence, as we have shown in the preceding chapter, the International Labor Organization.

The Organization consists, then, of two essential elements: one, so to speak, legislative, the General Conference of Representatives of the Members; and the other, executive, an International Labor Office, headed by a Director and controlled by a Governing Body.

THE CONFERENCE

First in importance, therefore, is the Conference or Assembly of Representatives as it initiates the measures eventually to be enacted into international laws. To this Conference each member nation sends four delegates, two representing the government, one representing the employers and one the workers. It seemed but right that the governments, responsible for the general well-being, be given a larger representation than those who stand naturally for sectional interests.

The employers' and workers' delegates are chosen in agreement with the industrial organizations which are most representative of employers or working people in their respective countries. If no such organizations exist, as is the case in some countries of recent industrial development, a difficult situation arises which has been met in various ways. Sometimes only government delegates have attended. Sometimes only government and employer delegates. Thus frequently delegations have been incomplete. This provision of the Treaty that worker or employer delegates must be nominated in consultation with the most representative organizations of employers or workpeople has greatly furthered the formation of national organizations of employers and employed. However, whether the delegations are complete or not the balance of power between employers and workers is preserved by a clause of Article 390 which provides that when only one of the two groups is nominated, the other may sit and speak at the Conference, but may not vote.

Each delegate may be accompanied by advisers, not to exceed two in number, for each item of the agenda of the meeting. This is universally considered an excellent provision as it permits particularly well qualified persons to take part in the debates. The advisers may speak to the assembly when asked to do so by the delegate, and one of them may even take his place for a whole session and vote in his stead.

The delegates are entitled to vote individually, and not as heretofore, in similar conferences, only by national units, upon all matters which come up for deliberation in the Conference.

When questions especially affecting women are to be considered, at least one of the advisers is to be a woman.

The meetings of the Conference may be held as occasion requires but must take place at least once a year. The duration of the Conference has varied between ten days and a little over three weeks. At the eighteenth session of the Governing Body, in April, 1923, it was decided to hold the Conference in the spring instead of in October as previously. The 1924 and 1925 Conferences have been, therefore, held in June.

As one may readily see, even from the brief description we have just given, these conferences are a decided departure from the established tradition of both international congresses and national legislative assemblies. Fortunately so, think many, for this bringing together of government officials, employers, workers, experts, men and women, leaders of labor and industry from every quarter of the globe, voting individually and hence with a greater opportunity for independence, cannot but mark an important step forward in the broad and impartial treatment of our economic problems.

The purpose of the Conference, then, is to bring about a betterment of the conditions of labor through the enactment of international law. As it was not invested with real legislative power, whose decisions would be automatically binding upon the different states, it limits itself to the adoption of certain definite proposals. These proposals, when approved by a two-thirds majority, take the form either of a convention or of a recommendation. A convention, when formally ratified by the members, becomes international law. It is drafted in such a form that it can frequently be embodied practically without substantial alteration as a part of the national law of a state which ratifies it. A recommendation is a declaration of policy or principle submitted to the states for consideration that they may translate it into legislation adopted to their particular circumstances. Recommendations and conventions as soon as approved by the Conference are deposited with the Secretary-General of the League and communicated by him to each of the member states. Within a year or eighteen months at the most, they are to be referred by each government to the competent legislative or diplomatic authority. Once ratified, they are binding, and measures may be taken, in accordance with a specified procedure,[1] to secure their enforcement.

The Conference, like most legislative bodies, works through committees and commissions: Committee on Credentials, Committee on Resolutions, Drafting Committee, and so forth. All the commissions of the Conference are of a tripartite composition. Like the Conference itself, they include delegates from each of the three groups—government, employers, and workers. Unlike the Conference, however, the three groups are usually present in equal numbers upon those commissions which consider the draft conventions and the recommendations.

The agenda for the meetings of the Conference are settled by the Governing Body. Any state member or any or-

1 *Cf.* pp. 130, 131.

ganization of employers or workers, considered as the most
representative in that country, may suggest the inclusion
of a particular question on the agenda. Any of the governments of the members may request the exclusion of a
particular item from the agenda, but the request will
not be granted if the delegates, by a majority of two-
thirds, are in favor of considering it. The agenda of the
Conference is communicated to the member states several
months in advance.

THE GOVERNING BODY

The elaboration of future labor laws [2] is not the only
prerogative of the Conference. Another of its most important attributions is the appointment of the Governing
Body.

The Governing Body is composed of twenty-four members, of whom twelve represent the governments, six the
employers, and six the workers. Of the twelve members
representing the governments, eight are appointed by the
eight states of chief industrial importance, and the four
by the countries nominated for that purpose by all the
government delegates at the Conference, excluding those
of the eight states already represented. Any question arising as to which are the states of chief industrial importance
is decided by the Executive Council of the League of
Nations.

The members of the Governing Body representing employers and workers are elected by their respective delegates at the Conference. Each of them is given a substitute
appointed through a similar procedure.

The period of office of members of the Governing Body
is three years. If, meantime, any vacancies occur, the

---

[2] We shall further on study in detail the work accomplished by
the Conferences already held. *Cf.* Chap. VII.

method of filling them is determined by the Governing Body itself, subject to the approval of the Conference.

The Governing Body has been invested with considerable power:

It appoints the Director of the International Labor Office, issues instructions to him, and generally supervises the activity of the Organization (Art. 394).

It settles the agenda for all meetings of the annual Conference (Art. 400).

It decides upon the form and contents of the annual reports that each of the members is to make to the International Labor Office regarding the measures taken to carry out the provisions of conventions to which it is a party (Art. 409).

It possesses judicial and discretionary powers in relation to the enforcement of these conventions and the sanctions to be applied to the defaulting party (Art. 397).

It frequently acts as intermediary between the governments and the Labor Office (Art. 397).

It elects its own chairman, regulates its own procedure, and settles the dates of its meetings (Art. 393).

The Governing Body was constituted for the first time by the Washington Conference in 1919. Considering its power and influence, it is well to know what was then its constitution.

States of Chief Industrial Importance

Belgium, represented by.......E. Mahaim
France, represented by........A. Fontaine
Germany, represented by......Dr. Leymann
Great Britain, represented by..Sir Montaigue Barlow
Italy, represented by..........G. de Michelis
Japan, represented by.........Katsutara Inuzuka
Switzerland, represented by....H. Rufenacht

United States, place occupied by Denmark, awaiting ratification of Treaty by United States

States Nominated by the Conference

Argentine, represented by.....de Alvear
Canada, represented by........Hon. James Murdock
Poland, represented by........F. Sokal
Spain, represented by.........Viscount de Eza

Employers' Delegates

Carlier (Belgium)   Pirelli (Italy)
Guérin (France)   Schindler (Switzerland)
Hodacz (Czechoslovakia)   Sir Allan Smith (Great Britain)

Workers' Delegates

Stuart Bunning (Great Britain) Legien (Germany)
Draper (Canada)   Lindquist (Sweden)
Jouhaux (France)   Oudegeest (Netherlands)

Chairman: A. Fontaine
Vice Chairmen: Jules Carlier
Jan Oudegeest

The first Governing Body was hardly appointed when its membership became the object of vigorous protests on the part of India, the Netherlands, Czechoslovakia, and Poland. These countries took exception to the list of the eight states of greatest industrial importance, as accepted by the Conference. Several non-European states objected also to the small representation granted to extra-European nations. We have already seen that it pertained to the Council of the League to decide which are the states of the greatest industrial importance. In view of the above protest, a mixed committee was appointed in 1920 composed of representatives of the Council of the League and of the Governing Body of the International Labor Office. It was to examine carefully the criteria which should be adopted in the determination of the industrial importance of states. The Committee decided to apply provisionally, while economic conditions remained unsettled, the following criteria, which are simply, in a revised and improved form, the criteria drawn up by the Organizing Committee of the Washington Conference:

1. Total industrial production including mining and transport industries

2. The proportion which the industrial population bears to the whole population

3. Total horse-power, not including locomotives and vessels

4. Horse-power per head of population

5. Total mileage of railways

6. Length of railways per thousand square kilometers of territory

7. Development of the mercantile marine

The Council of the League acting on this report upheld the claim of India and assigned to it the seat hitherto occupied by Switzerland. It was felt, however, that in order to satisfy the claims of all concerned, a reform of the constitution of the Governing Body was imperative. An amendment to that effect was therefore placed upon the agenda of the Conference of 1922.

As the exact determination of which are the eight states of chief industrial importance had proved so difficult, the Governing Body had, during the course of the year 1922, drafted a new article to replace Article 393 of the Treaty of Versailles, providing for a total membership of thirty-two and attempted to elude the difficulty of selecting the eight states of chief industrial importance by substituting six named states (France, Germany, Great Britain, Italy, Japan, United States) which would be permanently represented, the other vacancies to be filled by election.

The Conference, upon the representation of India and Canada, rejected the proposed article.[3] Finally, a new wording for Article 393 was adopted by eighty-two votes for, with two votes against, and six abstentions. If it is ratified by the Council of the League of Nations and by three-fourths of the members of the League, it will effect the following changes:

---

[3] *Cf.* Minutes of the Conference, fifteenth sitting, Geneva, 1922.

Instead of a total of twenty-four members there will be thirty-two, of whom one half will be persons representing governments, one-fourth persons representing employers, and one-fourth persons representing the workers. Of the states upon the Governing Body, eight will be, as before, the eight states of great industrial importance (Belgium, Canada, France, Germany, Great Britain, India, Italy, Japan) ;[4] the remaining eight will be selected by the government delegates present at the Conference, excluding the delegates of the eight members mentioned above.

The workers' and employers' representatives will be chosen, under the new as under the old scheme, by the workers' and employers' delegates respectively. The demands for additional representation on the Governing Body repeatedly made by extra-European countries are met in the new Article by provisions that six of the government representatives and two each of the employers' and workers' representatives shall belong to non-European states.[5]

Awaiting ratification of the amendment by the League of Nations, the Conference endeavored in the measure of its power, to meet the objections raised regarding representation on the Governing Body. Consequently, the result of the 1922 election was as follows:

States of Chief Industrial Importance

Belgium (E. Mahaim)	Great Britain (Boyd-Carpenter)
Canada (Hon. J. Murdock)	India (Sir Louis Kershaw)
France (A. Fontaine)	Italy (G. de Michelis)
Germany (H. Leymann)	Japan (H. Danke)

---

[4] There is a new factor which will undoubtedly again upset these arrangements, namely, the decision of the Permanent Court of International Justice by which agricultural workers are included in the terms "industrial workers." Some day China may therefore take the place of Belgium; and Brazil and Argentine may also claim a seat on the Governing Body by reason of their agricultural importance.

[5] Cf. Minutes of the Conference, fifteenth sitting, Geneva, 1922.

States Nominated by the Conference

Chile (A. Quezada)   Poland (F. Sokal)
Finland (N. A. Mannio)   Spain (de Altea)

Employers' Representatives

J. Carlier (Belgium)   James Lithgow (Great Britain)
W. Gemmill (S. Africa)   G. Olivetti (Italy)
F. Hodacz (Czechoslovakia)   R. Pinot (France)

Workers' Representatives

Léon Jouhaux (France)   Jan Oudegeest (Netherlands)
Th. Leipart (Germany)   E. L. Poulton (Great Britain)
Tom Moore (Canada)   A. Thorberg (Sweden)

One can see, therefore, that greater satisfaction has been already given to the non-European states; four out of the twelve government seats have been allotted to them; the employers and the workers likewise have allotted one of their six seats to non-European representatives. The list of the eight chief industrial states is also slightly modified as Canada and India are found among them. These changes have made necessary the elimination of Switzerland. It is a matter of universal regret that the country which had been a pioneer in international labor legislation and in international organization should no longer be represented. The contemplated reform of the constitution of the Governing Body will, no doubt, make her election again possible. The mandate of the members of the Governing Body elected in 1922 expired in 1925. At the June Conference of 1925, however, only two changes were made. In the government group, Argentina and Norway replaced Chili and Finland respectively; the employers' and workers' sitting representatives were reëlected without change.

Up to the present, January, 1926, the Governing Body has held thirty sessions. Its meetings generally take place at the seat of the League. It consents to hold its sessions in towns other than Geneva only if the state which invites it pays all the cost involved. It meets approximately every three months but a special meeting may be held if a written request to that effect is made by at least ten members of the Governing Body.

THE DIRECTOR AND THE LABOR OFFICE

The Governing Body cannot evidently discharge unassisted its manifold executive duties. Therefore, at its first session, at Washington, November, 1918, it proceeded at once to make provisions for the establishment of the International Labor Office. Albert Thomas, Minister of Munitions for France, during the War, whose foresight and energy were largely responsible for supplying in due time one of the indispensable requisites of victory, was appointed provisional director. He was authorized to take the preliminary steps towards gathering a staff and carrying out the work resulting from the Washington Conference. He immediately chose as deputy director, H. B. Butler, formerly of the British Ministry of Labour, who had just served as a secretary-general of the Conference. For his staff, Mr. Thomas drew largely at first from those who had been connected with the Commission on International Labor Legislation and the Washington Conference.

In June, 1920, the Office was temporarily established in Paris. The March following it was transferred to London, the temporary seat of the League of Nations, for by virtue of Article 392 of the Treaty of Peace, the Office must be established at the seat of the League. In June of the same year, it moved to Geneva, shortly in advance of the Secretariat of the League which took up quarters there in the month of November. Until January, 1926, it has occupied the premises of Thudictum College.

A beautiful site on the shore of Lake Geneva was given

by Switzerland in 1922 and the Assembly of the League of Nations voted $600,000 for the erection of a building. The new office is to be officially dedicated in June, 1926. An interesting feature of the undertaking is the contributions made by the various nations toward the new building by providing, after consultation with the architect, building materials, furnishings, ornaments, or works of art characteristic of their national genius.

The Governing Body, then, has as its executive agent, the Director. Naturally it lays down the general lines of the policy he is to pursue, intrusts him with such special tasks as the needs of the moment require, and supervises his activity. The Director, on the other hand, enjoys considerable initiative and independence. One of his most important duties is the organization of the Office and the proper selection and supervision of the personnel. This is indeed a grave responsibility, for upon the choice of an efficient staff depends, in a large measure, the success of an organization.

Speaking generally, it may be said that the main task of the Director is the collection and distribution of international information on labor problems and the use of this information toward the establishment of the best possible conditions of work in all countries. It is evidently with that end in view that he has planned his office.

The Labor Office has grown with the development of the institution. It was reorganized in 1922, and since that date only minor changes have been instituted. There are now, in 1926, three main divisions in the Organization. The Diplomatic Division is responsible for all relations with governments; it also provides the secretariat of the Conference, of the Governing Body, and of the committees. The Relations Division keeps in touch with the employers' and workers' organizations and with public opinion in general. The Research Division is a laboratory of international research on social questions. In addition to the three great divisions, and working for them, there are: the Editorial Section, which makes the results achieved known to the general public; the Administrative Section, which regulates the internal work of the Office and sees that its resources in staff, material, and finance are properly administered; and finally, there is the Cabinet, which assists the Directorate in its work.

The Directorate.—In the Directorate we find a Private Secretariat and an Administrative Section. The chief function of the Private Secretariat is to insure that the Director's instructions are exactly understood and carried out, and to prepare and organize the personal work of the Director. To the Private Secretariat is attached the Press Service.

The duties of the Administrative Section are twofold. Responsible directly to the Deputy Director, it assists him, on the one hand, in the coördination of the activities of the various divisions and sections and, on the other hand, in the centralization and direction of the general administrative work of the Office. It comprises the Registry, Typing, Financial Control, Accounts Branch, Staff Branch, Material Branch, and Household.

The Editorial Section comprises all the services dealing with the editing, translating, printing, and sales of the various publications of the office.

The Diplomatic Division.—The Diplomatic Division is at present composed of three sections: the General and Conference section, the Conventions Section, and the Legal Section. The duties of the General and Conference Sections are to prepare the work of the Conference, of the Governing Body and the commissions; to carry on the official correspondence with the governments and the League of Nations; to supply a secretariat for the Conference, the Governing Body, and the various commissions.

The Conventions Section examines the effect given to the decisions of the Conference from the point of view of ratification and execution of the conventions and is also responsible for the publication of the *Official Bulletin* and of the Final Record of the Conference.

The Legal Section studies the legal problems in the working of the Organization.

The Emigration Service is attached to the Diplomatic Division.

The Research Division.—The Research Division includes three Research Sections, each of which deals with a clearly defined question or set of questions. The first section deals with strictly statistical studies and those principally based on statistics. The second section is concerned with legislation and regulations on labor matters, and with studies mainly based on such legislation and regulations. The third section is responsible for all general social studies which are not strictly statistical or legal in character.

The Intelligence or Relations Division.—The Intelligence or Relations Division is composed of two large sections: the International Information and Liaison Section and the National Intelligence Section. The first includes (1) the Employers' International Organization Service which deals, from the international point of view, with the relations of the Office with employers; (2) the Workers' International Organizations Service, which carries out similar duties with regard to workers' organizations; (3) the Coöperative Organizations Service, which examines questions relating to coöperation and maintains relations with coöperative societies. To this section is also attached the Library and the Documents Service. The second or National Intelligence Section includes the groups of officials intrusted with relations with the national correspondents of the Office—Spain and Latin America, Northern Europe, and Eastern Europe.

CONSTITUTION OF THE INTERNATIONAL LABOR ORGANIZATION

Conference
- Government Delegates
- Employer Delegates
- Worker Delegates

The Governing Body
- Government Delegates
- Employer Delegates
- Worker Delegates

INTERNATIONAL LABOR ORGANIZATION

Directorate
- Private Secretariat
- Deputy Director and Administrative Section
  - Central Services
    - Registry
    - Financial Control
    - Typing
  - Establishment
    - Accounts
    - Staff
    - Household

Diplomatic Division
- General Conference
  - Conference
  - Governing Body
  - General Correspondence
- Conventions
  - Ratification
  - Application
- Legal Section
- Migration

Research Division
- Statistical Studies
- Legal Studies
- General Social Studies

Intelligence and Liaison Division
- International Information and Relations
  - General Organizations
  - Employers
  - Workers
  - Coöperative Societies
  - Library
  - Documents
- National Information and Relations
  - National Correspondents
  - Spain—Latin America
  - Northern Europe
  - Eastern Europe

In June, 1925, the staff numbered three hundred and fifty employees, representing twenty-eight countries; ninety-four employees, however, were British.[6] The proportion of women is a little less than 50 per cent. They occupy positions in almost every grade from chief of section

---

[6] Great Britain, 86; Ireland, 2; Canada, 3; Australia, 1; New Zealand, 1; South Africa, 1.

to messenger.   The Office is conducted on a civil service basis.

In order to keep in closer touch with the principal industrial countries, national correspondents have been appointed who serve as intermediaries between the Office on one hand and the governments and the employers' and workers' associations on the other.   They are already at work in Berlin, London, Paris, Rome, Tokio, and Washington.[7]   It is intended to have them in all the large countries as soon as funds are available.

In addition to these correspondence offices, through which the Office keeps in daily touch with national events, several countries have permanent social attachés in Geneva to enable them to keep in still closer contact with the International Labor Office.   Representatives of Albania, Bulgaria, Chile, China, Denmark, Finland, Greece, Hungary, Italy, Japan, Poland, Czechoslovakia, Venezuela, and Ecuador have already been appointed in that capacity. The Japanese government has a permanent delegation to the International Labor Office composed of seven members. According to a Japanese official statement, it was set up as "a tangible sign of the interest which the Japanese government takes in Labor questions, and of its desire to keep in close and constant touch with the International Labor Office, it having recognized that not only direct but also personal contact was necessary."[8]

"LEGISLATIVE" PROCEDURE

Having described the mechanism of this new institution, it behooves us to show how it is going to function.   The essential task of the International Labor Organization is

---

[7] The national correspondent for the United States is Leifer Magnusson, Washington, D. C.

[8] See E. B. Behrens, *The International Labour Office*, Leonard Parsons, London, 1924.

to see how the principles embodied in the Treaty of Peace can be made a reality; to make possible, therefore, an appropriate system of labor legislation and to secure its acceptance and application by all the member states.

In the realization of that aim, the Organization does not enjoy unlimited powers or freedom. The method it is to pursue has been clearly defined by the Treaty of Versailles.[9] For a fuller understanding of its character, we must recall the double movement from which the Organization sprang in 1919.[10]

On the one hand, there was the movement for the international legal protection of labor, foreshadowed almost from the beginning of the nineteenth century and culminating in the founding, in 1900, of the International Association for Labor Legislation, whose activity was rewarded by the successful Berne Conferences of 1905, 1906, and 1913.[11]

On the other hand, there was the trade-union movement throughout the period of the War and the Peace Negotiations which, in the Congresses of Leeds, 1916, Berne, 1917, London, 1918, and Berne, 1919, stood for an international labor code enacted by representative international conferences and binding without any further government intervention.

The procedure adopted for the Conference of the International Labor Organization is a compromise between the demands of the trade-unions and the method illustrated by the International Association for Labor Legislation. The Berne Diplomatic Conferences were not qualified to impose upon governments any obligations other than those of a moral nature. For reasons of political expediency or for worthier motives, the governments might even omit to sub-

---

[9] *Cf.* Part XIII of Treaty of Versailles, Art. 405. *Cf.* Chap. V, pp. 89–97.
[10] *Cf.* Chap. IV, pp. 64–71.   [11] *Cf.* Chap. IV, pp. 70, 71.

mit to their parliaments bills authorizing the ratification of the conventions drawn up by the Conferences.

After the War, Labor could no longer be satisfied with such a problematical way of securing a fair and rapid settlement of their grievances; therefore several of the members of the Labor Commission of the Peace Conference, particularly the Italian delegation, firmly insisted that the new organization, if it were to have any meaning, should be invested with final legislative powers.[12] The Commission felt, however, that the time had not yet arrived for so radical an innovation. The Treaty provides merely that each of the members undertakes to bring the recommendations or draft conventions before the authorities within whose competence the matter lies, for the enactment of legislation or other action (Art. 405). No nation is thus bound without its consent.

Greater regard is still shown for the opinion of governments by the official interpretation given to Article 405. Albert Thomas, the Director, in a letter to the governments, says that the Treaty ''does not impose on them any obligation to recommend to competent authorities the adoption of the decisions of the Conference. They are fully at liberty to make any observation as to the desirability or otherwise of adopting them.''[13] Great Britain and Switzerland have already acted on that interpretation.[14]

The difference, however, between the Berne procedure and that of the International Labor Organization, although trifling on the surface, may prove of considerable moment. In the case of the former conferences at Berne, the governments were in no way obliged to inform their parliaments of the decisions taken; that is to say, they were not bound

---

12 *Cf.* Chap. V, pp. 90, 91.

13 *Official Bulletin* of the International Labor Office, Vol. VI, No. 26, p. 606.

14 *Ibid.*, February 15, 1922, pp. 106-107; *ibid.*, January 5, 1921, p. 4.

to consult public opinion on that particular question. It is, however, precisely upon public opinion that the founders of the present organization relied to bring pressure to bear upon parliaments in order to secure the ratification of conventions. G. M. Barnes, in his address to the members of the Peace Conference,[15] when he presented the report of the Labor Commission, properly dwelt upon the importance of this new feature. Undoubtedly, if public opinion, and particularly the opinion of Organized Labor, is wide-awake and active, the process of ratification will be considerably hastened.

Therefore, even if the mechanism does not function as provided and expected, the resolutions of the Conference may acquire a significant persuasive authority—something like the influence which the Commission on United States Law has exercised for about twenty-five years on state legislation, chiefly in commercial matters. If the American example is in point, we might look forward to the formation of a substantially uniform body of law with such local modifications in detail as may be required.

ENFORCEMENT OF LABOR LAWS AND SANCTIONS

Difficult though it is to devise and enact appropriate labor legislation, it is still more difficult to secure its honest and consistent enforcement. The difficulty is further increased in the international order by the sensitiveness of the respective states regarding any foreign interference with questions of interior administration. And still, the Labor Commission felt that, without some definite provisions to insure the carrying out of the ratified conventions, the whole system would prove a pitiful failure. Many states might, with the greatest ease, place the new laws upon their statute books and let things run their course. The Treaty

---

[15] *Cf.* Chap. V, pp. 109, 110.

of Peace ruled therefore that each state shall present to the International Labor Office an annual report on the measures which it has taken to give effect to conventions duly ratified.

Additional guaranties of efficient enforcement were provided in the following form. Any one of the members has the right to file a complaint with the International Labor Office against another member for nonobservance of a convention. The Governing Body may thereupon communicate this complaint to the government concerned, or immediately refer the case to a Commission of Inquiry. The Commission of Inquiry, appointed according to a special procedure,[16] prepares a report embodying its findings on all questions of fact and containing recommendations regarding the steps that should be taken to meet the complaint, or the coercive measures, of an economic character, that may be applied against the defaulting government.

The defaulting government may appeal to the Permanent Court of International Justice of the League of Nations which acts as a supreme court and whose decision is final. If a defaulting government fails within the time specified to carry out the recommendations of the Commission of Inquiry or, as the case may be, the decision of the Permanent Court of International Justice, the plaintiff state may take against it the measures of an economic character indicated in the report of the Commission or in the decision of the Court.

Eager as the Commission was to insure the adequate enforcement of international labor laws, abundant provision is made for the defaulting state to remedy any grievance alleged against it before any question of penalty can arise. It is evident that the Commission did not believe in coercive measures to secure the observance of the conventions agreed upon by the contracting states. National honor, public

---

[16] Cf. in Appendix, Art. 412 of the Treaty of Versailles.

sentiment, international moral sense, and friendly representations are primarily relied upon and should prove sufficient.

Indeed, an important feature of the Organization, as we
have already pointed out,[17] is its reliance upon public opinion, to secure the efficiency of the entire system. This is
again particularly apparent in the provision by which any
properly constituted industrial association of employers or
workers in a member state can make direct representations
to the International Labor Office regarding the failure of
any state to carry out its obligations. The Governing Body
may communicate this representation to the government
complained against and invite it to make a statement on the
subject. In case of no reply or of an unsatisfactory reply,
the Governing Body has the right to make the entire case
public. This cannot but quicken public interest in social
reform, and bring the pressure of public opinion to bear
upon the proper observance of conventions.

Recent experience has shown that the impartial presentation of the facts in any industrial dispute has wielded an
appreciable influence. When the White Régime was introduced in Hungary in 1920, it was charged that freedom of
association was abolished and that trade-unionists were
prosecuted. The Hungarian Minister of Foreign Affairs
agreed therefore that the International Labor Office should
send out a Commission of Inquiry to ascertain the facts in
the case. The findings of the Commission were published
by the International Labor Office. As a result the Hungarian government was forced to adopt measures on various
points to which attention had been drawn by members of
the Commission.

A complaint on similar lines was made by the Spanish
General Union of Workers of Spain against the violation
of the freedom of association in that country. The Inter-

[17] *Cf.* Chap. VI.

national Labor Organization published the statement made by the Spanish trade-unionists and the reply from the Spanish government.

In Persia, likewise, the attention of the Labor Office was called to the deplorable conditions of labor in the weaving industry in Kerman, where children were employed at the age of five. As a result of careful diplomatic action on the part of the International Labor Office the Persian government was influenced to take quite severe measures to stop such abuses.[18]

THE PERMANENT COURT OF INTERNATONAL JUSTICE

We have spoken of the legislative and executive powers of the International Labor Organization and we have just seen that the Court of International Justice supplies, in a measure, the other attribute it should possess properly to fulfill its mission: a judiciary power.

The Permanent Court of International Justice, to which the judges were appointed by the Second Assembly of the League of Nations, held its first session in 1922. The Court is of special importance to the International Labor Organization. First, it acts as a supreme court whose decision is final with regard to the conclusions of the Commission of Inquiry, or culpable negligence of any member in meeting its obligations. Further, the Court is competent in all questions or difficulties relating to the interpretation of Part XIII and of the draft conventions concluded in virtue of it.

In response to the desire expressed by the International Labor Office, the Assembly decided that a chamber of five judges should be constituted as a special body within the Court for considering all labor questions. These judges are to be assisted by persons of recognized competence in

---

[18] See E. B. Behrens, *op. cit.*, pp. 38, 39.

labor matters, who would attend in the capacity of assessors.[19]

The Constitution of the Permanent Court of International Justice and its special Labor Chamber thus completes the legal system which is necessary for an efficient International Labor Organization.

This analogy between the legislative, executive, and judiciary powers of the International Labor Organization and the corresponding powers of independent states has aroused the fears of the champions of unimpaired state sovereignty.[20] The above prerogatives are indeed the essential attributes of sovereignty. As possessed by the International Labor Organization, however, they are manifestly insufficient to raise the institution to the rank of a superstate.[21]

It would be dishonest to hide the fact that whenever the nations enter into international understandings, and *a fortiori* when they establish international institutions, they thereby place some limitations upon their complete freedom of action. But such restrictions are the inevitable concomitance of any international relationship.

It may be said, therefore, with proper qualifications and reservations, that the states have, in this case, surrendered a certain amount of their sovereignty in the sense that they have contracted some very definite obligations. The states, for instance, are reminded every year by the Office that they must send delegates to the Conference, that they must choose them in accordance with the stated procedure, that they must submit conventions and recommendations to their parliaments, that they must send in an annual report on the execution of conventions, that they must contribute to the support of the Organization and so forth.

---

[19] Report of the Director, 1921, par. 113; *ibid.*, 1922, pars. 96-98.
[20] *Cf.* René Courtin, *L'Organisation Permanente du Travail et son action*, pp. 319-327.
[21] Maurice Guerreau, *L'Organisation Permanente du Travail*, pp. 41-60.

There is no doubt, then, that something new in international relations has been created. The Organization is a great deal more than merely an advisory commission or a diplomatic conference, but it is by no means a superstate, for its competence is carefully restricted to a precisely circumscribed field of activity, and even within that field it is clearly limited.[22]

As to whether this foreshadowing of an international power or of a superstate indicates really the present trend of political evolution and foretells serious impending adjustments between national sovereignty and international sovereignty now in the making, is a question of political science well worth studying.

MEMBERSHIP IN THE ORGANIZATION

The states which are members of the International Labor Organization are the thirty-two states signatories of the Treaty of Versailles, the states invited to adhere to the Covenant of the League of Nations, and Germany, invited although not granted as yet membership in the League of Nations.

In principle, therefore, the composition of the International Labor Organization is identical with that of the League of Nations, with the special case of Germany which is but a temporary arrangement.

The member states of the International Labor Organization are now fifty-six in number.

At the present moment only the following among self-governing states are outside the Organization:

The United States of America, Mexico, Turkey, Egypt, Russia and the Soviet Republics associated with her, certain very small states such as Liechtenstein, Monaco, San Marino, Fiume, one or two states of slight importance in-

---

[22] *Cf.* Chap. V, pp. 89–99.

dustrially such as Abyssinia and Nepal.[23] These small
states are never likely to be admitted to full membership;
they very likely will be allowed to be represented by some
other state.

Mexico has under consideration a request to the Conference for admission into the International Labor Organization.

General Calles, the new president, is deeply interested in
improving the condition of Mexican workers. Immediately
after his election, he made a tour of investigation in Europe, and met the Director of the International Labor
Office. General Calles assured the Director that as a demo-
crat and an enthusiast for social reform, he was greatly
interested in the progress of international labor legislation.
Shortly after taking office, he sent a representative to
Geneva to investigate the work of the Office and study ways
of coöperation.

The two great problems which remain are, however, those
of Russia and the United States of America. It is the absence of these two countries which prevents the International Labor Organization from acquiring its proper character of universality.

The United States,[24] a leader both from an industrial and
social standpoint, would have been gravely missed if her
employers' associations had not kept in touch with the Office and her Labor organizations lent their assistance and
encouragement.

As to Russia, the Organization has never lost contact with
her. A special section was created in 1921 for the study of
Russian questions. In 1920, the Governing Body planned
to send a mission of inquiry into Russia, but the Soviet
government refused its consent. Through the Conferences
of Genoa and The Hague, the International Labor Organi-

---

[23] See Report of Director, 1922, p. 12.
[24] For the United States see Chap. IX.

zation has been able to maintain certain relations with Russia. It is true that the declarations of the Third International with regard to the International Labor Organization remain as hostile as they were in the past to the "capitalistic" League of Nations, and that the government has not seemed any more disposed than hitherto to allow the dispatch to Russia of a mission of inquiry.

The Office feels that it should exercise great prudence in this connection.[25] The Organization is not as handicapped in her work by the absence of Russia as its critics imagine. Although Russia is a great storehouse of raw materials and a large potential market, she cannot be of great assistance to Europe in her present plight. The great fall in production, the financial catastrophe, the general impoverishment of the whole country, the dispersion, one might almost say the destruction, of the industrial working class, have rendered Russia powerless for several years to come. But when the time for reconstruction comes, the International Labor Organization, which is now the best informed body on Russian affairs and, no doubt, the most disinterested friend of Russia, will play a useful part in the resumption of her normal economic life.

In 1924, in view of the fact that several countries had recognized the Soviet government, the Labor Conference adopted a resolution instructing the Governing Body to enter into relations with the Russian government by the means and methods which it considered most appropriate. The Governing Body decided to leave it to the Director to choose the opportune moment for such a move. The Director, however, has shown himself very cautious. Eager though he is to develop closer relations with Russia, he said in his last report:

If it were not for the diplomacy of chicanery and *volte-face* pursued by the Soviet government whenever it is not negotiating

[25] See Director's Report, 1922, p. 15.

with Communists, it might have been possible to make some
advances.   The tentative efforts which have been made showed
that this was out of the question.   The Office might have fared
as others have fared.   The official representative of the Soviet
government might at any moment have dropped the mask and
appeared as the fanatical delegate of the Communist International.   The reëstablishment of secure and mutually beneficial
relations can only come through a natural evolution in Russia
itself, as that country becomes increasingly conscious that it is
necessary to take part in the life of the world as a whole, and
that, even though it may consider its own system superior to that
of any other country, it cannot in practice stand alone.

A large membership is not sufficient to impart strength
and efficiency to an organization; an active and earnest
membership is indispensable.   At the Conference of Genoa,
Mr. Tchitcherine made the declaration that the states, members of the International Labor Organization, were less
enthusiastically in favor of the Washington Conference
than Russia.

It must be admitted that the enthusiasm of the states for
labor reform is less now than it was at the close of the
War.   We have already alluded to the reactionary movement which has taken place in nearly all the countries of
the world.   It is interesting, therefore, to see what coöperation, whether genuine or not, the International Labor Organization receives from the various nations.   It is by their
participation in the General Conference and by their collaboration in the work of the International Labor Office
that the state members are able to display their interest in
the purpose of the Organization.   Forty-two states attended the first session of the Conference at Washington,
1919, twenty-seven at Genoa, 1920, thirty-nine at Geneva,
1921, thirty-nine at Geneva, 1922, forty-two at Geneva,
1923, forty in 1924, forty-six in 1925.

That participation cannot be truly effective unless the
states send full and competent delegations.   These delega-

tions, however, have often been incomplete either because the members sent only one government delegate or because they omitted to send employers' and workers' delegates. At Washington, in particular, sixteen states had appointed only government delegates and this fact called forth protests on the part of the workers' delegates who considered that the position of the workers at the Conference was thereby materially weakened. It is certain that the absence of employers' and workers' delegates from certain countries alters the general complexion of the Conference and disturbs the equilibrium which should be maintained between the interests represented; but it is quite clear that if the countries in which employers' and workers' organizations are in process of development were obliged to send complete delegations, there would be grave risk of their employers' and workers' delegates being ill qualified to represent the special interests of the employers or workers, and, although called employers' or workers' representatives, they would be nothing more than government representatives. Although, if employers' or workers' organizations do not exist, the member states are not under obligation to appoint delegates, the problem of securing the fullest measure of representation at the Conference must remain the constant care of all.

Better than long commentaries, the accompanying table will show the real interest taken by the various nations in the Organization.[26]

There is, then, a wide difference among the nations in their effective participation in the work of the International Organization of Labor. The eighteen Latin-American states send hardly any delegates. At the Washington Conference, the American governments were fairly well represented, and there were seen also some employers' and workers' delegates. The representation of the Latin-American

---

[26] *Cf.* pp. 140, 141.

REPRESENTATION OF MEMBER STATES

MEMBER STATES	WASHINGTON CONFERENCE, 1919			GENOA CONFERENCE, 1920			GENEVA CONFERENCE, 1921			GENEVA CONFERENCE, 1922		
	Government	Employers	Workers	Government	Employers	Workers	Government	Employers	Workers	Government	Employers	Workers
British Empire												
Great Britain.........	2	1	1	2	1	1	2	1	1	2	1	1
Canada..............	2	1	1	2	1	1	2	1	1	2	1	1
South Africa..........	1	1	1	..	..	..	2	1	1	1	1	1
Australia.............	..	..	..	2	1	1	1	1	1	..	..	..
New Zealand.........	..	..	..	..	..	..	..	..	..	..	..	..
India................	2	1	1	2	1	1	2	1	1	2	1	1
Occidental and Central Europe												
France...............	2	1	1	2	1	1	2	1	1	2	1	1
Italy.................	2	1	1	2	1	1	2	1	1	2	1	1
Spain................	2	1	1	2	1	1	2	1	1	2	1	1
Portugal.............	1	1	1	1	1	1	1	..	..	1	..	..
Belgium..............	2	1	1	2	1	1	2	1	1	2	1	1
Luxemburg...........	..	..	..	..	..	..	2	1	1	..	..	..
Netherlands..........	2	1	1	2	1	1	2	1	1	2	1	1
Switzerland..........	2	1	1	2	..	..	2	1	1	2	1	1
Hungary.............	..	..	..	..	..	..	..	..	..	1	1	1
Germany.............	..	..	1	2	1	1	2	1	1	2	1	1
Czechoslovakia	2	1	1	2	1	1	2	1	1	2	1	1
Poland..............	2	1	1	1	..	..	2	1	1	2	1	1
Austria..............	..	..	..	..	..	..	2	1	1	1	..	..
Scandinavian States												
Denmark.............	2	1	1	2	1	1	2	1	1	2	1	1
Sweden..............	2	1	1	2	1	1	2	1	1	2	1	1
Norway..............	2	1	1	2	1	1	2	1	1	2	1	1
Balkan States												
Jugoslavia............	2	1	1	2	..	1	2	1	1	2	1	1
Roumania............	2	..	..	1	1	1	1	..	..	2	1	1
Bulgaria.............	..	..	..	..	..	..	2	..	..	2	..	..
Greece...............	2	1	1	2	1	1	2	1	1	1	..	..
Albania..............	..	..	..	..	..	..	1	..	..	1	..	..

NOTE.—At the 1923 Assembly there were present 74 government delegates, 24 employer, and 24 worker delegates. They were accompanied by some 70 technical advisers. Ireland, newly admitted as a member of the League of Nations and hence of the International Labor

AT THE GENERAL CONFERENCE FROM 1919–1922 *

MEMBER STATES	WASHINGTON CONFERENCE, 1919			GENOA CONFERENCE, 1920			GENEVA CONFERENCE, 1921			GENEVA CONFERENCE, 1922		
	Government	Employers	Workers	Government	Employers	Workers	Government	Employers	Workers	Government	Employers	Workers
Baltic States												
Finland	2	1	1	2			2	1	1	2	1	1
Esthonia							2	1	1	2	1	1
Latvia							2	1	1	2	1	1
Lithuania										2		
Latin America												
Cuba	2	1					2			2		
Haiti	1											
Guatemala	2	1	1				1			1		
Salvador	1											
Honduras												
Nicaragua	1											
Costa Rica												
Panama	2	1	1									
Venezuela	2			1			1			2		
Colombia	1						1			1		
Ecuador	2											
Peru	2	1	1									
Brazil	2		1				2			2		
Bolivia	1						1					
Paraguay	2									1		
Uruguay	2			1			2			2		
Argentine	2	1	1	1	1	1						
Chili	2			1			1			2		
Africa												
Liberia												
Eastern Countries												
Hedjaz												
Persia	2											
China	2						1			2		
Siam	2			2			2			2		
Japan	2	1	1	2	1	1	2	1	1	2	1	1
TOTAL	73	25	25	47	19	20	68	25	25	69	22	22

Organization, sent delegates for the first time. In 1924 there were present 69 government delegates, 29 employer delegates, and 28 worker delegates. In 1925 there were 80 government delegates, 32 employer delegates, and 32 worker delegates.

* The proportion of representation did not change substantially after 1922.

Republics, therefore, is much more political than economic.[27] While the cost of sending complete delegations may contribute to this state of things, there is little doubt that it reveals also on their part a lack of interest in international labor legislation.

As this has been the case as well for Oriental countries like Persia, China, Siam, and Hedjaz, the representatives of the governments have been in overwhelming majority. This of course tends to create a condition which might run counter to and finally defeat the original purpose of the Organization.

THE BUDGET AND RELATIONS WITH THE LEAGUE OF NATIONS

The financing of an institution is oftentimes the measure of its influence. Fairly autonomous in most other respects, the International Labor Organization is in this matter closely dependent upon the League of Nations. It has no income of its own. The idea has been to have a general budget for all the international institutions grouped within the League and to allow certain of these institutions a comparative measure of autonomy. The Labor Conference therefore is not empowered to discuss the budget. The budget is entirely within the competence of the Assembly of the League; its administration, on the other hand, falls to the Governing Body appointed by the Conference.

All possible guaranties for wise expenditure and strict economy have been provided. First, the budget is prepared in draft form by the Director. The Finance Commission examines this draft and submits its proposals to the Governing Body. The draft budget, as drawn up by the Governing Body, is submitted to the Commission of Control

---

[27] Albert Thomas, the Director, visited South America in the fall of 1925 and received assurance from the various South American states that they would hereafter send to the International Labor Conference more representatives and fuller delegations.

which acts for all the institutions of the League. The Commission of Control makes its recommendations and, according as circumstances require, proposes reductions or increases. The Governing Body meets again and gives its opinion on the recommendations thus made. The budget is presented to the state members by the Secretary-General of the League and finally it is the Assembly which votes the budget after having referred it to its Fourth Commission for examination.

The budget for the year	1921	amounted to	8,762,500	Swiss francs.
" " " " "	1922	" "	7,959,325	" "
" " " " "	1923	" "	8,544,212	" "
" " " " "	1924	" "	6,942,295	" "
" " " " "	1925	" "	7,199,595	" "
" " " " "	1926	" "	7,135,000	" "

The Organization lives within the limits laid down at the time of its foundation in 1920. Its development is obviously checked by the necessity for economy which the governments constantly impress upon their delegates. While every state is restricting expenditures, international organizations can hardly hope to be treated generously. And yet, is it right to place the latter on the same footing as national institutions, most of which are now firmly rooted? Primarily on the insistence of Great Britain, the budget for 1924 was materially reduced as may be seen above. During 1924 a marked improvement took place in the payment of annual contributions and the general financial situation is now more favorable.

Considering that these new international organizations have been intrusted with the mission of organizing the world for peace and regulating industrial relations in order to eliminate the waste of labor conflicts and of a demoralizing competition, is not the constant curtailment of their budgets a shortsighted policy? It might lead us to a severe commentary regarding the sincerity of our humanitarian declarations if we were to dwell upon the fact that the entire budget of the International Labor Organization does not represent a quarter of the cost of a dreadnaught, and there are fifty-six states contributing to this outlay.

The financial dependence of the International Labor Organization upon the League is not their only point of contact. The two institutions, although the result of two entirely different movements, are often brought together in close coöperation, either by the terms of their constitution or because of the complex character of the problems which come before them for study or solution.

The Treaty of Peace provides, for instance, that the International Labor Office shall form a part of the institutions of the League of Nations; that it shall be established at the seat of the League; that the meetings of the Conference as a rule shall be held at the seat of the League; that the Director shall be entitled to the assistance of the Secretary-General of the League in any matter in which it can be given. Moreover, this Secretary-General registers all the draft conventions and recommendations of the Labor Conference.

The humanitarian interests of the League are so vast that they cannot but frequently affect the welfare of Labor. Impressed by that fact, Mr. Oudegeest, in January, 1921, placed before the Governing Body a proposal to the effect that the Director should attend meetings of the Council of the League in order to express his opinion on all questions concerning labor. The Council of the League has agreed to communicate to the Director a copy of the agenda of its meetings. The Director, then, informs the Secretary-General as to the items of special interest to the Labor Office and the Council decides whether the Director should be heard.

The Director has been regularly consulted by the Council of the League on matters affecting the Office; for example, in January, 1922, concerning Russian refugees, and in

May, 1922, in connection with the long controversy about the competence of the International Labor Office in agricultural matters.

Moreover, the Office is represented on all commissions of the League of Nations whose work, in any way, is of interest to Labor, such as the Commission on Hygiene or even the Commission on Disarmament. Similarly, the League takes part in the work of the Commission set up by the Governing Body, whenever the problems under discussion are akin to the general purpose of the League.

In his report to the 1925 Conference, the Director remarks that these friendly relations maintained by the League and the Labor Organization "have preserved for the League of Nations the good will, and the confidence of the Working Classes who now closely associate the International Labor Organization with the general work of the League of Nations for consolidating peace."

This collaboration has given the best results. Its advantages have been particularly evident in regard to questions concerning international intellectual coöperation, disablement, health, the white-slave traffic, transit, mandates, Russian refugees.[28]

Though closely allied in their structure and their activity, it would be erroneous to conclude that the International Organization of Labor is but a section of the League. On the contrary, it is a fairly autonomous body; it has the power to initiate its own policy and to carry it out in almost complete independence. We are now about to see what use the Organization has made of its prerogatives and opportunities.

---

[28] *Cf.* Director's Report, 1921, pp. 39-44; *ibid.*, 1922, pp. 65-72.

CHAPTER VII

THE International Labor Organization had been launched with a minimum of opposition. It had been planned along logical enough lines and while essentially dependent upon the League and the member states, it had been invested with sufficient powers to show whether it justified the confidence the world was ready to place in it. Its opponents were eagerly awaiting the first deliberations, which, they thought, would vindicate their thesis that the international regulation of labor is a dangerous venture doomed to an early failure, or capable of a great deal of mischief, and its friends were anxiously watching its first steps, knowing full well the thousand pitfalls of the road. It can be said, without hesitation, that the first have not seen their hopes realized, while the anxiety of the latter still persists.

The activity of the Organization manifests itself principally in two ways: through the annual Conferences and through the daily work of the Office. A rapid survey of their respective records will show us whether they have thus far supplied sufficient proof of their usefulness and any assurance of survival in spite of the many odds against the undertaking.

ANNUAL CONFERENCES OF THE ORGANIZATION

The Washington Conference.—The first session of the General Conference was held at Washington toward the close of 1919. It was presided over by the Hon. W. B. Wilson, United States Secretary of Labor, and met in the

Pan-American Building where had been convened the Disarmament Conference. Called in the fervor of a crusade for social justice in March, 1919, it met in the October following under rather unfavorable auspices. President Woodrow Wilson, its most illustrious protagonist, was ill and unable to attend. The United States had not ratified the Peace Treaty and the Senate seemed prepared to reject it altogether. The relations between Labor and Capital were embittered by the steel strike, and were destined soon to grow even worse through the miners' strike. An Industrial Conference,[1] called by the President to adjust pending labor conflicts, had failed. Under these circumstances, the general public might well look askance at this newly-born polyglot institution, trying to bring about an industrial peace which was eluding the search of the experienced leaders of the nation.

And still never did an international assembly prove richer in promises and in actual achievement. The generous hospitality of the American people, the unfailing courtesy of the Washington officials, as well as the competence and sympathy of the Secretary of Labor, created an atmosphere favorable to the success of the Conference. Altogether, thirty-nine nations were represented;[2] the governments sent one hundred and twenty-three delegates, the employers' and workers' organizations twenty-five each. These in turn were assisted by one hundred and

---

[1] Cf. Monthly Labor Review, November, 1919, pp. 40-49; ibid., January, 1920, pp. 60-68.

[2] Germany and Austria were not yet members of the League; it was thought, however, important to admit them to the International Labor Organization. The Organizing Committee recommended "that in anticipation of their admission to the League of Nations and in view of their expressed willingness to coöperate in the work of the labor organization; Germany and Austria are hereby admitted to membership in the International Labor Organization with the same rights and obligations possessed by the other members according to the terms of the Treaties of Peace signed at Versailles on the 28th day of June, 1919, and at St. Germain on the 10th day of September, 1919." Minutes of the Conference, p. 21.

fifty advisers, of whom twenty-three were women. An invitation was extended to American employers and unions to send unofficial representatives. The American Federation of Labor accepted [3] and appointed Samuel Gompers. The veteran Labor leader attended but one sitting, during which he took an energetic part in the discussion regarding the eight-hour day, contending spiritedly that production was increased rather than diminished by the shorter work-day. He created a sensation by declarations of the temper of those which follow:

First let me say that so far as discussing the question of the length of the work-day is concerned, unless the eight-hour day, under normal conditions, shall be the maximum of the day's labor, you might as well abandon the discussion of this subject, for Labor of America and Labor of Europe and Labor of all countries, which has some intelligence and understanding, will not consent to a work-day longer than eight hours in each day. . . . There is something not yet understood by employers, and that is that a long work-day does not yield the greatest product. . . . We are not going back, nor are we going to be driven back. The whole purpose and worth of the International Labor Commission, of the Draft Conventions and of the International Labor Conferences was to bring light into the lives of the working people of the world, and not to take from them, by indirection or otherwise, the advantages which they have gained. [4]

Mr. Gompers clearly realized that the eight-hour day was the cornerstone of the entire labor program. If the Conference embodied it in an international convention it would be the most fruitful victory Labor had ever won. The con-

---

[3] Labor's interest in the Conference was shown by the calling, at about the same time, of an International Federation of Trade-Unions Congress and the first International Congress of Working-Women attended by representatives of more than twenty countries. The American Federation of Labor was also to hold its conference in Washington a short time afterwards.

[4] Minutes of the First Annual Meeting of the International Labor Conference, 1919, Government Printing Office, 1920, pp. 44-45.

vention was adopted and marks the most significant step the Organization has taken in industrial reform.

We cannot follow day by day the deliberations of the Conference, although there are few documents more interesting and instructive than the minutes of these annual gatherings. A concise statement of their resolutions, as one usually reads, is a very colorless account, failing to picture, as it does, the strong personalities of the leaders, the constant clash, sometimes comical, sometimes dramatic, of convictions, interests, and prejudices, the puzzling interplay of ethical, economic, and political influences, and withal the evident good will and earnestness that usually inspire the debates. In these pages, we must limit ourselves to a cold analysis of practical achievements.

After a month of concerted efforts, the Washington Conference adopted six draft conventions dealing with: [5]

(a) The application of the principle of an eight-hour day and a forty-eight-hour week
(b) The question of preventing or providing against unemployment
(c) The employment of women before and after childbirth
(d) The employment of women during the night
(e) The minimum age of employment of children in industry
(f) The night work of young persons employed in industry [6]

It also agreed upon the following six recommendations concerning:

(a) Unemployment
(b) Prevention of anthrax
(c) Reciprocity of treatment of foreign workers
(d) Protection of women and children against lead poisoning
(e) Establishment of Government Health Services
(f) Application of the Berne Conventions of 1906, on the prohibition of the use of white phosphorus in the manufacture of matches [7]

---

[5] *Ibid., loc. cit.*   [6] *Ibid.*, pp. 256-261.
[7] *Ibid.*, Appendix, pp. 261-264.

The Genoa Conference.—It is interesting to note that the second annual Conference had really an American origin. Throughout the sessions of the Labor Commission Mr. Gompers had been particularly anxious to safeguard the rights already acquired by American Labor. In virtue of the American Seaman's Law, the sailors of the American merchant marine enjoy a unique privilege. They are guaranteed the right of leaving their ships when these are safe in harbor. Mr. Gompers was eager to make that right one of the fundamental principles of the new "Charter of Labor."

He was strongly opposed by the British delegation. Thereupon, M. Fontaine, the French delegate, suggested that inasmuch as the question implied not only the liberty of the seamen but also the rights of the traveling people and was thereby a delicate one, it would be wiser to refer it to a special session of the International Labor Conference.[8]

The Washington Conference intended its conventions and recommendations to apply more particularly to manufacturing industries. Still the interest aroused by Mr. Gompers in the welfare of seamen had not subsided and the International Labor Organization felt it could not long leave out of consideration the right of a large class of workers whose occupation more than any other seems to require international regulation. It was, therefore, resolved that the "provisions relative to transport by sea and on inland waterways shall be determined by a special conference."[9] Accordingly, the Governing Body of the International Labor Office decided to convene the second session of the International Labor Conference at Genoa, on June 15, 1920, as a special seamen's conference. Twenty-seven na-

---

[8] Minutes of the Labor Commission, thirty-eighth sitting, pp. 359*ff*.

[9] *Cf.* draft convention of the Washington Conference limiting the hours of work in industry, Art. 1 (*d*).

tions sent representatives. There were eighty-seven delegates, of whom forty-seven represented the governments, twenty the shipowners' and twenty the seamen's organizations.

The Genoa Conference presented greater difficulties than the Washington Conference because no previous attempt had been made to bring about international agreement on questions affecting the employment of seamen.

Three draft conventions and four recommendations were adopted:

Conventions

    (*a*) Fixing the minimum age for admission of children to employment at sea

    (*b*) Concerning unemployment indemnity in case of loss or foundering of the ship

    (*c*) Establishing facilities for finding employment for seamen

Recommendations

    (*a*) Concerning the limitation of hours of work in the fishing industry

    (*b*) Concerning the limitation of hours of work in inland navigation

    (*c*) Concerning the establishment of national seamen's codes [10]

    (*d*) Concerning unemployment insurance for seamen

It has often been argued that special circumstances in certain countries and industries prevent the formulation of international rules. It would seem, then, that these inter-

---

[10] The Conference requested the Office to make the necessary studies preparatory to that end. The work accomplished has been summarized in a pamphlet entitled "The International Seamen's Code." The five following subjects have been suggested as susceptible of immediate codification: articles of agreement; lodging of seamen on board; discipline; conciliation between seamen and their employers; social and industrial insurance for seamen and the possibility of international reciprocity in this matter. *Cf.* Report of the Director, 1921, p. 202.

national regulations could be easily accepted in the case of maritime navigation, for there the conditions of labor are so much alike.

The agreements concluded at Genoa represented solid achievements. Nevertheless, the Conference is regarded in a sense as a failure, because no solution of the question of working hours was reached. This question was considered the most important item on the agenda. The main issue was whether the Conference should adopt the British government's proposal for a fifty-six-hour week at sea and a forty-eight-hour week in port or the French proposal of a forty-eight-hour week with unlimited overtime compensated by additional wages or by extra time off in port. The seamen's group were in favor of the French system. A large majority of the shipowners were hostile to both alternatives. The decision then rested with the government delegates, who were sharply divided. The final vote was forty-eight for and twenty-five against the draft convention embodying the French proposal. It failed of the necessary majority by two-thirds of a vote. As the governments of several of the most important countries voted in the minority (Great Britain, Japan, Norway, Spain), it is probable that the convention would not have been ratified by these countries, even had it been carried.

First Geneva Conference, 1921.—It soon became evident that the Washington draft conventions and recommendations would have to be extended to the largest and most important class of workers, the agricultural workers. The Governing Body decided to devote the 1921 Conference to that question. A determined opposition rose from various quarters, and was firmly voiced by the French government.[11]   Not only was the appli-

---

[11] For an excellent summary of the whole controversy see Report of the 1921 Conference of the Director to the Geneva Conference of 1922, pp. 73-85.

cation of the eight-hour day and forty-eight-hour week
to agriculture vigorously denounced, but the whole question of the competence of the Organization anent agricultural labor was raised. The Conference scheduled to take
place in Geneva in April, 1921, was postponed to the fall
of the same year and opened on the 25th of October, with
thirty-nine nations represented. The delegates numbered
one hundred and eighteen, and they were accompanied by
some two hundred and thirty technical advisers; of the
delegates sixty-nine represented the governments, twenty-
four the employers, twenty-five the workers. Lord Burnham, of Great Britain, ex-member of the House of Commons and proprietor of the *London Daily Telegraph,* was
elected president of the Conference. After many stormy
sessions, the Conference decided the fundamental question
of jurisdiction in the affirmative.[12] It clearly favored that
agricultural labor regulations should come within the scope
of the International Labor Organization. It was later sustained in that opinion by a ruling of the International
Court of Justice.[13]

The question of the adaptation to agricultural labor of
the Washington declarations concerning the regulation of
the hours of work failed of the necessary two-thirds vote
and was withdrawn from the agenda, but the resolution was
passed that "the regulation of the hours of work in agriculture be inserted in the agenda of a future session of the
Conference."

The third Conference is looked upon as a very successful
one. Seven draft conventions and eight recommendations
were adopted:[14]

---

[12] *Cf.* Geneva, 1921, pp. 18-76.
[13] *Cf.* Report of the Director to Geneva Conference of 1922, pp.
72-85.
[14] International Labor Conference, third session, Geneva, 1921,
Appendix, pp. 832-863.

Conventions

(a) The right of association for agricultural workers
(b) The extension of workmen's compensation laws to agricultural workers
(c) The employment of children in agriculture
(d) The prohibition of the use of white lead in painting
(e) The employment of young persons under eighteen as trimmers and stokers
(f) The medical examination of children and young persons employed at sea
(g) Weekly rest in industry

Recommendations

(a) The development of vocational agricultural education
(b) The prevention of unemployment in agriculture
(c) Insurance of agricultural wage earners against sickness, invalidity, old age, etc.
(d) The night work of children in agriculture
(e) The night work of women in agriculture
(f) The employment of women in agriculture before and after childbirth
(g) The living-in conditions of agricultural workers .
(h) The weekly rest day for workers in commercial houses

Though the majority of the decisions of this Conference dealt with agriculture, one of its most significant decisions was undoubtedly that with regard to the prohibition of the use of white lead in painting. Thus was settled a question of the gravest importance and which had been the subject of bitter controversy for the last fifty years.

Second Geneva Conference, 1922.—In view of the difficulty of securing ratification of the draft conventions already adopted, particularly under the present unsettled economic and political conditions, it was thought wiser in 1922 not to continue to add to the list of impending obligations of the nations. The three preceding Conferences had adopted thirty-six decisions to be submitted to the legislative authorities of the

various countries—not a small task, indeed. It was undoubtedly better to mark time for a while. Moreover, it
was necessary to devote some thought to questions of internal organization [15] and the Conference of 1922 was a
welcome opportunity to do so.

The Conference met in Geneva, which thereafter was to
be the regular meeting place. Lord Burnham was again
chosen as its president. Thirty-nine countries were represented.

An amendment to Article 393 of the Treaty of Versailles, referring to the constitution of the Governing Body,
was adopted by the Conference. We have dealt at considerable length with the history of that reform in the
preceding chapter.[16]

Only one recommendation was adopted, referring to the
communication of emigration and immigration statistics to
the International Labor Office.[17] Information concerning
emigration, immigration, repatriation, and transit of emigrants should be communicated every three months, and,
within six months of the end of the year to which they
refer, should be communicated the total figures of emigrants and immigrants, specifying sex, age, occupation, nationality, country of last residence, country of proposed
residence. The adoption of uniformity in issuing identity
papers and recording statistical information was also recommended.

Third Geneva Conference or Fifth Session.—The fifth
session of the annual Conference, held in Geneva, October
22 to 29, 1923, dealt exclusively with the vital problem of
factory inspection. The Organization had been long pre-

---

[15] International Labor Conference, fourth session, Geneva, 1922,
Appendix, pp. 1-15.
[16] *Cf.* Chap. VI, pp. 116–122. Amendment given in Appendix I,
p. 290.
[17] International Labor Conference, fourth session, Geneva, 1922,
p. 395.

occupied with the question of inspection. Factory inspection had been brought up repeatedly at previous sessions of the Conference. The Treaties of Peace themselves had taken note of its importance and issued the warning that no lasting benefits would be derived by the workers from labor legislation unless provision was made for an adequate system of inspection.

During the 1923 Conference the question was divided, in order to permit a thorough examination, into four principal sections: (1) scope of factory inspection; (2) nature of the functions and powers of factory inspectors; (3) organization of factory inspection; and (4) inspection reports. This examination revealed a great diversity of practice among industrial countries but this diversity did not prevent an agreement upon general principles. These principles were embodied in a single recommendation which ought to prove a most valuable guide in the organization and perfecting of factory inspection.

The Sixth Session of the Annual Conference.—The International Labor Conference held its sixth session at Geneva, from June 16 to July 5, 1924. There were in all two hundred and ninety-one members of the Conference; sixty-nine of them were delegates of governments, twenty-nine represented the employers' associations, and twenty-eight the workers' organizations of their respective countries; and there were one hundred and sixty-five technical advisers.

The Conference unanimously chose as its president Hjalmar Branting, who has played such a brilliant part in the affairs of Sweden and on the wider stage of international politics.

The Conference adopted a draft convention concerning equality of treatment for national and foreign workers as regards workmen's compensation for accidents, a draft convention on night work in bakeries and a draft convention concerning the weekly suspension of work for twenty-four hours in glass-manufacturing processes where tank furnaces are used. It adopted a recommendation concerning the development of facilities for the utilization of workers' spare time, and an additional recommendation concerning equality of treatment for national and foreign workers as regards workmen's compensation for accidents, two very important matters.

The development of facilities for the utilization of workers' leisure is of much greater importance than it at first appears. Many have feared that the new-found spare time might be used in ways not conducive either to the wellbeing of the worker or to the prosperity of the community. While avoiding excessive paternalism, much could be done in a constructive way to facilitate the pleasant and useful employment of spare time. The recommendation which resulted from the long discussion of this topic deals successively with the preservation of spare time (by the prohibition or discouragement of supplementary employment, and the better organization of transport to avoid waste of time); the relation between spare time and social hygiene, including the problems of drink, tuberculosis, and venereal disease; housing policy; institutions for the utilization of spare time (e.g., gardens, allotments, sport, education) which should be encouraged; and finally the free use of institutions and the coördination of local action in the matter. The Committee further adopted a resolution asking the International Labor Office to keep in constant touch with the governments on the questions discussed and to publish regularly reports on the action taken and the results obtained.

On the whole the delegates were proud of the results of the sixth Conference. The conventions and recommendations adopted represent a solid achievement, and if finally ratified, they will mark a substantial advance in international labor legislation.

During the sixth session was also debated the problem which had for some time past troubled the Office of facilitating the ratification of conventions. It has seemed, in many cases, as if a slight amendment to a convention would make it possible for a particular government, whose legislation differed in what was perhaps a minor point, to register its ratification. A provisional procedure was therefore decided upon, namely, to send the text of a convention or recommendation, before a final vote is taken upon it, to the governments of the members, which will be entitled "to submit such amendments as they consider necessary to facilitate their ratification." These will be examined at the succeeding session of the Conference before the delegates proceed to the final vote. Therefore, the sixth session adopted provisionally the three draft conventions referred to above.

The Seventh Session of the Annual Conference.—The seventh session of the International Labor Conference was held in Geneva, from May 19 to June 10, 1925. Doctor Edward Benes, Minister of Foreign Affairs of Czechoslovakia, was unanimously elected president. The delegates felt honored to work under a man who had won the respect of all in the councils of Central Europe and who, as a member of the Committee on International Labor Legislation at Paris, in 1918, had assisted to shape its charter in the Treaties of Peace. Forty-six countries (the highest figure yet reached) were represented at the seventh session. There were in all one hundred and forty-four delegates present, of whom eighty represented their governments, thirty-two the employers, and thirty-two the workers.

The first part of the agenda of the seventh session demanded final votes upon the proposed draft conventions and recommendation provisionally adopted in 1924. In addition to this legacy from the sixth session a new item appeared on the agenda, the question of workmen's compensation. Moreover, the term of office of the Governing Body had come to an end and it was necessary that new elections be held.

The seventh session finally adopted the draft convention provisionally accepted by the sixth session concerning equality of treatment for national and foreign workers as regards workmen's compensation for accidents. The practical value of this convention was evident. A worker who is employed outside his own country and who is injured in the course of his employment frequently benefits by the compensation legislation of neither his own land nor that in which he works. This convention will put an end to that anomaly and in these days when much immigration is taking place it will be of immediate benefit to many thousands of workers.

The draft convention forbidding night work in bakeries was adopted, after a revision of the original text and a discussion which occupied eleven sittings.

The draft convention concerning the weekly suspension of work for twenty-four hours in glass-manufacturing processes where tank furnaces are used, provisionally adopted by the sixth session, was lost.

Finally the seventh session opened up the whole subject of social insurance, which next to the eight-hour day is the most vital part of a social welfare program.

A draft convention was adopted regarding workmen's compensation for accidents, and another regarding workmen's compensation for occupational diseases; also recommendations concerning (1) the minimum scale of workmen's compensation, (2) workmen's compensation for occupational diseases, (3) jurisdiction in disputes on workmen's compensation, (4) equality of treatment for national and foreign workers as regards workers' compensation for accidents.

The most important act of the Conference was the laying down of international standards in workmen's compensation legislation. The object of the convention is to secure that workers "who suffer personal injury due to an industrial accident or their dependents are compensated for loss of earnings." The convention applies to all workers, including apprentices, whether in a public or a private enterprise.

The draft convention on occupational diseases is in the nature of a supplement to the accident compensation convention. It shows how far the nations are ready to go in the way of assimilating industrial diseases with industrial accidents. The convention, however, gives only three types of industrial diseases which shall be considered as industrial accidents, namely, lead and mercury poisoning and anthrax infection.

As to legislative procedure, the Conference refused to continue the practice of the sixth conference, namely, to postpone a final vote until the following year. It definitely abandoned the second reading plan.

For May, 1926, the Governing Body has called two sessions of the Conference. The first, that is, the eighth session, would be the normal session to deal with the general questions and if necessary take a final vote on the draft convention on workmen's compensation discussed by the 1925 session, and one new question, namely, the simplification of the inspection of immigrants on board ship. The second session is to deal with the maritime questions and will therefore be largely a session of specialists. Its agenda will be (1) the international codification of rules relating to seamen's articles of agreement; (2) general principles for the inspection of the conditions under which seamen work and live.

In order that the scope of the International Labor Organization and the importance of the task they set out to accomplish may be more evident, we will classify the conventions and recommendations so far adopted under their appropriate headings. It is only then that one can fully appreciate the work done by the Conferences.

LEGISLATION OF THE ORGANIZATION

THE FAMILY

The broad humanitarian purpose of the Organization appears first in the interest it has taken in that most fundamental social unit, the family, by furthering legislation for the protection of maternity, women, children, and young persons in industry. If they had achieved nothing more than to bring before the parliaments and the public opinion of the world that great social duty to make possible a happy and healthy family life, they would have justified their existence.

Women have always taken a prominent part in the work of the International Labor Organization. Women had a share in shaping its constitution. Women delegates have attended all its general conferences. Women constitute almost half the permanent staff of the International Labor Office. Women's organizations maintain close contact with it. An important part of its work has been concerned with the conditions of employment of women.

Most of the questions on which the International Labor Conference has adopted decisions concern men and women equally, and the decisions themselves apply equally to women and men without distinction. For example, the important draft convention providing for an eight-hour day and a forty-eight-hour week applies equally to men and to women, and so do the conventions providing for the establishment of free employment agencies and for a weekly rest in industry. Aside from these the Organization has taken a special interest in the welfare of women and children.

I. *Maternity*

For the protection of maternity, the following measures have been proposed: [18]

1. Draft convention passed at Washington, 1919, applying to women employed in commerce and industry providing (*a*) that no woman shall be permitted to work during the six weeks preceding her confinement; (*b*) that she shall have the right to leave her work upon production of a medical certificate stating that her confinement will probably take place within six weeks; (*c*) that each woman, so absent, irrespective of age or nationality, whether married or unmarried, shall be paid benefits sufficient for the full and healthy maintenance of herself and of her child, provided out of public funds or by a system of insurance; (*d*) that such women shall be further entitled to the additional benefit of free attendance of a doctor or certified midwife; (*e*) that women workers nursing their children shall be allowed half an hour twice a day during the working hours for this purpose.

2. Recommendation voted at Geneva, 1921, that measures be taken to insure to women wage earners in agricultural undertakings protection before and after childbirth similar to that provided by the Washington Convention for women employed in industry and commerce.

3. Resolution adopted at Washington, 1919, inviting the governments to study appropriate means to relieve nursing mothers from the necessity of supporting themselves through factory work.

---

[18] All conventions, recommendations, and resolutions are found *in extenso* in the Appendix which follows the Minutes of the Annual Sessions of the Conference, published yearly in the Official Report of the International Organization of Labor.

II. *Protection of Women and Children*

(*a*) *Night work*.—1. Draft convention voted at Washington, 1919, providing that women without distinction of age shall not be employed in any industrial undertaking during the night.

2. Draft convention of Washington, 1919, providing that persons under the age of eighteen shall not be employed during the night in any public or private industrial undertaking, except where only members of the same family are employed.

3. Recommendation voted at Geneva, 1921, regulating the employment of women wage earners in agricultural undertakings during the night in such a way that they shall be assured a period of rest compatible with their physical necessities, and consisting of not less than nine hours which should, when possible, be consecutive.

4. Recommendation voted at Geneva, 1921, to regulate the employment of children under fourteen engaged in agricultural undertakings during the night in such a way as to assure them a rest period of not less than ten consecutive hours and of young persons between the ages of fourteen and eighteen similarly engaged so as to assure them a rest period of not less than nine consecutive hours.

5. Resolution voted at Geneva, 1921, requesting the governments, which would not judge it possible to apply immediately to the devastated regions the draft convention of Washington regarding the night work of children, to endeavor to apply it dating from December 31, 1923.

(*b*) *Minimum age for admission to industrial employment*.—1. Draft convention of Washington, 1919, providing that children under fourteen years of age shall not be employed in private or public industrial undertakings.

2. Draft convention of Genoa, 1920, providing that children under fourteen shall be prohibited from employment

or work on vessels, except where only members of the same family are employed.

3. Draft convention of Geneva, 1921, providing that children under fourteen years of age may not be employed nor may they work in any public or private agricultural undertaking except outside the hours fixed for school attendance. If employed outside the hours of school attendance, the employment shall not be such as to prejudice their attendance at school.

4. Draft convention voted at Geneva, 1921, providing that young persons under the age of eighteen shall not be employed as trimmers or stokers on any vessel engaged in maritime navigation, whether publicly or privately owned, exclusive of ships of war, school ships, and training ships approved and supervised by public authority, and vessels mainly propelled by other means than steam.

5. Draft convention of Geneva, 1921, providing that the employment of any child or young person under eighteen years of age on any vessel engaged in maritime navigation, exclusive of ships of war or vessels on which members of the same family are employed, shall be conditional on the production of a medical certificate attesting fitness for such work.

6. Draft convention of Geneva, 1925, providing that no young person under the age of eighteen shall be employed in night work in bakeries even when such authorization is granted for adults.

Hours of Work and Rest

Vital to society as the protection of women and children may be, workers had laid more emphasis upon the amount of time which should be devoted to labor in justice to themselves, to their families, and to society. For many years, the shortening of the working day had been the goal of their highest aspirations and represented the most concrete results of their intensive campaign since the War. In truth, we have reached here the very core of the great labor problem. While the statement of this reform is exceedingly simple, there is none that carries with it so many perplexing implications. It cannot be an isolated reform; it is but the first chapter of an entire social renovation. For five years now, it has been the subject of debate in every country. In the United States, for instance, through the years 1918-1920, the National Industrial Conference Board has issued several reports on hours of work.[19] Employers, the world over, have grown much concerned about it. They wonder whether humanity is not going astray on that question, whether it is not our standard of civilization that is ignorantly threatened, for our civilization is based on a high economic productivity, and the theory of the eight-hour day seems to them a danger to production.

Any one who has ever dealt with the problem admits how difficult it is to regulate the hours of labor on any uniform basis, even within national frontiers. Exceptions and qualifications must be provided for to meet the exigencies of trade, of climate, of certain customs and traditions. As soon as we attempt a like regulation on an international scale, the intricacy of the problem grows apace. Delicate as the task was, the International Organization of Labor felt bound to approach it with all the daring that the post-War enthusiasm permitted. Its decisions are summed up in the following declarations:

I. *Length of the Working Day*

1. Draft convention of Washington, 1919, limiting the hours of work in industrial undertakings to eight in the day and forty-eight in the week.

---

[19] *Cf.* publications of the National Industrial Conference Board, Research Reports Nos. 4, 7, 11, 12, 16, 18, and 27.

2.   Recommendation of Genoa, 1920, to the effect that each member shall, in consultation with the organizations of employers and workers concerned, enact legislation limiting in this direction the hours of work of all persons engaged in the fishing industry with such special modifying provisions as might be necessitated by the conditions surrounding the fishing industry in each country.

3.   Draft convention of Geneva, 1925, providing that the working of bread, pastry, or other flour confectionery during the night is forbidden.   Reasonable exceptions to insure weekly rest or to deal with national necessities are approved.

II.   *Weekly Rest*

1.   Draft convention of Geneva, 1921, providing that the entire staff employed in any industrial undertaking, whether public or private, shall in every period of seven days be allowed a rest period of at least twenty-four consecutive hours.   This rest period shall, wherever possible, be granted simultaneously to the entire staff of the undertaking, and shall, wherever possible, be fixed so as to coincide with the traditions and customs of the country and district.   Exceptions may be made in the case of undertakings in which only persons of one single family are employed.

2.   Recommendation of Geneva, 1921, providing for a rest period of twenty-four consecutive hours in every seven days for the entire staff employed in any commercial establishment, public or private.   Wherever possible, this rest period shall be granted simultaneously to the entire staff of each establishment and should be fixed so as to coincide with the days already established by tradition and custom in the country or district.

3.   Resolution voted at Geneva, 1921, asserting that it is the duty of member states to encourage the adoption of

a weekly day of rest for all workers of their respective countries, this rest to be extended to thirty-six hours through collective agreements between the employers' and workers' organizations.

4. Recommendations of Geneva, 1925, concerning the development of facilities for the utilization of workers' spare time, it providing for the preservation of spare time and studies the ways and means for the best utilization of the leisure of workers.

UNEMPLOYMENT

Unemployment is the great nightmare of Labor and a most trying economic problem. Credit must be given to the International Labor Organization for its full realization of the importance of this evil and its earnest desire to coöperate in the discovery of suitable remedies. The problem, however, looms up so vast and so complex that it frequently appears insoluble. It cannot be solved unless through international coöperation. The situation has been aggravated by post-War economic and political conditions, such as lack of international confidence, instability of exchanges, curtailment of consumption due to reduced incomes, so that the crisis of unemployment has reached in the last four years unheard of proportions. At the Conference which was held in September, 1921, at the invitation of President Harding, official estimates of the number of unemployed in the United States varied between 3,500,000 and 5,700,000.[20]

These figures, while showing the severity of the crisis, reveal also the inadequacy of the means at present available to obtain reliable data. In 1924 and 1925 the situation

---

[20] William L. Chenery, "The President's Conference and Unemployment in the United States," *International Labor Review*, March, 1922.

in the United States has greatly improved as a result, it would seem, of the double policy of credit control and immigration control. For a time, however, unemployment ever in our midst, was a distressing reality. If we are to devise any corrective or palliative measures, more exact and detailed statistics are needed. At its very first Conference, the International Labor Organization had emphasized that great need, and on the basis of such data as were then available it began to suggest remedies of a more general character as are embodied in the following recommendations:

1. Draft convention of Washington, 1919, to have transmitted to the International Office, at intervals of not more than three months, all available information relating to unemployment and the measures taken to combat it. Each member further agrees to establish a system of free public employment agencies under control of a central authority.

2. Recommendation of the Washington Conference, 1919, that each member of the International Labor Organization take measures to prohibit the establishment of employment agencies which charge fees or which carry on their business for profit. Where such agencies exist, it is further recommended that they be permitted to operate only under government license and that all practical measures be taken to secure their abolition as soon as possible.

It is also recommended that the execution of all public work shall be coördinated with the view to reserving as much of it as is practicable for periods of unemployment and for districts most affected by it.

3. Draft convention of Genoa, 1920, providing that the members organize and maintain an efficient and adequate system of public employment offices for finding without charge employment for seamen, and to maintain such public employment offices either under the direct control of the

state, or of representative associations of shipowners and seamen jointly, or under the control of a central authority. Existing agencies of a commercial character may be permitted to continue their work temporarily under government license, but practical measures should be taken to abolish them as soon as possible.

4. Recommendation of Geneva, 1921, that each member shall consider measures which will have as their object the prevention or provision against unemployment suitable to their respective agricultural or economic conditions. Six different measures are suggested to obtain this end.

(a) Adoption of modern technical methods to bring under cultivation land either not now worked or worked partially, but which could be made to yield an adequate return.

(b) Encouragement of adoption of improved systems of cultivation and more intensive use of land.

(c) Development of facilities for land settlement.

(d) Taking steps to render work of a temporary nature accessible to unemployed agricultural workers by means of the provision of transport facilities.

(e) Development of industries and supplemental employments that will employ agricultural workers suffering from seasonable unemployment.

(f) Taking steps for the encouragement of the creation of agricultural workers' coöperative societies for working, purchase, or operation of land and for this purpose taking measures to increase agricultural credit in favor of coöperative agricultural associations of land workers having as their object the use of land for production.

5. The two following resolutions were passed upon at Geneva, 1921:

(a) The Conference, considering that the question of the world distribution of raw materials is closely connected with the most important labor problems, especially that of unemployment, instructs the Governing Body to study the problem and to submit its conclusions to the next conference.

(*b*) Resolution to instruct the International Labor Office to institute a special inquiry on the national and international aspects of the unemployment crisis, and on the means of combating it, to instruct the Governing Body to take every step within its power to secure the summoning of an international conference which shall consider the remedies of an international character to put an end to the crisis of unemployment.

6. Draft convention of Genoa, 1920, relating to the unemployment indemnity in case of loss or foundering of the ship. All persons employed on any vessel engaged in maritime navigation, exclusive of ships of war, shall, in case of loss or foundering of the vessel, be paid an indemnity against unemployment at the same rate of wages at which they were employed. The total indemnity to any seaman may be limited to two months' wages.

7. Recommendation of Washington, 1919, that each member undertake to establish an effective system of unemployment insurance to associations whose rules provide for the payment of benefits to unemployed members.

8. Recommendation of Genoa, 1920, with a view that each member of the International Labor Office establish for its seamen an effective system of unemployment insurance whether such unemployment arises from shipwreck or any other cause and that such insurance shall be paid by the government or by means of government subventions to industrial organizations whose rules provide for payment of benefits to unemployed members.

These various measures have been highly commended almost universally. Archibald Crawford, the secretary of the South African Industrial Federation, speaking before the Sixth Annual Convention of the South African Federated Chamber of Industries held åt Cape Town on April 24-25, 1923, said: "The Conventions, Recommendations and Resolutions of the International Labor Conference on the subject of unemployment were the real foundations of a permanent solution of this great problem." [21]

In a careful study of the problem conducted recently by the International Labor Office, this conclusion is reached:

There is no panacea for unemployment. Its origins are many and it can be effectively checked only by a variety of methods. One of these, however, is stabilization of the price level. A further object would seem to be the progressive elimination of the difficulties of international trade, a process which would unquestionably lead to a higher general level of employment and the consequent avoidance of much individual privation and distress. The prevention of unemployment demands, in brief, a policy of international coöperation to secure better organization of production and exchange, such a policy involving, as a primary step that of securing stability in the value of all media of exchange.[22]

EMIGRATION

Closely connected with unemployment is the question of emigration. Not only the evil of unemployment cannot be efficiently counteracted but production may be seriously hampered and social reform considerably delayed, unless we have an intelligent international distribution of the forces of labor. Dependable previsions and calculations in economics become almost impossible unless we can secure a certain equilibrium in the factors of production. For no country, perhaps, this problem presents an importance equal to that which it has assumed in the political and economic life of the United States.

---

[21] *Cape Times*, April 26, 1923. *Industrial and Labor Information*, Vol. VI, No. 12.

[22] "Unemployment in 1924 and 1925," *International Labor Review*, August, 1925, p. 224.

In Washington a resolution was passed moving the creation of an international permanent commission intrusted with the study of emigration and notably the international coördination of various national legislations.

The second Geneva Conference of 1922 voted a recommendation to communicate emigration and immigration statistics to the International Labor Office with a view to paving the way to future international action regulating conditions of emigration.

INDUSTRIAL HYGIENE AND SECURITY

It is a most evident duty on the part of society not to demand products the manufacture of which threatens the health of the workers, or, if they be necessary, to devise efficient measures to protect the workers engaged in these dangerous industrial processes. Compliance with that duty should be prompted as well by the most elementary conception of the truest interests of the community, as the life, strength, and health of the workers are a most valuable asset. Considerations of humanity and sound economics moved the International Labor Organization to resume the efforts already put forth by the International Association for Labor Legislation, and it has made the following contributions to this worth-while movement.

I. *White Lead*

A draft convention of Geneva, 1921, (*a*) prohibiting the use of white lead and lead sulphate and all products containing these pigments in internal painting of buildings; (*b*) regulating the use of it in operations for which their use is not prohibited; (*c*) forbidding women and male persons under eighteen years of age to engage in any painting work where white lead, lead sulphate, or their products are used; (d) providing that morbidity and mortality statistics shall be obtained.

II. *White Phosphorus*

The Washington Conference recommended that those members who have not already indicated their adherence to the Berne Convention of 1906 relating to the prohibition of the use of white phosphorus in the manufacture of matches shall do so.

III. *Lead Poisoning*

The Washington Conference adopted the following recommendation: In view of the danger involved for both women and children, it is recommended that women and young persons under the age of eighteen be excluded from employment in which there is danger from lead poisoning. It is further recommended that the employment of women and of young persons under the age of eighteen shall be permitted in processes involving the use of lead compounds only where adequate provisions are taken for their efficient protection.

IV. *Anthrax*

1. Recommendation of Washington, 1919, that arrangements shall be made for the disinfection of wool infected with anthrax spores, either in the country exporting such wool or, if this is not practicable, at the port of entry in the country importing such wool.

2. Resolution voted at Geneva in order that the study of the prophylaxy of anthrax be intrusted to a special commission.

V. *General Protection*

1. Recommendation of Washington, 1919, that the members of the International Labor Organization shall institute a system of efficient factory inspection, if they have not already done so, and shall in addition establish a government health service for the purpose of safeguarding the health of the workers.

2. Creation of a Consulting Commission of Experts, with the mission of studying questions of industrial hygiene.

3. Recommendation of Geneva, 1921, that each member extend to agricultural wage earners the benefit of its laws and regulations instituting systems of insurance against sickness, invalidity, old age, and other similar risks, on conditions equivalent to those prevailing in the case of workers in industry and commerce.

4. Convention of Geneva, 1921, extending to all agricultural wage earners its laws and regulations which provide for the compensation of workers for personal injury by accident arising out of or in the course of their employment.

5. Recommendation of Geneva, 1921, that measures be taken for the regulation of living-in conditions of agricultural workers. These conditions refer to proper housing, heating, moral and physical hygiene.

6. Draft convention of Geneva, 1921, undertaking to secure to all those engaged in agriculture the same rights of association and combination as to industrial workers and to repeal any statutory or other provisions restricting such rights in the case of those engaged in agriculture.

7. Draft convention of Washington, 1919, providing that members of the Organization who have systems of unemployment insurance in effect on satisfactory terms make arrangements whereby their nationals, working in the territory of another member, shall be admitted to the same

rates of benefit as prevail in the country in which they are employed.

8. Recommendation of Washington, 1919, providing that the members of the International Labor Organization shall, on condition of reciprocity upon terms to be agreed between the countries affected, admit foreign workmen, together with their families employed within its territory, to the benefit of its labor laws and regulations as well as to the same rights of lawful organization enjoyed by its own workers.

9. Draft convention of Geneva, 1925, concerning the quality of treatment for national and foreign workers as regards workmen's compensation for accidents.

10. Draft convention of Geneva, 1925, concerning workmen's compensation for occupational diseases, providing that compensation shall be payable to workmen incapacitated by occupational diseases or in case of death from such diseases to their dependents.

11. Draft convention of Geneva, 1925, concerning workmen's compensation for accidents, insuring that workmen who suffer personal injury due to an industrial accident, or their dependents, shall be compensated on terms at least equal to those provided by this convention.

12. Recommendation of Geneva, 1925, concerning the minimum scale of workmen's compensation.

The above record shows undisputedly that neither the Office which prepared this legislation, nor the Conferences which elaborated it in commission or public sittings, have incurred the reproach of idleness. Their critics have rather charged them with hasty procedure, untimely and excessive zeal.

No one, however, can deny that they have concentrated their efforts upon the most fundamental labor problems of our age. Nothing could exceed in importance the protection of mothers, women, and children, the elimination of unemployment, and the preservation and proper use of a man's energy for his highest good and the greatest advantage of the community.

The Conferences have done their part in the measure in which circumstances allowed. The work was undertaken with eagerness and conscientiously carried on. Every convention and recommendation is the product of close discussion by experts chosen by their trade-unions or their employers' organizations, or their national administrations for their knowledge of the subjects under consideration. It is true that many of the proposed reforms had been wholly or partially realized in some countries, but nowhere had they been extended to the laboring class as a whole, or strictly enforced. The Conferences were also ably conducted and, as a first experiment of an international parliament of nations, it is by no means a discouraging experience. In spite of the many differences of race, opinions, and class affiliations, the delegates have found it possible to work together and to come to definite agreements. They have done their part honestly, at least while at the Conference. We shall see later whether the governments have discharged their obligations equally well.

MORAL INFLUENCE

It is impossible to measure the influence exercised by the International Organization of Labor on national legislation, solely in terms of ratifications obtained. The entire movement has brought about a large volume of social legislation now before the national parliaments. It may even be stated that the decisions of the Conferences have almost everywhere constituted prototypes for the labor legislation adopted since the Washington Conference. The International Labor Organization is undoubtedly giving a new impulse to the effort for reform.

While we admit that, on the whole, labor legislation in the various countries has progressed along the lines suggested by the Industrial Labor Organization, we may ask whether this progress was due to the Organization or to other causes.

In the new countries like the Republics of South America and the British Dominions, the moral authority of the decisions of the Conference seems real. Chili is a very interesting illustration of it. Although poorly represented at the Conference, and with none of the proposed conventions admitted to the legislature, the Chilean government has nevertheless embodied in its labor legislation practically all the decisions of the Conference.

The countries of Europe and of the Orient seem still more influenced by these international deliberations. The Bulgarian government, in bringing up for ratification before its legislature the Washington conventions, said: "We must take into account what has been done by our nearest neighbours; we cannot expose ourselves to the charge that our country interferes with the policy of other states which wish to better the condition of the workers." [23]

In Japan, the government shows a sincere desire to improve the conditions of labor. An imperial decree, promulgated on January 15, 1923, prescribed the institution of a permanent Imperial Office abroad to deal with matters relating to the International Labor Organization.[24] It is composed of two secretaries under the control and direction of the delegate of the Japanese government to the Governing Body of the International Labor Office. The Labor representatives of Japan who attended the Conference have repeatedly stated how useful the declaration of principles formulated by the Labor Commission is for

---

[23] Cf. *Official Bulletin* of the International Labor Organization, November 13, 1921, p. 3.

[24] Cf. *Industrial and Labor Information*, International Labor Office, March 2, 1923, p. 5.

them. A measure which to us is commonplace, as, for example, the right of association, is full of importance to them in the conquest of their liberties.

The same thing is true for India. After the Washington Conference great hopes had been aroused in that country. They have not been in vain. It is a great pacific revolution which has taken place. It will make its influence felt in international relations.

In the Occidental countries, it seems doubtful whether the International Labor Organization has played a great part. The decisions of the annual Conferences are still inspired by the legislation already in existence in these countries, and it might seem therefore that these nations influence the Organization more than the Organization influences the nations.[25]

We should not overlook this other appreciable result, that through the International Labor Organization the conditions of the workers in Asia and Africa are considerably bettered and that consequently their demoralizing competition is less to be feared.

Moreover, there are certain classes of laborers, particularly seamen, which cannot improve their working conditions except through international understandings.

The Conference offers also a very special interest as an international forum. Through the public discussion of their claims and of their grievances, the Labor leaders arouse the attention of the world, influence public opinion or educate it in their respective countries. It is also of great educational value to all the representatives. Nothing could be of greater profit than to have representatives of Labor, Capital, and governments know each other, establish personal contact, learn to understand their respective problems and effectively to coöperate towards the promotion

---

[25] *Cf.* Max Lazard, *L'Organisation Permanente du Travail*, Paris, 1922, pp. 60-65.

of the public good. Thence, for the Organization to grow into an agent of industrial conciliation is but a step.[26]

Another lesson of great value is the fact that the workers are given here an opportunity to influence their governments. They are learning to resort to legal means, to use peaceful methods rather than force. Moreover, the thoughts and feelings of the masses are largely controlled by their wants. The satisfaction of these wants, in an equitable measure, is the great economic problem which is going to demand a scientific exploitation and distribution of the earth's resources. To that end, the Conferences already supply the nucleus of a world economic parliament which will teach men coöperation in the hard business of making a living, instead of a wasteful and inordinate competition which brings about a demoralizing accumulation of riches in one section of the globe and a deadly shortage of the essentials of life in another.

It is also true that these solemn declarations of principles which serve to express the unanimity of the aspirations of humanity have an immense value. It is impossible to measure the influence exercised by the Declaration of Independence and the Declaration of the Rights of Man in the evolution of modern civilization. Similarly, the declaration of principles which has been called the Charter of Labor is bound to exercise a noticeable influence upon the thought of the world.

That moral influence of the International Labor Organization appears also in the fact that the Economic Conference called by Lloyd George at Genoa, in 1922, felt that an international convention on reconstruction and unemployment, even though attended by nations not members

---

[26] Albert Thomas refers hopefully to the first case of international conciliation, through the International Labor Organization, between the shipowners and seamen, August, 1920, to January, 1921. Cf. *The International Labor Organization and the First Year of Its Work*, Geneva, 1921, pp. 29-31.

of the International Labor Organization, such as the United States and Russia, could not ignore the authority of the Organization in economic debates of that importance. Although the unexpected turn of events did not allow the Office to contribute as largely as they had hoped, it was a decided gain for the Organization to have received this new official recognition. It demonstrated that, whenever the need occurs, the Organization is both willing and competent to assist. It also shows that no great economic gathering can henceforth take place without availing itself of the information collected and the experience acquired by the International Labor Organization.

RESEARCH WORK OF THE ORGANIZATION

The International Labor Organization is not only intended to draft new laws of conventions; it is also a great clearing house of information with regard to all Labor, industrial, and social movements. In the words of the Treaty, its second task is "the collection and distribution of information on all subjects relating to the international adjustment of conditions of industrial life and labor" (Art. 396).

The efforts carried on in the last five years for the establishment of a system of legislation on an international basis as prescribed by the Treaty of Peace have revealed the urgent need for more exact and comparable information. To-day there exists hardly a country able to establish a system of social legislation without being in possession of accurate information regarding the work accomplished in foreign countries. In certain Labor Departments, it has been considered necessary even to create special sections for foreign information. The parliaments themselves have, besides, set up special services not only for labor questions but for mere general and political and economic matters. The International Labor Office endeavors to make a satisfactory reply to the questions asked, and one need hardly indicate the value of such services to newly developing countries, in particular to those which cannot provide the means for securing satisfactory information.

Even the larger countries sometimes consider it necessary, in order to save expenses, to use the Office, which has means at its disposal for the collection of information in different countries that is not available in any single country. In this way, it has been able to reduce the expenditure of various countries.

Employers' and workers' organizations have realized the importance of industrial information for the defense of their respective interests. This is of considerable value. But the information thus obtained is not always unbiased and does not always make for mutual understanding and conciliation. It is important to have a body of men devoted to the collection of strictly scientific investigation which can be placed within the reach of every one.

It is not unlikely, moreover, that the men who thus endeavor to study thoroughly these industrial problems should be able not only to supply information but to give to individual governments valuable advice and thereby prevent considerable waste and delay in experimentation.

The International Labor Organization discharges its duty as a clearing house of information in two ways: first, by careful preparation of the decisions of the International Labor Conferences; secondly, by furnishing all information required by governments and industrial organizations.

Since the reorganization of the Office, in 1922, this task of preparing and furnishing information has been intrusted partly to the Research Division and partly to the Intelligence and Liaison Division.

It may seem at first difficult to make a wise and efficient

distribution of labor between these two sections. But the purpose of the Directorate is very clear, inasmuch as it intends the Research Division to be able to concentrate entirely on pure research without any thought of serving any one group, or of obtaining any immediate results. It should deal with questions as objectively as possible in truly scientific fashion. On the other hand, the Directorate wishes the Intelligence Division to meet the more immediate needs and demands; it should be the daily dispenser of such information as is constantly required by all to further the work of international labor legislation. The requests for information from all quarters are becoming more numerous every month. During the past year, the Office has received inquiries from governments, employers' and workers' organizations, public and private institutions, as well as from individuals belonging to the following countries: Australia, Austria, Belgium, Canada, Chili, China, Czechoslovakia, Denmark, Esthonia, Finland, France, Germany, Great Britain, India, Italy, Ireland, Japan, Yugoslavia, Netherlands, Norway, Poland, South Africa, Spain, Sweden, Switzerland, United States of America.

The following is a list of some of the subjects on which the International Labor Office has supplied information, in answer to requests from governments since October, 1921:

Profit sharing and copartnership in various countries.

Swiss bill concerning apprenticeship.

Collective labor contracts in various countries.

Eight-hour day in Germany, Belgium, the United States of America and Great Britain.

Regulation of hours of work in commercial undertakings in different countries.

Technical education in Germany.

Classification on unhealthy occupations in various countries.

Holidays in industry and commerce in various countries.

Percentage of sailors and fishermen on board British merchant vessels and fishing boats.

Legislation in force in various countries for the regulation of working hours in hospitals.

Price fixing by laws of articles of necessity in various countries.

Organization and activity of British Civil Servants Associations.

New system of unemployment insurance in Great Britain.

Legislation in various countries concerning night work in bakeries.

Inquiry into the application of the forty-eight-hour week in Great Britain.

Statistics.—One of the most important sections of the Research Division is the Statistical Section. Every one who has at all dealt with economic problems knows that it is a distressing experience to endeavor to secure reliable data, intelligently presented, and methodically classified. Hardly any progress can be made, for instance, in the solution of the problem of unemployment until we have a coherent body of statistical information. The Statistical Section will be engaged not only in the collection of statistical information but in the working out of standard methods for compiling statistics concerning labor problems which will be internationally comparable. Thus it may be possible, for the first time, to deal accurately with some general economic problems.

The Basel International Labor Office had undertaken the collection of laws, statutes, and orders concerning labor and industry adopted in various countries. The International Labor Office carries on that task through the Labor Legislation Section. Most of the governments are supplying it with official documents and legislative acts concerning labor. These are translated, classified, and interpreted by judicial and administrative authorities so that they are readily available for use by any section or inquirer.

Library.—Closely connected with the research work is an adequate library; a large number of standard books on the history of labor legislation, economics, international law and other topics have already been acquired.

The nucleus of the library was formed by the purchase of the Basel Library of the International Association for Labor Legislation. The library possesses the most complete collection in existence of publications relative to industry and labor. This is due to several causes. First, the countries belonging to the Organization send their official publications: second, similar reports are obtained by exchange or purchase from countries which are not members; and finally, publishers send books relative to industrial questions to the International Labor Office for review. Nearly two thousand newspapers and fifteen hundred periodicals are received every week. Research students are going to Geneva in increasing numbers to avail themselves of such a large store of information. In comparison, however, with the well equipped and ably managed American university or public library it is quite deficient. But these shortcomings will undoubtedly be corrected in the more convenient quarters of the new building.

Inquiries.—The Office obtains information in diverse ways through the collection of documentary information appearing in the press, journals, and magazines, and the critical interpretation of it through such sections as the Statistical Section and the Legislative Section, also by sending out questionnaires.

Naturally, the most useful information is that which is obtained on the spot by trained investigators. This method has been followed several times by the Organization. Two of the best known investigations of that character are, "Production in the Ruhr," of May, 1920, and "Labor Conditions Among the Miners of Upper Silesia," of September, 1920.

Some particularly important inquiries are ordered by the Governing Body of the Conference and are called Special Inquiries—thus, the voluminous Inquiry on Labor Conditions in Soviet Russia, and the Inquiry into Production, which aroused so much opposition in certain quarters.

Publications.—The International Labor Office issues a number of very useful and interesting publications: the *International Labor Review,* the *Official Bulletin, Industrial and Labor Information,* the *International Labor Directory, Legislative Series,* and others.

The *International Labor Review,* a monthly, gives articles, statistics, and information relating to labor and industry, of interest and value to employers, workers, and governments. It contains contributions by well-known economists, employers, and trade-union leaders, as well as articles prepared by the International Labor Office. The *Review* has appeared since January, 1921, in both English and French, two thousand copies being in English and two thousand in French. In conformity with the Peace Treaty, it may also be published in other languages in the future.

The *Official Bulletin* is the weekly journal of the Office, and its purpose is to supply information regarding the activities of the International Labor Organization. It contains the text of official documents, reports of meetings of the Governing Body and of the various international commissions, as well as general information with regard to the progress of the work of the Office.

The *Industrial and Labor Information* contains brief notes on important current events relating to Labor and Industry. It is issued weekly, and fortnightly is published with it a *Russian Supplement* devoted entirely to Russian questions.

The *International Labor Directory* contains in a compendious form full information with regard to the organizations, both official and unofficial, which deal with industrial and labor matters throughout the world. It is published annually, in French, English, and German.

The *Legislative Series* contains reprints and translations of the texts of laws, decrees, orders, and regulations affecting Labor issued in the various countries of the world. The *Industrial Safety Survey* is published every two months and is intended to act as a link between those in all countries who are interested in the problems of accident prevention.

Further augmenting the scope and value of its publications, the International Labor Office has begun the publication of the *Encyclopedia of Industrial Hygiene,* which will be issued in two forms: first, a brochure edition comprising one or more articles dealing with a particular subject; and second, the volume edition, into which previously published brochures will be incorporated.

The purpose of the *Encyclopedia of Industrial Hygiene* is to gather and disseminate all information available concerning industries or processes which may be considered unhealthy. This work is planned to aid in the detection of occupational diseases, indicate steps for their cure and prevention and lay down general principles for the proper protection of workers.

One of the most comprehensive and instructive publications, if one wishes to follow both the growth of the Organization in all its phases, the development of the international spirit in labor legislation and the character of actual relations between the three factors of this new movement, namely, the governments, the employers, and the workers, is the Annual Report of the International Labor Conference. It contains in French and English, the always very complete report of the Director, the stenographic reports of the sessions of the Conference, and the official text of the draft conventions and recommendations adopted by the Conference. No one who has not perused this report can claim to comprehend the significance and purpose of the Organization.

Since 1922, the Governing Body has also authorized the publication in Italian of a small monthly review entitled *Informazioni sociali* which contains extracts from the periodicals of the office.

A little later a similar publication appeared in Spanish for Spanish and South American readers. The Berlin office issues likewise a monthly review called *Internationale Rundschau der Arbeit,* which is read in Germany and in Austria. A German edition of the *Legislative Series* and German translations of the most important studies and reports are published in Geneva.

Of great value to the student of labor and social problems are naturally the Studies and Reports published from time to time by the Office. Among the best, we may mention, besides those referred to above in connection with Inquiries: "The International Status of Seamen"; "The Application of the Three-Shift System in the Iron and Steel Industry"; "The Eight-Hour Law in the French Mercantile Marine"; "The Eight-Hour Law in Agriculture in Czechoslovakia"; "Methods of Compiling Emigration and Immigration Statistics"; "Legislation and Treaties Concerning Emigration and Immigration"; "Statistics of Unemployment in Various Countries, 1910-1922"; "Wages Changes in Various Countries, 1914-1921."

The effort made by the Office to inform the general public and to supply those specially interested in labor problems with thorough impartial and objective studies and investigations is most commendable. This publication section is undoubtedly one of the most important and the Office should consider well spent any funds devoted to a further increase in the number and competence of its staff.

It is a significant and encouraging fact to note, that although the United States is not a member of the Organization, it receives as large a number of the above publications as either Great Britain or France respectively.

Commissions.—To complete the enumeration of the means employed by the Office in the collection and utilization of the most complete and scientific information, the commissions must be mentioned.

The Research Division, eager though it be to cover the field, could not possibly do so unaided; the help of experts and specialists in the various departments of labor and industry is necessary. But it cannot expect to enroll in its service all the highest international authorities upon the infinite variety of questions with which it will have to deal. This result is, in a measure, secured through the organization of special commissions, permanent or temporary. In some cases, these commissions are exclusively scientific and composed of experts; in other cases, they are composed of representatives of employers and workers. In both cases, their resolutions are only advisory. The principal ones are the following:

The International Emigration Commission was established by resolution of the Washington Conference and met in August, 1921, under the chairmanship of Lord Ullswater. Its report was presented to the Geneva Conference of 1921. An item concerning emigration was inscribed on the agenda of the 1922 Conference and a recommendation on the subject was adopted by the Conference.

The creation of a joint Maritime Commission was decided upon by the Governing Body in March, 1920. The chairman of the Governing Body is chairman of the Commission which consists of two members of the Governing Body, five representatives of the shipowners, and five representatives of the seamen. It advises the Office on all maritime questions connected with its work.

An advisory Commission on Industrial Hygiene which was proposed by the Washington Conference, was provisionally constituted and met in October, 1921. In January, 1922, the Governing Body decided upon the definite constitution of this Commission, which is to consist entirely of experts, the greater part of the work of the Commission is to be carried on by correspondence.

An advisory committee for the study of questions relating to anthrax was proposed by the Geneva Conference, 1921, and is now constituted. The purpose of the Committee, which consists of experts from the chief countries interested, is to examine the problem of infection from anthrax spores in all its bearings. The Committee met in London from December 5 to 17, 1923, and has presented a report to the Governing Body.

A meeting of experts in social insurance was held at the International Labor Conference in September, 1921, to examine the means by which experts in various countries could best assist the International Labor Office and the manner in which a consultative committee could be established.

In September, 1921, the Governing Body authorized the Director to consult experts in all matters relating to men disabled in the War. A first meeting of experts in war-disablement relief was held at Geneva in March, 1922. It examined ways of organizing medical insurance and prosthesis, as well as insurance for disabled men living outside their own country.[27]

The second meeting of this Commission, held in July, 1923, studied the methods of finding employment for disabled men.

There was also appointed an Unemployment Commission which met on various occasions in 1920. With the assistance of technical experts from various countries, it

[27] Cf. *International Labor Directory*, p. 13.

put forward a series of proposals concerning the comparison of international unemployment statistics.

Lord Burnham, who filled the chair at two successive Conferences, in his closing speech in November, 1922, said:

The International Labor Organization is not meant to be a legislative machine for turning out Conventions and Recommendations. It is the servant and in some ways it may well be the teacher of Governments and Governors in undertaking the satisfactory and comparative treatment of industrial problems. I ask you what function could be more important for general progress and contentment than this, at a time when a round dozen of new states have been called into being or revived on the European continent, and when in other continents there are so many states whose statesmen and officials are always applying to us for the fullest intelligence of what is being done everywhere to promote the welfare and efficiency of the working people? [28]

It is a remarkable fact that from no country are more inquiries addressed to the Office than from the United States of America.

The Research Division, then, is that one element of the Organization which ought to remain of permanent interest. Even though the International Labor Organization were to fail, it seems as though some such center of industrial relations should be maintained. It is gratifying for us to see that it was brought to the present state of efficiency under the direction of an American, Dr. Royal Meeker.[29]

The necessarily incomplete survey we have attempted gives a sufficient idea of the efficiency of the organization —Conferences, Governing Body, and Office—to satisfy those who believe in the fundamental validity of the under-

---

[28] International Labor Conference, fourth session, Geneva, 1922, p. 441.

[29] Dr. Royal Meeker was appointed Labor Commissioner for the State of Pennsylvania in May, 1923, and resigned in 1924 to devote himself to research.

taking that its future is assured. Men well versed in the study of political institutions have spoken of it as one of the best pieces of constructive statesmanship. But a close observer of the general sentiment will soon notice that the opponents have not been routed, nor the skeptics convinced, nor the indifferent converted. As an institution of this character needs above all else the support of public opinion, it is well to consider, as objectively as possible, the arguments for and against, so we may act knowingly in our endorsement of, or in our opposition to, this significant international movement.

CHAPTER VIII

CRITICISM AND DEFENSE

IT would be most unusual indeed, and contrary to all historical precedents, if an organization which affects so directly the interests of millions of men and which is so novel as to demand a considerable readjustment of ideas, traditions, and institutions, were to come into being without encountering vigorous protests and begin to function without arousing criticism and opposition. The International Labor Organization is being submitted to the test which humanity has ever applied to all forms of innovation.

The friends of the Organization, far from resenting such criticism, should welcome it, nay, invite it, provided it is offered in good faith. The Organization is bound to be somewhat rudimentary at this stage of its development. It is a new departure and may fall into many errors. It may also be diverted towards private ends instead of remaining dedicated to the general good. Its life is going to be a process of unceasing adjustment. It needs constant watching and patient care. With the desire of making clear its value and practicability, we shall see how it stands in the opinion of the world, and attempt as complete as possible a statement of the charges brought against it, following them up immediately with such refutations as seem convincing, and such amendments as would be likely to disarm loyal opposition.

In the course of the preceding chapter, we gave the International Labor Organization due credit for its untiring activity. But no matter how willing and how industrious may be the Director, the Office, the Governing Body and the delegates, the final proof of the worth of the institution is the bills actually passed by the national legislatures upon the initiative of the Conferences. The draft conventions and recommendations adopted by the annual assemblies are, as we already know, to be submitted to the member states for ratifications within a year, or in exceptional cases within eighteen months. Up to the first of April, 1925, however, the number of ratifications registered by the Secretary-General of the League of Nations was nearly one hundred and forty-six. Further, in thirty-three cases, ratification had been authorized but not yet communicated, and in twelve cases ratification had been recommended to the competent authority by the government, but approval has not yet been signified. Really then, out of a total of approximately nine hundred possible ratifications only one hundred and forty-six have been received.[1]

Moreover, many of these ratifications come from states of small industrial importance like Bulgaria, Greece, Roumania, and Esthonia, and the conventions which have been the most readily ratified are those which simply confirm a state of things already in existence in many countries. For instance, the Washington convention on the night work of women has been ratified by nine countries, while the convention which applied to the eight-hour day had been ratified, three years after its appearance, only by France, Czechoslovakia, Bulgaria, and three states for which special provisions had been granted, Greece, India, Roumania, and conditionally by Austria and Italy.

The most confident could not call this showing a remarkable success. Such is the state of things which arouses now the greatest amount of skepticism on the part of governments and the general public, emboldens the opposition,

[1] *Official Bulletin*, Vol. IX.

and causes no little anxiety among the defenders of international labor legislation.

The workers, being the most immediately concerned, have expressed their indignation at the slow pace of ratifications. The Congress of the International Federation of Trade-Unions, which met in London in November, 1920, manifested their bitter disappointment in the presence of the failure of international labor legislation. At the Geneva Conference of 1922, the workers' representation was particularly incensed to see the eight-hour day convention ignored by the great industrial states. Labor leaders voiced their resentment in no uncertain terms. M. Jouhaux, the President of the French Confédération Générale du Travail, declared: [2]

If the workers come to the conclusion that the International Labor Office cannot, even in a small degree, satisfy the just aspirations of the workers, just aspirations consistent with the general interest, what will follow? The result will be a return to force. It will mean that the workers will have to use the strength of their organizations and resort to force. Either the International Labor Office must secure the necessary powers to bring about ratification or else the procedure adopted at Washington must be declared an absolute failure and a return to methods of compulsion is inevitable.

M. Martens, the Belgian workers' representative, was not less disturbed. In a long and impassioned address he declared: [3]

Part XIII of the Treaty was signed as a charter of workers and we shall continue to defend the rights embodied in that charter to the utmost of our power, although we may be regarded as traitors by the extremists, while we are denounced as revolutionary by the reactionary party. [And again at the same sitting he said:] The day will come when the workers, grown

[2] International Labor Conference, fourth session, ninth sitting, Geneva, 1922.
[3] Verbatim Report of the Proceedings, International Labor Conference, Geneva, 1922, pp. 109-114.

stronger than they were before the world struggle, will again claim their rights and will be able to act in such a manner as to show the employers that resistance is useless.

These prominent speakers seemed to sum up the sentiment of the entire Labor delegation. For Labor, the causes of such an unjustifiable delay in ratifications were the selfishness and obstruction of the employers, and the hypocrisy of governments too subservient to the big interests. Unless it meets with a more sincere coöperation, Labor threatens to withdraw its support from the Organization and let things run their course.

The government delegates brought excuses and justifications for the slow progress of international legislation, and the employers replied to the charges of the workers by communicating to the Conference a joint declaration, read in English by Mr. Lithgow, representative of British employers. In view of the gravity of the charges made by Labor it is only fair to hear the case of Capital:

The employers' delegates at the Fourth International Labor Conference have attentively listened to the remarks of the workers' representatives.

Labor has appealed to the sense of justice and goodwill of the Employers. Upon these the workers can fully rely; the spirit which animated the Employers at Washington and which is the spirit of Part XIII of the Treaty of Peace still lives in them. Employers have never departed from their determination to do everything in their power to improve the lot of their fellow-workers; nationally as regards their own individual countries and also internationally through the medium of the Permanent International Labor Organization. But it must not be forgotten that it is above all upon employers that rests the responsibility of providing the means of national existence. It is not upon deficient production nor upon production at excessive costs that a nation can live, and it is not from these that a Government can procure the means of maintaining State Services.

What were the intentions of those who drew up the Washington Conventions and particularly that relating to the eight-hour day? In fixing a reduced working day, what they had in mind was the amount of effective work which could be done and further, that there would be granted the necessary provision for adjusting the new régime to meet the particular requirements of each particular case. After taking note of the objections which Governments have raised to the ratifying of Conventions one is forced to ask oneself whether sufficient account was taken of the conditions under which these Conventions would have to be applied.

Moreover at the close of the War there was a general feeling that the supply of the world's immediate material wants would lead to an era of economic prosperity. The artificial and transitory character of that prosperity, however, soon became evident and there arose the universal crisis which had been predicted in certain quarters but which public opinion had refused to anticipate.

Each country must coöperate to restore the financial strength and economic stability of the world. Each country must honor its signature by contributing to the creation of that wealth which alone will allow its obligations to be liquidated. That is a duty which involves the honesty and solidarity, not only of each country but of all countries. In this task each citizen must contribute his share. Present-day conditions which impose upon employers constant sacrifices to keep their works open and to provide work for their employees should not less impose upon Governments the obligations to pursue resolutely a policy of strict economy. The same conditions ought also to encourage the workers to play their part. All that employers have done, whenever possible, to improve their plants and methods of working has not proved sufficient to make up for the undeniable falling off of output.

The signatories of the Peace Treaty in setting up the International Labor Organization to assure better conditions for the workpeople, also intended that no country should be penalized in its competitive trade through its having given improved conditions to its workpeople. The situation, to-day, had to be faced anew. Certain countries are so placed that the forcing of them to give effect to the conditions prevailing in the more fortunate countries would be to involve them in the greatest risks and expose their workpeople to unemployment on a serious scale. It is for these reasons that the employers' delegates feel it their duty to state that while still remaining true to the high ideals of the Washington Conference, they must yield to the necessity which compels every country to require from its people the sacrifices which are inseparable from the process of reëstablishing its economic welfare and restoring the peace of the world.[4]

The case was put with greater vigor perhaps by Warrington Smith, of South Africa:

You cannot ask the Governments when they have the greatest difficulty in meeting their financial obligations to commence drafting ideal legislation for their citizens. To-day it is a question of living, of making both ends meet. Every class is suffering. The working class is not alone in that respect. When all trade is upset and half the world is not producing, you cannot expect that industries and governments will be able to organize the life of the nation as they should wish to do in ordinary times and so as to secure the maximum of efficiency from the short time of an eight-hour day. We all need the will to produce and the will to work. I believe the eight-hour day will come. I believe the Washington Convention is right, but do not hasten unduly. Do not ask for the impossible at a moment when the world is submerged in industrial and commercial chaos.[5]

The quarrel is not over. For the Hamburg Socialist Congress held in May, 1923, numbering more than six hundred delegates, severely condemned the attitude of the countries which had failed to fulfill the obligations they had undertaken towards the International Labor Organization. A resolution declared that the draft conventions represented the minimum demands of Labor and urged the workers "to oppose the many sinister attacks to prejudice the work of the International Organization of Labor by the various capitalist interests, which are always against the social betterment of the workers."[6]

The situation, as merely indicated by the above declarations, is then critical enough. The Organization is going

---

[4] *Ibid.*, pp. 127-128.   [5] *Ibid.*, p. 131.
[6] *Industrial and Labor Information*, Vol. VI, No. 10.

through trying days and some wonder whether it will survive the ordeal.   The enactment of international legislation is after all the *raison d'être* of the Organization and if the present state of affairs were long to endure, no matter how many and valuable services it might have rendered in other fields, the question of the continuance of the International Labor Organization would undoubtedly be raised.

It must be conceded that apparently unjustifiable delays have occurred in obtaining the expected ratifications.   But if we consider this regrettable situation dispassionately we shall find for it several attenuating circumstances.   Parliamentary life offers many examples of similar disappointments on the part of the promoters of very important and necessary measures of domestic policy.   It is not easy to secure the passage by our respective legislatures even of those labor bills which have been originated at home.   An international regulation will meet with still greater opposition or indifference.

General conditions, moreover, are not specially favorable to the enactment of legislation which adds to the task of post-War readjustment and to the financial burden of the nations.   Peace has not been firmly established, the problems of reparations and of interallied indebtedness are as puzzling as ever and the economic crisis has not abated. In view, then, of the general anxiety and of the pressure of vital affairs upon governments, is it so strange that parliaments should feel some reluctance towards including international labor conventions in their legislative program when these are still in the experimental stage?

"Moreover, all students of Labor Problems know that there are two principal conditions necessary to the progress of social legislation: a certain degree of economic prosperity and an active labor policy," [7] or, at least, a fairly

---

[7] Report of the Director, Geneva, 1922, p. 99.

strong current of sympathetic public opinion. The former element, that of economic prosperity, is now surely wanting, and as to the latter, it is quite evident, speaking of Europe generally, that Organized Labor is neither so strong nor so popular as in 1919. Politically, we all know that for a diversity of motives, some honorable, some less so, a reaction has set in, a reaction against the spirit of Versailles and of Washington, a reaction against all enthusiasm for social conciliation and generous reforms. The workers are unanimous in denouncing the European "political reaction."

These obstacles, serious though they are, could in a measure be overcome if the great industrial states felt deeply the urgency of labor regulation to even up the charges of production in international competition. To-day, however, the former relation between the terms of international competition have been substantially modified and in world trade the dominant and perplexing factors are not labor costs but rather political stability, exchange and transportation.

Altogether, then, we are going through a period decidedly unpropitious to the development of international labor legislation, irrespective of the merits or demerits of the International Labor Organization. Time is required to alter these conditions. Meanwhile, it might be inquired whether, perchance, the Organization could not, through some amendments to the prescribed procedure, facilitate the task of the well disposed parliaments.

In that connection, Warrington Smith, of South Africa, made an enlightening declaration:

There were two distinct reasons why ratification had been difficult regarding the Hours Convention: firstly, in South Africa, our law was in general conformity with the Convention but there were details which needed adjusting and annoying modifications, and it was inevitable therefore that our Parliament and

Government would be reluctant to take steps to make the small almost verbal alterations necessary. . . . The second great difficulty was the world crisis.[8]

At the same Conference, Mrs. Kjelsberg, a delegate from Norway, felt that one reason for nonratification was that, at Washington, the Conference had gone into too much detail in the different provisions of the convention. Certain countries like Norway had national legislation on many of the subjects covered by the draft conventions and would have been able to ratify all of them, had they been authorized to make the minor alterations necessary in each particular case.

Great Britain has raised the question whether the texts of the conventions really correspond to the average possibilities in each state, and whether they have been drawn up in such a way that adaptation of national legislation could be made comparatively easy; in a word, whether the texts of the conventions themselves have not constituted an obstacle to ratification.

In some cases, ratifications are delayed because the existing legislation has to be amended before the conventions can be ratified, in order to avoid contradictions in their code, or because the diverse legislation of the component units of a newly created state must be previously unified, as is the case of Yugoslavia.

Finally, it may well happen that the objections of a government are well founded, in the sense that some conventions were not perhaps sufficiently studied, because the information necessary to draw up such a general agreement was not at hand. In such occurrences, amendments and revisions are quite in order, and when realized, ratifications will be more numerous.

Ratifications might be hastened also if they could be

_____

[8] International Labor Conference, fourth session, Geneva, 1922, pp. 130-131.

made with reservations. While the procedure of ratification with reservations bearing upon the essential articles of a convention was not contemplated by the authors of the Treaty and could, if tolerated, gravely endanger the efficiency of the Organization, reservations regarding accidental features of a convention are held permissible. Reservations of this kind were made by Bulgaria as regards the draft convention on hours of labor when she indicated that the provisions of the convention would be applied in Bulgaria only after July, 1924. Another type of reservation recognized as legitimate is that of ratification conditional upon ratification by one or more other members of the Organization. Undoubtedly other cases will arise in which the reluctance of governments to ratify will be overcome by the recognition of reservations, wherever these do not oppose the spirit of the convention or rob it of its efficacy.[9]

In spite of every effort, the slowness of ratifications may remain a cause of deep anxiety and finally impose upon the Organization the policy suggested by G. M. Barnes. The British Labor delegate advocated the limitation of conventions to reforms that have already been adopted by the principal powers and which would consequently obtain their support. Even then the results for the workers' welfare would be worth while. In countries where the legislation does not exist, it would be a clear gain for Labor, and in the others the consecration of the national progress by international agreement would represent added security by giving a guaranty of permanency.

It may happen, therefore, that through an improvement in economic conditions, through fitting amendments to the actual procedure, ratifications of conventions and recommendations by the national legislatures will take place in much larger numbers. And still that expectation may not

[9] Report of the Director, International Labor Conference, Geneva, 1922, p. 1011.

materialize unless Labor and employers deal with the entire problem with good faith, with a real intelligence of their respective positions and a fair regard of their essential rights.

Labor's indictment of Capital is, no doubt, unduly severe. It is an evidence of superficial reasoning sweepingly to ascribe to selfishness and ill will the attitude of the employers. There are some, who, without question, have gladly returned to a class struggle psychology and are anxious to regain some of the positions recently lost to Labor. They are ready to take advantage of a fairly general political reaction, of the present embarrassment of Labor, and of the weakness and anarchy of the trade-unions to further their own ends.

But this state of mind does not satisfactorily explain the present crisis. The worker must not lose sight of the fact that the employer almost irresistibly is brought to lay stress upon a set of economic principles quite at variance with the philosophy of Labor. During the last few years, for instance, the thought behind the policy of employers' associations has been the reduction of the cost of production in order to increase trade. They hold that a longer working day is one of the most efficient means of lowering that cost. Hence their opposition to the eight-hour day arises in part no doubt from an honest conviction. Again in dealing with wages, the employer will tend to fix wages on the basis of what industry can bear rather than on the cost of living, and what industry can bear is not determined by his personal likes or dislikes but by the condition of a world market.

Not unfrequently employers feel also a collective responsibility for the economic prosperity of the nation, which is the guaranty of the strength of the state and of the welfare of the citizens. And they are, no doubt, in a measure sincere when they bring up the present unsettled condition of the world as a well-nigh insurmountable obstacle to the carrying out of social reforms or economic betterment.

And still, when all is said to exonerate the employer, the impartial observer is bound to recognize that there exists a real hostility towards the International Labor Organization.[10] There is evidence that the employers, whether in good faith or otherwise, are exercising no inconsiderable pressure upon governments and parliaments to prevent ratifications. They also seek to limit the competence of the Organization or interfere with its operation as is evidenced by their concerted opposition to the extension of the competence of the International Labor Organization to agricultural questions, their denunciation of certain official inquiries, particularly those into the problems of unemployment and of production,[11] and their charges of wasteful administration.[12]

The diffidence and hostility of the employers [13] and their sympathizers seem to rest upon two sets of reasons, some of a mere general character which might be true of any international agency, and others special to the present International Labor Organization. Considering the question in its more general aspect, they hold that the *sovereignty of the states,* of the larger ones particularly, sovereignty so important to the establishment and pursuance of an intelligent and efficient policy, is *seriously threatened.* The individual nations who alone are quite aware of their real

10 *Cf.* Georges Scelle, "La quatrième conférence internationale du travail," *Revue politique et parlementaire,* January, 1923.

11 *Cf.* Pierre Waline, *ibid.,* December, 1922.

12 *Cf. Daily Mail,* London, May 31. 1923.

13 The majority of Labor is in sympathy with the Organization, aside from the fact that they would wish for a larger representation for the workers and greater powers for the Organization. We leave out of consideration, here, the opposition arising from the Third International or the whole of the Communistic movement, for a refutation of that hostility involves a criticism of the entire revolutionary program. The International Labor Organization is based on the assumption that the present economic system is substantially worth preserving.

and permanent interests, and better than any one else know the inherent difficulties of their economic and social life, will not submit to the decisions of a world parliament whose majority may be, in thought and feeling, quite at variance with them.

They also hold that it is folly to endeavor to enact universal labor legislation in face of the present diversity of national conditions. This diversity may be first physical: a rule applicable to workers in a temperate climate would not be equally applicable to those of a warmer zone; laws relating to child labor would not be suitable in all cases since children of some lands mature more quickly than those in others. Abolition of night work for women may be objected to on the score that in tropical countries the only cool period of the day is after sunset; differences in soil, in rainfall, in seasonable changes with their effects on products raised or goods manufactured, may also militate against international regulation.

Again this diversity may be one of economic organization or of social advancement. Various countries of the world are going through different phases of economic development. First, as to their economic organization: some states are in the stage of provincial or city economy, others still within the period of national economy and others have reached the international stage. Second, as to the standards of living of their workers: some countries are high-labor standard countries, others low-labor standard and the transition from the one level to the other is difficult. Labor legislation must naturally be adapted to that degree of economic development and therefore the *regulation of labor is essentially a domestic question.*

Besides, as there is a close relation between the organization of labor and economic development, and still closer relation between economic development and political development, and as the political development of the various countries is clearly unequal, can we consistently consider the universalization of labor legislation a possibility?

Then again, we cannot touch labor legislation without affecting as well the entire social life of a community. You cannot regulate the employment of children and not provide corresponding educational facilities and make laws to render that education compulsory. It is not enough to legislate in that one sphere, there is an entire social evolution that goes along with labor legislation. Likewise, the unemployment problem is related to any number of economic and political problems. In a word, the whole social question is a unit, and these various phases of it are so interwoven that a modification of any one inevitably reacts upon all the others.

Employers have always resented the *immixture of national parliaments in economic questions* at home as being both incompetent or partisan. They are therefore even more violently opposed to such interference at the hands of a world assembly which will repeat all the evils of parliaments, made even worse by national rivalries and class struggles.

They observe also that the fundamental principle itself may work great injustice, for instance, by denying a nation, through the rigid enforcement of the eight-hour day, the opportunity to make up a temporary deficiency in production. It truly was intended to protect the most progressive nations against a disloyal competition, to equalize the expenses of production of every nation. But such a policy might prove a serious detriment to some one country. France and Belgium, half ruined by the War, cannot accept that their present inferiority be rendered permanent; just like a family or an individual, a nation which has suffered a misfortune must retain the right to make up her losses through extra labor. It would seem that, in such a case, the International Labor Organization might work a real injustice and decidedly interfere with the manifest right and even the duty of self-respecting and enterprising peoples.

With more explicit reference to the International Labor Organization of the League of Nations, they hold against it that it is primarily a Labor organization, as its name indicates, founded to promote the policies and defend the interest of workers. Why should the employers be asked to support it and contribute to its success?

As for the benefit it claims to bring to the employers, that benefit cannot materialize under present conditions. It was hoped that by international labor legislation, it would do away with that fear of disastrous competition always within the power of those countries which do not assume the financial burden of labor protection and of social reform. For the heavier charge upon production is ever the labor charge, constantly increased by the cost of reform. But this *primary purpose can never be fully attained* when two absent states, *Russia and the United States of America,* nearly equal, by their industrial population and their normal production, one half of the total membership.

When it is reported that the United States and Russia will ultimately join, the European employers reply that this situation could hardly be remedied by the entrance of the United States as it enjoys a favored status. Being a federal state, with limited jurisdiction in labor questions, it can treat any convention as a recommendation and is not subject to the formal obligation which the other states assume.

Their diffidence is also based on the fact that the world *does not show any genuine enthusiasm* for, or any great faith in, the International Organization of Labor, and more than anything else the support of public opinion is necessary to such an organization. This is evidenced by the incomplete delegations sent by several states. Out of fifty-six states, forty-six were represented at Geneva in 1925, and only twenty-nine of these sent complete delegations. So out of two hundred and twenty-four possible delegates, there were present only one hundred and forty-four, distributed as follows: eighty representing governments, thirty-two representing employers, and thirty-two representing Labor. Another proof of indifference is found in the delay in paying assessments. The proportion of nonpaid contributions was 7 per cent in 1920, 19 per cent in 1921, and 45 per cent in 1922.

The employers also object to the *excessive activity of the Conferences*. In less than seven years, the Conferences have dealt with the most vital problems: industry in 1919 at Washington, seamen at Genoa in 1920, agriculture at Geneva in 1921, emigration at Geneva in 1922, factory inspection in 1923, workmen's compensation for accidents, and occupational diseases in 1924 and 1925. Briefly then, twenty-one draft conventions and twenty-four recommendations seem to many an excessive demand upon the various states, while they were busy with after-War reconstruction and overburdened with problems of unusual complexity. According to them, the fear that was expressed earlier in this chapter about the dangerous curtailment of state sovereignty by any international organization, is clearly exemplified in the present occurrence. The Governing Body and the Conference are clearly endowed with legislative, judicial, and elective prerogatives which heretofore have been the exclusive attributes of independent states.

Moreover, the decisions of the Conferences are taken by a majority vote and not by a unanimous vote as is the case with the League of Nations, and therefore a nation may be required to do things which she absolutely disapproves.

Similarly, the presence of small states and their equality with the larger states in the Conference has given rise to no little apprehension. The large states fear that their interests might be controlled by small states which had nothing to lose in the decisions taken. This became particularly evident at the Genoa Conference. If the convention on hours of work in reference to seamen had been adopted, in spite of the opposition of large states possessing a merchant marine of several million tons, by a majority of small states possessing either a very small or no merchant marine, the authority of the Organization could have been endangered, as the parliaments of the larger nations, sensing the injustice, would never have ratified those directions.

Even if wise laws could be passed and their ratification universally obtained, the most important feature is still their loyal enforcement. The best means of supervising the enforcement is through the unions and inspectors. The International Labor Organization seems to think that these inspectors should hold international conferences to unify their system. But this would be, it seems, going beyond the powers conferred by the Treaty of Versailles to the International Labor Organization. It is evident that the Organization tends to extend its authority much too far, clearly into the field of production which the employer is determined to keep to himself. It will inevitably attempt to become a superstate or at best a superparliament of Labor, invading all economic fields, first under the pretext of making investigations therein, and then enacting laws for their regulation.

They finally object to the personality of the Director whom they look upon as a politician with strong Socialistic leanings, who is bound to permit the Organization to be used for Socialistic world-wide propaganda.

Having brought together as complete a list of the charges

usually made against the Organization, let us now examine their validity.

We have seen that the employers endeavor to discredit the International Labor Organization on the grounds that it infringes upon the sovereignty of the states and tends to erect itself into a superstate in the domain of economic relations. The Organization certainly, as now constituted, does not lend foundation to such a fear.

It is generally admitted that the League of Nations does not represent a superstate. The component governments retain their entire independence and the unanimity of votes is required to arrive at binding decisions. In the International Labor Organization, it is true, a majority of the votes is sufficient and it would seem, at first, as though a state could be bound by decisions which it has opposed and deems contrary to its interests. We must confess that the Organization is invested with powers which constitute a real departure in international procedure and possesses some of the prerogatives which would of necessity belong to a superstate. We discover in it a foreshadowing of legislative, executive, and judiciary powers. But the atmosphere of complete independence and the character of finality are still wanting, nevertheless. The authority and independence of the law-making bodies of the member states remain unimpaired, and no convention or recommendation becomes a law without their explicit assent.

Advocates of the International Labor Organization sometimes argue that the governments have little to fear because in the Conferences they can, practically speaking, control a majority. That would be correct enough if the governments were to be of one mind upon labor problems, but considering the great difference which exists between them in political and economic development, this presumed concordance is not likely to be realized, and a certain group of governments, the conservative group, for instance, might hap-

pen to be overruled by a coalition of the more progressive
states. The fear of a like possible grouping of some states
against others prompts the objection of employers against
the equal representation of small and large states in the
Conference. It may be said, in reply, that all states have
indeed an equal voice in the Conference. The vote of each
representative has the same value. It is, however, important to remember the guaranty afforded by the very constitution of the Organization. Under the terms of Article 40,
it is the duty of the Governing Body to prepare the agenda
for the sessions of the Conference and the Governing Body
thus exercises an effective control over the actual activities
of the Conference. In this assembly, the eight chief industrial countries of the world, namely those countries for
which the decisions of the Conference have the most serious
consequences and imply the heaviest financial burdens, occupy a preponderating position. It should further be re-
membered that the experience of three years goes to show
that, in fact, the fears which were expressed have not been
realized.

The objections drawn from the intrinsic impossibility of
building up a body of international labor legislation in view
of the diversity of conditions the world over is stretched
unduly.[14] The Office is fully aware that many of the draft
conventions and recommendations cannot be applied in their
entirety to areas where industrial organization is practically
nonexistent.[15] Part XIII of the Treaty has clearly recog-

---

[14] *Cf.* Low, *The International Protection of Labor*, New York,
1921, pp. 74*ff*.

[15] Still the following comment of H. B. Butler, Deputy Director
of the International Labor Office, throws an interesting light on
this problem: "In the various Commissions appointed at the Washington Conference, it was not possible to have the majority of the
Governments represented as it would have hindered the efficient
transaction of business. Many thought that the reports of the
Commissions would be subjected to much criticism on the part of
the non-represented Governments. It happened, on the contrary,
that they were easily accepted." Mr. Butler emphasizes a point

nized that "differences of climate, habits, customs, economic opportunity and industrial tradition make strict uniformity in the conditions of labor difficult of immediate attainment," and both Articles 405 and 421 indicate that in such cases special modifications may be required. If complete uniformity is a dream, we can at least endeavor to attain an approximate equality in the charges of production which would make the international labor legislation a real protection against disloyal industrial competition.

As for the threatened invasion by the Labor Office of certain economic fields, like the field of production, invasion deeply resented by the employers, we may as well admit that it is well-nigh inevitable. Friction can be avoided, however, if the Office takes care not to extend its activity to these domains unless under the pressure of circumstances, at the invitation of interested parties, or when officially so directed by the League of Nations. To any one who realizes the close interdependence of all economic problems, it is evident that artificial limits, once set to the activity of the Office, cannot have a permanent and inflexible character. Tact and judgment on the part of the Governing Body and the Director should considerably allay the fears of the employers; it does not follow, however, as argued by the employers, that such an extension of activity could substantially alter the now subordinate character of the institution and lift it to the rank of a superstate.

The employers have reminded us that the claims of the International Labor Office are unacceptable because an entire social reconstruction is involved in the enactment of such a body of labor legislation as it contemplates. To that the Organization should plead guilty, if indeed it were an offense. We must not be afraid to admit that labor laws

which became constantly clearer as the Conference proceeded, namely, that industrial problems and the possible solutions of them are surprisingly similar in all countries. *Cf.* Solano, *Labor as an International Problem*, p. 204.

imply or demand a parallel adjustment of the social conditions, and to us it should be an additional motive, rather than a deterrent, to promote laws which thus contribute to the raising of the general social level. The main thing is to proceed cautiously, for indeed social reorganization must be carried on with knowledge and care.

The objection drawn from parliamentary evils can be met by saying that precisely, in this Organization, it is hoped that a different spirit will preside over the enactment of laws. The International Labor Conference marks a complete departure from traditional legislative assemblies; it is an interesting experiment in political theory and practice. We are all agreed in condemning excessive state interference. With the development of strong organizations of employers and workers, we can leave to direct negotiations between them the settlement of many industrial disputes. They cannot, however, dispense with the guidance and support which the authority of the state affords them. The International Labor Conference is the embodiment of that truth. It attempts to combine an official conference, whose decisions are cast into the form of laws and international treaties, with a conference between employers and workers, in contact with the everyday facts of industry and the actual needs and claims of the people. We then find here a new method, more objective, more impartial, a rather unusual parliament not directly subservient to political interests, vivified by the presence of experts, and strengthened by the cumulative wisdom of the various races and civilizations. So far the experiment has been justified. Undoubtedly it is too early to pass final judgment upon it but the criticisms of domestic parliaments may not hold good in relation to the Labor Conference.

We now come to the contention that the acceptance of international legislation by nations impoverished by the War may seriously interfere with their economic recovery, that no limit should be put to their willingness to repair the damage of the War through extra exertion. It is replied that when circumstances very clearly point to its necessity, special and temporary concessions could be granted to nations in unusual economic stress. But it must also be remarked that the claim that labor and social legislation work to the economic loss or detriment of the nation which adopts it, is certainly not true in the long run.

One of the most harmful interpretations we have to deal with is that the International Labor Office is entirely for the benefit of workers and that employers, therefore, need not go heartily into it; the most that can be expected of them is a passive attitude. One cannot too vigorously combat such a theory. The Organization is intended naturally to promote the welfare of Labor, but we should feel that what is Labor's rightful gain is the gain of the whole political body and that indirectly the Organization serves the employers fully as much as it serves Labor by promoting industrial peace and coöperation. It also helps them directly by generalizing labor legislation and protecting them against disloyal competition. Moreover, the social gains, gains in which Capital has a predominant share, are immeasurable, the principal being perhaps the education of the workers in the relation of the concrete industrial reforms they seek to the whole field of general, social, and economic problems, thereby winning the workers over to a policy of improvement of social conditions by the moral forces of conciliation, reason, and law.

The employers are deeply impressed by the nonparticipation of Russia and the United States, and see in it an evidence of the near failure of the International Labor Office, as, without the accession of these large industrial states, it cannot fulfill its primary purpose. It would seem that, here again, they have given the facts too pessimistic an interpretation.

Russia will inevitably come into the League of Nations and the International Labor Office. Moreover, although large and populous, she is not presently a great factor in the industrial world, and, as she resumes her place in the world of production and exchange, she will be drawn into the circle of international organizations.

As for the United States, the decision of its electorate is not irrevocable and there is growing in our midst a strong movement for a closer coöperation with existing international institutions. Regarding the favored status which this country would enjoy, if it chose to go in, this, according to Samuel Gompers, would not matter greatly because the United States is not likely to lag behind in any legislative movement which is really conducive to the general welfare.[16]

The present development of labor legislation in the United States does not seem to justify the confidence of Mr. Gompers. This, however, is true that while other great industrial nations have gone farther in labor legislation than has the United States, much legislation will have to be adopted by the International Labor Organization before American standards are reached by a majority of the members of the Organization. Meanwhile there are many features of the activity of the International Labor Organization in which American coöperation exists and can be developed, particularly in the field of research.[17]

With regard to the absence of some twenty states out of fifty-six at the annual Conferences, it may be said that the great industrial states are always represented, and considering the financial crisis which has existed for several years and the distance which separates Geneva from some of the countries, the average attendance of thirty-five states is by no means an alarming record.

16 *Cf*. Minutes of the Labor Commission, p. 280.
17 *Cf*. Chap. IX.

Incomplete delegations are not the result of any ill will; there is no hostility to the principle involved. Some delegations are incomplete because workers' or employers' organizations hardly exist in those countries.

Employers have taken exception to the excessive activity of the Conferences. Under post-War conditions there was some justification to their contention. The 1922 Conference gave them satisfaction in a measure by deciding that, thereafter, every other Conference would be a Conference of preparation. The proposed recommendations or conventions would be studied at the preparation Conference and voted upon only at the next Conference, a year later. This should reduce substantially the volume of labor legislation submitted to the national parliaments. Comparatively few conventions have been adopted since 1922.[18]

As for the charge of propaganda, if trying to arouse interest in the welfare of the working classes and in the promotion of social and industrial peace through legislation may be branded propaganda, then the Office will have to plead guilty to the offense, or cease to be a living force. A reprehensible propaganda it would be, if the Office were to use its influence for the promotion of theories subversive of the present political and economic system. Of that, however, it is surely innocent. The entire Organization is really based upon the assumption that the capitalistic system is to endure; it is primarily intended to help it to function with the highest degree of harmony and efficiency.

As to whether the syndicates or Socialist parties consider it as the goal of their ambitions, or as a mere stage in their gradual conquest of power, that is another question which should, in no way, cast a shadow upon the value and usefulness of the Organization.

Regarding the Director, every one knows that he is too deeply convinced of the importance and value to the world

[18] See table of ratifications, facing p. 326.

of the Organization as constituted, not to avoid scrupulously anything that would threaten its existence, as Socialistic or Communistic propaganda would certainly do. A sufficient proof of his impartiality is in the attacks he is the object of from extreme representatives of Capitalism and Collectivism, and, as well, the unanimous expression of confidence that he has repeatedly received from the Conference and the Governing Body.

We may have failed to dispel the skepticism or diffidence of some of our readers. No doubt, there are objections in their minds which we have not fully met. But life, with its great power of adaptation and adjustment, will take care of those. We cannot present to them an institution acceptable to all from every point of view. Of such there are none in existence and none within our human powers of conception or organization. But the present general principle is sound and it should rally the peoples and nations of good will.

The tendency toward international organizations cannot be stopped. Labor feels that something must be done internationally to improve conditions. There are international organizations in existence which appeal to them and which they may join unless we offer them a saner and better way of reaching the desired goal.

Moreover, it would be inconsistent to endeavor to bring about peace among nations and perpetuate the causes of social war. We must make law prevail, a law if you wish that will adjust itself to changing conditions, but we must institute a rule of law to guarantee orderly progress, a rule of law among nations, a rule of law among individuals. War is not a reasonable or efficient way of obtaining justice, nor is the strike or the lock-out which are weapons of economic warfare. For such means as tend to act through the fear of death, of ruin, of hunger, of bodily harm, must gradually be substituted others of a juridical kind. The progress of the twentieth century is going to consist in the creation of a complete and working code, honestly accepted, of labor legislation and of international legislation.

Truly, an international organization cannot succeed unless it is supported by an international spirit, and the international spirit is very feeble as yet. But the spirit and the institution will grow apace, supporting and strengthening each other along a curve of evolution very similar to the process by which the national spirit came into being.

The International Labor Office has an assured future. It will live because it serves vital material interests and satisfies high social ideals. After all, the greatest treasure of humanity is work, and work we should ever try to render honorable, healthy, and fruitful. That inescapable duty we cannot fulfill, however, without the assistance of international organizations. Moreover, the International Labor Office is in the great evolutionary movement and will endure. Even if it were temporarily wrecked by hostile interests, it would reappear in some similar form like the democratic institutions of the nineteenth century which all autocratic régimes struggled in vain to suppress.

In a word, we should like to tell Americans that the International Labor Office is really a serious business. The delegates we saw there gave us the impression of men of ability and good will. Yes, there were difficulties to overcome, individual and national selfishness, but they had to yield gradually to international self-respect. What we saw in Geneva is a structure resting upon a firm foundation, resting on something which, in spite of the skepticism of the age, lies deep in the human heart—goodness.

CHAPTER IX

IN order better to solve the problem of the participation of the United States in the International Labor Organization, it would be enough for the American people to ask themselves a few simple questions: "Is the International Labor Office useful to the world? Do we personally need it? Is there any obligation on our part to join it? What sacrifices of sovereignty or otherwise will it demand of us? Is it efficient or does it promise to become so?" It would not be difficult to reply satisfactorily and convincingly to every one of these questions. The subject matter of this study contains at least a general answer to the above queries. It remains now to consider more particularly American conditions and American participation in this world effort.

On the general proposition of standards of living for workers we are all agreed in America. We wish them to be high, because they condition the quality of our citizenship. We are proud of the record made in that direction by our industrial organization. We believe that workers in our country enjoy a greater measure of comfort, freedom, and opportunity than they do in any other land and we glory in it.[1]

---

[1] "American Labor on the whole enjoys the benefits of the most wealthy and prosperous country; it has the highest wages and the best mechanical appliances in the world." *Cf*. Sherwood Eddy, *The New World of Labor*, 184. An investigation conducted by the *Man-*

And still, if we come down from the serene sphere of
general statements, we cannot fail to discover shocking
abuses, inexcusable negligence, and unwarranted disregard
of ascertained methods of increasing the efficiency [2] and the
security of our labor, particularly of lower classes of
workers.

The United States of America is a world in miniature, so
to speak. We find within our frontiers a great diversity of
climatic conditions, of economic development, of racial
characteristics, of religious and political ideals. We have,
therefore, put to us the problem of creating that unity of
policy which efficiency and justice demand while preserving

---

chester Guardian reveals the following comparative tables of wages in
America and Europe: *

RELATIVE REAL VALUE OF WORKERS' REMUNERATION MEASURED BY
ITS POWER TO PURCHASE CERTAIN ARTICLES OF FOOD
(GREAT BRITAIN—100)

Occupation	Great Britain	Germany	France	Belgium	United States
Bricklayer...........	100	41	55	50	300
Carpenter...........	100	41	60	50	240
Unskilled labor.......	100	62	58	51	86
AVERAGE........	100	48	57.6	50.3	208.6

RATES OF MONEY WAGES FOR 48 HOURS' WORK, APRIL, MAY, 1922

Occupation	United States	Great Britain	France	Germany
Bricklayer...........	$60.06	$19.54	$11.88	$3.48
Carpenter...........	54.00	19.54	15.26	3.48
Unskilled labor.......	14.40	13.54	8.79	3.40
AVERAGE........	42.83	17.54	11.976	3.45

* "Reconstruction in Europe," *Manchester Guardian*, October 26, 1922, pp.
512-544. The accuracy of this table is very relative but may be accepted for a
purpose of general comparison.

2 *Cf.* Report of Federated Engineering Societies, 1922.

that diversity of ways and means which physical and human nature seem to require. We have before us, in the unification and codification of our national labor laws, a problem quite similar to the one which the International Labor Office has undertaken to solve. In that attempt, no doubt, we can lend each other invaluable assistance.

Not only are we very far from having settled that important problem, but it does not seem that we have even begun to consider it on anything like a scientific basis. It is evident also that much progress remains to be accomplished in matters of protection of workers, of women and children, of the development and extension of adequate systems of insurance, and so forth. So far is this true that unfriendly critics have been able to state that the boasted welfare of our working classes is not due to any superior organization of our industry or to higher social ideals but to the special circumstances, such as the available free lands, the abundance of natural resources and raw materials, the large and diversified domestic market, which have interfered with the operation of the economic laws that, in a less favored Europe, under the same economic system, have brought misery and want to millions of workers.

Whatever truth this interpretation may contain, one thing remains certain and it is that we are not entitled to the credit, too readily claimed by many, until we have devised and realized an economic organization free from some of the blemishes which mar our economic order and which are well within our power to remove.

About twelve years ago we were fully a generation behind Europe in any adequate governmental protection of the health and welfare of nearly thirty millions of workers. The night work of women and children seemed to be steadily increasing; only three states of the forty-eight had any workmen'ε compensation laws; none had any state insurance against sickness, old age, invalidity, death, or unemployment. Preventable ill health was reckoned to entail for the nation an economic waste of at least one hundred and ninety-three million dollars each year. The world's record for the killing and crippling of men, women, and children in industry was conceded to be held by the United States, whose fatal accidents were variously numbered at from fifteen thousand to fifty-seven thousand five hundred per annum. According to conservative estimates, four million five hundred thousand employees were regularly engaged in seven-day labor, and therefore deprived of Sunday rest.[3]

It is true that conditions have changed greatly since 1913, as most of our effective labor laws are the fruit of the past dozen years. And still, as John B. Andrews wrote recently, "with a vast army of child laborers who ought to be in school, with peonage persisting in even one State, with scores of thousands of women still employed by parasitic industries for long hours at wages below the level of decent existence, with the lurking danger of industrial poisons ever on the increase and for the most part still unreported and uncompensated, with many thousands of coal miners being killed three times as fast as they kill them in Great Britain, and with millions involuntarily unemployed during each turn of the business cycle,"[4] surely the need is still urgent for further progress in labor legislation in America.

While private organizations and many generous employers have earnestly tried to better the condition of the working class, we feel that permanency and security in that improvement is attained only through labor legislation within the limits we have stated in earlier chapters. In that field, generous recognition for their signal services

---

[3] Cf. Low, *The International Protection of Labor*, pp. 80ff.
[4] Cf. *American Labor Legislation Review*, June, 1923, p. 122.

must go to the American Association for Labor Legislation, the National Consumers' League and the Child Labor Committee. However, no matter how eager their members and how generous their ideals, these bodies are not in a position to carry the movement they have initiated into the international sphere where it must, in order to bring its full fruitage, find its ultimate consecration.

During the War we were the first to realize the necessity of making justice and not war diplomacy preside over the eventual deliberations of peace. We became convinced of the unity of the whole problem. More, perhaps, than any other people we hated war, not because we lacked the courage or the strength to face confidently such an ordeal, but because we knew it had been and was one of the scourges of humanity, and of that form of humanity which had special claims upon our interest—the people. We understood the complex intermingling of the economic and political problems, and while no one was more in favor of the independence of peoples than were we, we realized keenly their growing modern interdependence. Hence our higher self was convinced that the hour had struck for the organization of institutions which would study, provide, strengthen, and safeguard the most appropriate means to secure international peace and justice.

It is in that spirit that we took such a prominent part in the work of the Commission for International Labor Legislation. In the chapter on the Birth of the International Labor Office, we have followed, step by step, the work of the American delegation and we have seen that, in the words of Mr. Gompers, "America wrote into the labor section the heart and soul of that section." The first Conference, and the most fruitful, was held in Washington, at the invitation of our President, and presided over by our Secretary of Labor.

Then, all of a sudden, after a bewildering political debate, we withdrew our coöperation. Nothing, perhaps, has given a greater shock to the world, aside from the War itself, than that hasty and unforeseen retreat of American forces of idealism from the devastated fields of Europe. And still our presence in these new organizations is absolutely indispensable for their true effectiveness.

It is rather pathetic to hear some of the officials of the International Labor Office comfort themselves with the thought that their institution may safely go on without the presence of America. But these optimistic utterances are simply prompted by the desire not to cause the members of the Organization to lose heart while further developments are anxiously awaited.

It is true that the absence of the United States has been less keenly felt at this time than it is likely to be at a later period. The factors of international competition have been upset. The unheard of depreciation of exchange interferes with the normal operation of economic laws. This, however, cannot but be a temporary phenomenon. Competition will be resumed on a pre-War basis and the factor of labor standards will again be a dominant one in the problem of production for the international market.

It is of the essence of such institutions to be world-wide. They cannot possibly fulfill their mission unless they bind together all the states of industrial or political importance. This is still more true in the case of an economic organization. So conscious of it were the founders of the International Labor Office that they decided to accept Germany and Austria into its membership before considering their admission into the League of Nations.

It was felt, of course, above all else that no sacrifices were too great to secure the adherence of the United States. We find an evidence of that sentiment throughout the deliberations of the Commissions and particularly in the concessions that were made regarding the ratification of con-

ventions by federated states. The delegates really modified
the very nature of the Organization in the hope of better
days and divested it of all legislative authority in order to
win the assent of the United States.[5]

It is true they were greatly disappointed by our
failure to ratify the treaties but we all know that the
American decision was not based upon the merits or demerits of the International Labor Office. No one who reads
history and is abreast of the times believes that our isolation is meant to be permanent. Officially we are marking
time. Our people, anxious to help without sacrificing any
of the essentials of their political stability and of their
economic prosperity, are now being educated into the ways
of international coöperation; the door is ajar. Under the
pressure of public opinion, at no distant date, it will open
wide to permit the abundant and, this time, constant flow
of generous assistance to the solution of the trying problems of man, for service is, according to Secretary Hoover,
the moral and political ideal of the American citizen.

It is not within our purpose to analyze the motives
political and economic which actuated that momentous decision. Both the League and the International Organization of Labor suffered from their too close connection. As
some opposed the League through fear of the International
Organization of Labor, others opposed the International
Organization of Labor because it might lead to the League
or to the World Court. The reluctance of the United States
to participate in the International Organization of Labor
is perhaps more satisfactorily explained by the conflict of
two industrial philosophies—the one sponsored by the

---

[5] Australia and Canada are also organized under the federal plan,
and therefore are not able to ratify directly but must secure action
through the federated provinces. In the case of Canada this difficulty is increased by reason of the nearness of the United States.
There would be much greater activity in ratifications of conventions
in Canada and greater interest on the part of the provinces were
it not for the American policy of nonparticipation.

working classes and reflected in the International Organization of Labor and the other represented by American tradition. Reference has been made to them already but it may be helpful to restate them at this time.

Not infrequently Labor has to meet in employers, governments, and courts a philosophy of extreme individualism and laissez faire such as obtained in England in the latter part of the eighteenth century. The standpoint of employers' opposition is that of the doctrine of natural rights, free competition, freedom of contract, and inviolable property rights. It is assumed that a harmony of interests prevails in society and that the employers' interests are identical with the interests of society. Therefore, labor legislation is to be condemned when it interferes with employers' interests. The employer gives work to Labor and can hire and fire as he will. He has a right to manage his own business, for it is his. It is further assumed that free competition is always in the interest of society and therefore the employer has the right to bargain individually with Labor and to refuse to bargain collectively. All the above rests on a social philosophy of God-given, inalienable, absolute natural rights and is the old classical individualistic laissez-faire position of the eighteenth century.

American courts have been condemned for incorporating the same point of view in their decisions. Thus, according to Professor Watkins of the University of California, "American courts have been condemned as antiquated in viewpoint and method, basing their decisions on logic rather than on the current facts of economic life, individualistic rather than socialized, protecting property rights rather than personal rights and exaggerating private right at the expense of public right and welfare, ultra conservative, basing their decisions upon eighteenth century legal philosophy and failing to meet the needs of a changing industrial society." [6]

---

[6] *Introduction to the Study of Labor Problems,* p. 617.

To that philosophy of the employer there is opposed the philosophy of Labor. Sherwood Eddy describes it thus:

Labor and the progressive thinkers rest upon the evolutionary rather than the absolutist philosophy, upon the rights of persons as paramount to those of property. Labor takes its stand against autocracy in industry as well as in government. It believes that there is a harmony of interest between workers and that they owe a supreme duty to one another and to society as a whole. They believe that they give profits to the employer as truly as the employer gives work to them; that it is necessary for the welfare of the mass of labor to bargain collectively and that the individual worker without capital, tools or means of livelihood is utterly helpless before the employer or group of employers who possess an overwhelming advantage over him as an isolated individual. They believe that they have as much right to representatives of their own choosing within or without their own works as have the employers to utilize the assistance of outside employers and legal counsel. They believe that they have the same right to protect the standards of their class as a whole as have employers, business or professional men.

They believe that while a selfish individualist philosophy may claim the right of the individual laborer to work where, when and for whom he pleases regardless of the welfare of his fellows, that a larger view of social relationships and obligations in an organic society must look beyond the isolated action of the individual to the final test of social well-being. . . . They may not always realize or be able to express this philosophy, but a real idealism and a real philosophy of life underlies this movement of modern labor throughout the world.[7]

These two opposing philosophies exist in this country but it would not be correct to say that either one of them adequately represents the employers' group or the laborers' group. Not a few employers have adopted a more progressive policy than the one described [8] and many workers have not been converted to the modern labor program.

It is evident that the International Organization of La-

---

[7] Sherwood Eddy, *op. cit.*, p. 191.
[8] Herbert Hoover, *American Individualism, passim.*

bor, although not strictly a Labor organization, as Labor claims only one-quarter of the representatives, is more inclined toward the evolutionary than toward the classical philosophy of property and personal rights. And to the extent in which that is felt and feared by the American employers there arises a corresponding opposition to a movement for international labor legislation under the inspiration and guidance of the International Labor Organization of the League of Nations.

While the controversy is going on regarding the real motives which moved the United States to decline membership in the new international organizations, it may be worth while to relate the cases of unofficial coöperation between the United States and the International Labor Organization, which, minor though they be, are of special significance as they may prepare the way for closer relations in the future.

The International Labor Office has not been entirely ignored by the United States. First, a correspondent's office has been established in Washington since 1920. Ernest Greenwood was the first correspondent appointed. He directed his efforts towards making known the aims of the International Labor Organization to the national organizations of employers, and in the American press. He endeavored to bring about direct relations with the American Chamber of Commerce and to secure such coöperation as might be possible from the United States government. Mr. Greenwood resigned at the end of 1923 and was succeeded by Leifur Magnusson, formerly of the United States Department of Labor at Washington and for nearly three years one of the officials of the Scientific Division of the International Labor Office at Geneva.

Mr. Magnusson has lately told us how he understands his mission in the United States. The Washington Branch exists primarily for the purpose of interpreting the industrial and labor situation in the United States for the central office. Obviously the International Labor Organization needs to know the experience of the United States as the largest industrial country in all matters of labor legislation and industrial relations and conditions. To that end the Washington Branch collects Federal and state government publications in the field of labor and industry and sees to it that they are regularly dispatched to Geneva. It prepares memoranda in response to specific inquiries from the central office. Larger researches have also been undertaken and published as studies of the International Labor Office. Among these may be mentioned a study of the housing situation in the United States, the use of leisure time by industrial workers, the status of health insurance and old age pensions in this country.

For associations and individuals in this country, the Washington Branch exists to give information concerning the work of the Office at Geneva. It also publishes monthly a press release that summarizes happenings in the world of labor abroad as chronicled in the publications of the International Labor Office or reported in special communications prepared at Geneva.

The work of the International Labor Office has been followed with keen interest by the American workers and employers. Relations have been maintained with universities and with the American Federation of Labor and with great employers' associations such as the National Association of Manufacturers, the National Industrial Conference Board, the Chamber of Commerce of the United States, Chambers of Commerce in various states and cities.

The Chamber of Commerce of the United States of America asked the International Labor Office in 1922 to supply it with statistics concerning wages in the most important industries and trades for the chief industrial countries of the world.

The National Industrial Conference Board [9] and the Chamber of Commerce of the United States have made thorough inquiries into the Organization. Their representative, Magnus W. Alexander [10] visited Geneva in 1922 and wrote an extensive report on the International Labor Organization. It is a very honest and scholarly treatment of the subject of International Labor Legislation. Mr. Alexander's appreciation of the accomplishments of the Organization reveals naturally the employer's point of view, but a genuine spirit of fairness dominates the entire investigation. One might, however, take exception to the emphasis given, seemingly, by way of criticism, to certain statements of officials of the Labor Office which show the keen interest of Labor in the Organization and the desire of the Office to retain Labor's confidence and support, but which in no way prove the office to be under the influence of European Socialism. Whatever form of Socialism may be represented in the International Labor Organization, it has no connection with Moscow but stands in practice for a progressive program of social reform. Mr. Alexander seems to fear also that the United States may submit itself to a legislation imposed from without. In this he is rather unmindful of the safeguards provided by Article 405, or skeptical concerning their efficacy. He finally opposes the social philosophy of the United States to that of Europe, considering that the practice of collective conventions cannot be adapted to a régime of labor legislation.[11] Time may well demonstrate the contrary.

---

[9] The National Industrial Conference Board is a federation of employers' associations representing over 50,000 undertakings employing 7,000,000 workers.

[10] Magnus W. Alexander, "The International Labor Organization of the League of Nations," Research Report No. 48, 1922, p. 160. A new edition is forthcoming.

[11] Recently he seems to have grown even less friendly to the Organization. He now argues clearly for a policy of continued isolation, urges coöperation from the outside and not a participation

And his own fears are somewhat modified or allayed in his very outspoken belief in coöperation with the International Labor Organization opposed though he may be to active participation. In a personally signed article in the *New York Times*, Mr. Alexander wrote as follows: "The problem of our relationship to the International Labor Organization is 'Participation or Coöperation.' Calm reflection would seem to point to the latter as the immediate requirement without prejudice as to what the experience of the next few years or a decade may teach."

Elliott Goodwin, as vice president of the Chamber of Commerce of the United States, also visited Geneva in 1922 and wrote a very favorable report.

When the Chamber of Commerce of the United States held its congress in May, 1922, the Director of the International Labor Office was invited to attend and present the case of the International Labor Organization. This visit, however, had to be postponed.

The National Association of Manufacturers is the only organization of employers which has definitely gone on record as opposed to the participation of the United States government in the International Labor Organization. At their convention in May, 1924, held in New York City, their Statement of Principles contained the following paragraph:

As Industrialists, we are unwilling that the United States should become a party to the International Labor Organization as now organized and administered. We believe this Organization is developing a philosophy in which individual freedom is largely sacrificed to federated control of individual and industrial liberty. We cannot surrender our interest in working out these problems by the exercise of the largest of individual free-

which might hamper production, conflict with individual initiative, with the open shop policy and deprive employers of some of their present privileges and emoluments. *New York Times*, February, 25, 1923, quoted by *American Labor Legislation Review*, March, 1923, p. 87.

dom of contract and employment necessary to achieve the best welfare of both the individual and the nation.

This declaration is obviously based on the misunderstanding of the nature of the Labor Office and of the work which it is doing. In earlier chapters we have already discussed this industrial and social philosophy which the National Association of Manufacturers so persistently defends.

The Office has, of course, remained in constant contact with the American Federation of Labor. The President of the Federation, Samuel Gompers, who had served as chairman of the Commission on International Labor Legislation which framed the constitution of the International Labor Organization during his presidency of the Commission on International Labor Legislation in Paris, always followed the work of the Office with close interest. The Federation of Labor has submitted the publications of the Office to careful study and considerable correspondence containing useful and instructive criticism is exchanged by the two organizations.

More recently the *American Federationist,* the official organ of the American Federation of Labor, has carried each month international items of interest to Labor, while the August number contained an account of the latest, or seventh, conference of the Office, by the Director of the Washington Branch of the International Labor Office. A most interesting item appears in the Report of the Executive Council of the American Federation of Labor for 1925, to the effect that the American Federation of Labor has solicited contributions among its membership for furnishing a room in the International Labor Office building at Geneva, which it is expected will be dedicated early in 1926.

It was at the request of American employers and engineers that the Office undertook an inquiry into the three-shift system as applied in the iron and steel trade. Toward the end of 1920, the Taylor Society of the United States of America, an association of production managers, labor managers, and engineers engaged in the study of production and labor problems in industry, asked the International Labor Office to undertake an inquiry in the application of the three-shift system in the iron and steel industry.

Since the steel strike of 1919 in the United States and the report published by the Inter-Church World Movement upon it, a considerable force of public opinion had demanded that the possibility of profitably adopting the three-shift system in preference to the two-shift system should be adequately investigated. The Taylor Society was carrying on such an investigation. The International Labor Office drew up and circulated a questionnaire in English, French, Italian, German, and Spanish to the governments and representative associations of employers and workpeople in its state members.

The questionnaire was intended to determine how far the three-shift system had replaced the two-shift system, the effects of it upon output, the quality of production, labor costs, the accidents rate, the health and efficiency of the workers, the employment of their leisure.

The answers brought out the fact that the two-shift system was now almost entirely replaced by the three-shift system throughout Europe, but the change has been so recent and has taken place under such abnormal industrial and political conditions that a definite comparison between the two systems cannot be attempted. The workers welcome the change but on the whole the employers regret it. The governments feel that when tried under more normal conditions, the system may become more acceptable to employers.

The information obtained was communicated by the Washington representative of the Office to Mr. Hoover,

United States Secretary of Commerce, with a view to being of assistance to a large industrial conference which was to deal with this subject.

Moreover, the report was of great assistance to those who were interested in securing action by President Harding in support of introduction of the eight-hour day in the iron and steel industry. The very fact that it was disclosed that the steel industry of the world was on an eight-hour day, cannot help but have had its influence in bringing home to the officials of the American steel industry the backwardness of their own position in that respect. In any case, the three-shift system has become effective in the United States.

The Washington Conference of the International Labor Organization, in 1919, moved the establishment of an International Emigration Commission. This Commission, while showing due regard for the sovereign rights of each state, was to consider and report what measures should be adopted to regulate the migration of workers out of their own countries and to protect the interests of wage earners residing in countries other than their own.

In order to obtain the most complete information for the preparation of the report, a questionnaire was sent by the Office in 1920 to all governments as well as to the most representative organizations of employers and workers. Thirty-one governments replied. The United States government had contemplated representation on the International Emigration Commission and, although finally no official representative attended, the United States government supplied the Office with a very full answer to the questionnaire issued in connection with the work of the Commission. Several large American associations requested and obtained permission to follow the work of this Commission.

One of the representatives of these organizations, Miss

Kellor, a well-known authority on emigration problems in the United States, was a witness before the House of Representatives Committee on Immigration and Naturalization in December, 1921, and at the close of her evidence asked the permission of the chairman to draw attention to certain inaccurate information which had been published in the United States regarding the proceedings of the International Emigration Commission. She presented to the Committee on Immigration and Naturalization a copy of the resolutions adopted by the Emigration Commission and the Committee decided to insert these resolutions in its record. Miss Kellor also informed the Committee that the most scrupulous courtesy had been observed by the Emigration Commission in discussing matters concerning the United States.

The Commission recommended the creation of a permanent committee assisted by experts for following the general development of emigration problems. The Governing Body expressed the opinion that the committee should include, if possible, an American expert. The correspondent of the Washington Office brought the proposals unofficially before the Emigration Service of the United States and the Commissioner-General of Emigration decided in February, 1922, to nominate Fred. C. Croxton as an American expert to serve on this committee. The commission has not been appointed as yet.

Due to various upsets, but more particularly on account of the aggressiveness of the Italian government to capture the direction of international conferences on migration, the work of the International Labor Office was delayed. The principal result of the Commission's activities was to bring the matter out of the state of preliminary discussion by the Commission into the program of the Conference. The eighth Conference, for example, in June, 1926, will discuss the simplification of the inspection of emigrants on board ship. Plans have gone through and the Governing Body has appointed from its membership a committee of three representing the three groups in the Organization—government, employers, and workers—and then will create in different countries a panel of experts, among whom it is expected several Americans will be included.

The International Labor Office has set up another commission whose work is of considerable interest to the United States, namely the Anthrax Advisory Commission. Before the Washington Conference, most countries had endeavored by means of veterinary or factory regulations to deal with anthrax infection, but the experience of some of the more important manufacturing countries, and particularly of Great Britain, was that regulations were entirely inadequate to cope with the evil. It was felt that international action to control the exportation and transport of wool, horsehair, hides, and skins was the only means of preventing the disease being carried from animals to men. The Conference decided to request the coöperation of the United States. It expressed the hope that in view of the important scientific work carried on by the United States Department of Agriculture for the purpose of preventing the spread of anthrax in the United States, and in view of the important researches conducted by the United States Bureau of Labor Statistics, the United States may find it possible to collaborate in this international endeavor which has for its object the amelioration of hygienic conditions and the protection of the workers against disease.

On October 6, 1922, the Office received from the American Legation at Berne a communication to the effect that the government of the United States had decided to send a representative to the Anthrax Advisory Commission in an unofficial and consultative capacity and had nominated for this purpose Dr. Marion Dorset, chief of the Biochemic Division, United States Department of Agriculture.

Dr. Marion Dorset took part in the meetings of the Advisory Committee on Anthrax at London, in December, 1922, and made valuable contributions to the findings of the Committee. His appointment by the United States government was the first step towards a special form of cooperation between the United States and the League. Since then, the United States government has been officially represented on the League commissions dealing with the traffic in women and children and the traffic in opium, on the Health Committee, on the committees dealing with Greek refugees, and at the Customs Conference for the suppression of traffic in arms. Miss Alice Hamilton is a member of the Correspondence Committee on Industrial Hygiene of the International Labor Office and it was in that capacity that she was invited to sit on the Health Committee of the League of Nations. Miss Grace Abbott, chief of the Children's Bureau of the Department of Labor, is a member of the League's committee on traffic in women and children.

As a further example of that policy of seeking outside advice and collaboration, there is to be cited the International Conference of Labor Statisticians, which met for the first time in 1923. A second meeting convened in Geneva in April of 1925. These conferences have had for their purpose the standardization of methods of statistics, to bring about an international comparability of labor statistics and information. Thus far the Conference experts have agreed on the minima of information and presentation for statistics relating to industrial accidents, wages and hours, cost-of-living index numbers, certain limited comparisons of real wages, and unemployment statistics. If everything goes well as a result of the second Conference of Statisticians, new household budget inquiries not later than 1928 may be expected in countries which have made none since 1920 or 1921, and it is quite possible that most countries will accept a new and uniform base, namely, 1930, for their calculation of cost-of-living index numbers. The great task ahead is the securing of the acceptance of the proposals of the Conference.

At the meeting of the Inter-Parliamentary Union, held at Stockholm in August, 1921, a resolution was adopted urging the members of the Union to promote, within the parliaments of the world, legislation towards the realization of the conventions and recommendations adopted.[12] On March 18, 1922, Senator Walsh, of Montana, on behalf of the American Group of Inter-Parliamentary Union, presented to the Senate the draft conventions and recommendations adopted at the three sessions of the International Labor Conference and asked that they should be referred for consideration to the Committee on Education and Labor of the Senate. Senator Walsh, after having given a brief description of the functions of the International Labor Office, asked that his communication of the draft conventions and recommendations should not "be considered in the nature of a formal presentation of the resolutions of this character but that they should have the considerate attention of the Committee on Education and Labor." The conventions and recommendations were referred to the Committee on Education and Labor without objection and thus the United States, in a way, of its motion fulfilled the procedure which Article 405 of the Treaty of Versailles lays upon the state members as an obligation.

Further, the Office, through its correspondent at Washington, had been able on various occasions to place at the disposal of the United States a considerable amount of industrial information. In particular, on the occasion of the Unemployment Conference convened in 1921 by Mr. Hoover, Secretary of the Department of Commerce, the

[12] A somewhat similar resolution was considered by the session of the Inter-Parliamentary Union in Washington, October, 1925.

Washington correspondent had supplied Mr. Hoover with a complete review of the unemployment situation in other countries and of various measures which had been taken by other governments to meet the situation.

From day to day, the Office was receiving from the United States full information as to the conditions of labor in this country and more numerous requests for information with regard to conditions of labor and social problems elsewhere. It is noteworthy that the employers' organizations of the United States were asking the International Labor Office for information far more frequently than the workers' organizations. A large number of employers had, moreover, evinced a keen personal interest in the Office and its work.

It is worth recording that during the first six months of 1921 and in addition to what may be called commercial correspondence, the number of letters received from the United States reached 1,124, while during the same period the number of letters received from France and Great Britain respectively was 1,398 and 1,101.[13]

This brief survey indicates that the importance of the Office as a clearing house for industrial and social information was being more and more appreciated in the United States and it was hoped that the United States would participate to an increasing degree in the scientific investigations undertaken by the Office. It was even thought that the hour was at hand for some type of larger participation.

Thus, Mr. Adatci, the delegate of the government of Japan, certainly expressed the sentiments of all present when, during the 1922 Conference, he moved the following resolution:

---

[13] Even to-day the volume of communications between the Office and the United States is third in importance. Great Britain is first on the list and France second.

The International Labor Conference, earnestly desirous of securing as soon as possible the effective collaboration of the United States in the work of the International Labor Organization, expresses its desire that the United States should seek some means of associating itself with this work independently of the provisions of Part XIII of the Treaty of Peace. The Conference recommends that the International Labor Organization shall take appropriate measures to obtain the effective collaboration of the United States in the work of the International Labor Organization.[14]

The Committee of Selection decided that it was not opportune to put to a vote the resolution of Mr. Adatci, who evidently intended to discover other means of coöperation with the United States aside from formal membership in the International Labor Organization.

The Director of the Labor Office, Albert Thomas, was equally eager to open the road to closer coöperation. In his report to the 1922 Conference, he said:

As American opinion gradually realizes that the International Labor Organization has no political aspect but is solely devoted to the scientific study of social and industrial problems and to the effort to secure improved standards, particularly in those countries where conditions are backward or in those trades and occupations in which workers are exposed to special dangers of accident or disease, the misunderstanding as to the real character of the Organization may be dissipated and the obstacles to the fuller association of the United States with the Organization may be removed. The problem in fact of the full participation of the United States in the International Labor Organization can only be solved in this way, *i.e.*, by a full understanding of its object and working.[15]

It is no doubt with that object in view that he undertook, in December, 1922, his visit to the United States.

The visit of Mr. Thomas was a delicate one, for although

---

[14] Minutes of the International Labor Conference, 1922, p. 150.
[15] Report of the Director, International Labor Conference, 1922, p. 21.

there was at that time, since the meeting of the Bankers' Association and the new declarations of the Farmers, in 1922, a revival of interest in international questions, still a foreign visitor could not handle but with great reserve a subject bearing directly or indirectly upon association with the League of Nations.

There was a point of contact, however, which presented no such objections, that was the scientific aspect of the work of the International Labor Organization. The exchange of information and the coördination of scientific inquiries, both for the sake of accuracy and economy, could prove as useful to the United States as to the Organization. Thereupon, Mr. Thomas entered into relations with the American Association for Labor Legislation which continues its most efficient and useful service as a branch of the International Association for Labor Legislation. He addressed the sixteenth annual meeting of the Association in Chicago, December, 1923, and praised their continued efforts in support of labor legislation. The Director visited also the universities of Harvard and Columbia with the intention of developing and encouraging collaboration with certain of their departments. The departments of social sciences of all our universities could not but derive great profit from a close coöperation with the Research Section of the International Labor Organization.

Perhaps the best work in social and scientific research in the United States is done under the auspices of some of our great private foundations. The Director was aware of their contributions and outlined plans for coöperation, for instance, between the Office and the Russell Sage Foundation which maintains a Department of Industrial Relations; similarly with the Rockefeller Foundation in its furtherance of Industrial Hygiene, and with the Division of Economics of the Carnegie Endowment for International Peace.

The Department of Labor of the United States enjoys the reputation of being one of the most efficient organizations of its kind, and through the initiative of Dr. Royal Meeker, once Commissioner of Labor Statistics and until June, 1923, head of the Research Division of the International Labor Organization, a friendly coöperation had been maintained between these two institutions. The Director called upon the heads of several departments such as the Women's Bureau, the Children's Bureau, the Bureau of Labor Statistics, the Bureau of Immigration, the Bureau of Naturalization, the Employment Service, to invite their further coöperation. It was the desire of the Secretary of Labor himself to extend the scientific collaboration of his entire department with the Organization in the "truest spirit of service to the cause of human betterment."

It seemed, therefore, to the Director that, under the head of scientific coöperation, the United States, as represented by all the organizations engaged in that type of work, was ready not only to recognize the value of the International Labor Office but to lend its assistance in the full measure of its power and also to learn and profit by the world-wide and daily tested experience of the Office.

The employers of the United States are too alert and too well informed to underestimate the importance of such an institution as the International Labor Organization. The National Industrial Conference Board, the well-known association of employers, had already manifested keen interest in the Organization and delegated its Managing Director, Magnus W. Alexander, to make an investigation of its character and activity. The Board expressed to Mr. Thomas the desire to coöperate with the Organization in their extensive work of economic research. Other bodies such as the National Association of Manufacturers and the Industrial Council were also willing to exchange information.

The Director confessed, however, that he had found it

difficult to awaken in the employers an interest in closer forms of coöperation. In his report, he said:

The awakening of this feeling appeared all the more difficult in view of the disfavor with which American employers regard collective action. At the same time, however, they attach great importance to their relations with their workers. They are very eager to discover the most efficient methods of securing in the interest of increased production closer coöperation between employers and workers. The real difficulty in establishing closer relations arises from the individualistic spirit of the American employer.

The employers' organization which had shown the greatest interest in international problems was the Chamber of Commerce of the United States, which had become closely associated with the International Chamber of Commerce by the election of Willis H. Booth to the presidency of that body. Julius N. Barnes, then President of the Chamber of Commerce of the United States, and E. H. Goodwin, its secretary, were in genuine sympathy with the work of the International Labor Office and had directed their Committee on Industrial Relations to seek possible avenues of coöperation with it.

At a dinner given on January 12 at the Metropolitan Club, Washington, D. C., to Albert Thomas, Julius Barnes said that there were times when national self-interest and international coöperation ran in parallel channels:

America has a considerable pride that its common standard of living is manifestly higher than that of any other industrial country. It desires to maintain and advance that standard, but as a surplus producing country selling in the export markets of the world there is a limit to the disparity in the living conditions and wage scale which cannot be wholly overcome even by American resourcefulness and American adaptability to large scale production through mechanical aids. . . . Manifestly, also, both in the interest of an increase in human standards and also in the self-interest of national production of our own standards, the

processes of equalization in wages and working conditions between ourselves and our industrial competitors should be one
of leveling up their standards rather than leveling down our own.
It is with this idea that the Chamber of Commerce of the United
States is seriously considering the advisability of participation
in the Employers' Section of the International Labor Office, so
that we may understand and influence comparative world industrial realizations.[16]

The workers of America have on the whole been in warm
sympathy with the Industrial Labor Organization. A certain number of prejudices still endure in some quarters, for
instance, the fear that adherence to the Organization would
gradually imply political entanglements, the fear that the
small representation (1 to 4) given to the workers in the
Conferences would interfere with the progress of social
legislation, the fear that the difficulty of raising the standards of backward countries might either lower the American standards or delay further progress. These objections,
however, do not stand close examination.

On the occasion of Mr. Thomas' visit to the United States,
Samuel Gompers in a communication to the press said that
he had been asked to make a definite statement as to the
attitude of the American Federation of Labor towards the
question raised by Mr. Barnes. This attitude had been
clearly defined at two conventions of the Federation : it was
one of indorsement of the International Labor Organization. Mr. Gompers recalled that he was the authorized representative of the American Federation of Labor at the
Paris Peace Conference and had been a member of the
Commission which drafted the Labor Charter under which
the International Labor Office was organized, and that
American Labor, having thus participated in laying the
foundation for the International Labor Office, was watching the development of that Office with the deepest inter-

---

[16] *Cf. Industrial and Labor Information*, Vol. V, No. 6.

est and with a desire to participate at the earliest opportunity. The statement continued:

The announcement made by Mr. Barnes seems to offer the opportunity for American employers and American workers to participate in the activities of their respective groups in the International Labor Office, even though the United States does not officially become a full member of the International Labor Organization.

Mr. Barnes, I am sure, speaks with authority and none is happier than I because of his declaration. His statement makes it possible for me to bring the whole matter before the February meeting of the Executive Council of the American Federation of Labor.

In view of the record, I feel sure that our Executive Council will welcome the opportunity to have the matter brought before its next meeting, and I am also certain that the action of the President of the United States Chamber of Commerce will be as welcome to the other members of the Council as to myself.

Perhaps there may be some who will wonder why it is necessary for employers and workers to act together on this question. The International Labor Organization, it should be explained, is composed of four delegates from each member nation. Two of these represent the Government, one represents the workers and one represents the employers. There are thus three kinds of delegates. Where a nation is not a member—and the United States is in that category—organized workers and organized employers may participate unofficially in behalf of those whom they represent; and that, I understand, is what Mr. Barnes has in mind.

I think such participation or collaboration will be decidedly helpful, and now that the effort has been begun it may be possible for both workers and employers of the United States to sit in the next annual meeting of the International Labor Organization in Geneva. This will be particularly gratifying because this is the one world organization that is actually functioning in a constructive, helpful manner.

It seemed for a while as though all that private initiative could do would be done on the part of employers and workers to secure a growing understanding and coöperation between America and the International Labor Organization. And still that is very far from the goal expected. Encouraged by these developments some began to think that a properly informed public opinion might sanction an official participation of the United States in the work of the International Labor Organization, particularly if it could be shown that such a move did not involve or imply a membership in the League of Nations.

The case of Germany, a member of the Organization although not a member of the League, had suggested that the United States might become a member of the International Labor Organization, a nonpolitical organization of an economic and social character, without ratifying the Covenant. That possibility is not positively excluded by the Treaty, still it would seem that such a measure would necessitate the approval of the Conference. Although the actual members of the League of Nations, anxious to secure the adherence of the United States to the League itself, might not countenance such a step, there is no fear that the annual Conference of the International Labor Organization would decline the coöperation of the United States upon that basis. The United States government, however, was not ready to go even that far. Was there then no other way of bringing about a closer coöperation? The Federal government had repeatedly sent observers to international meetings. Could it not likewise send an observer to the Conference? Hon. W. B. Wilson had presided at the Washington Conference, when Secretary of Labor, although the United States had not adhered to the League of Nations.

And if the government could not contemplate even such a remote participation, could not at least the workers and the employers send delegations which would attend the meetings, and take part in the discussion without the right to vote? Workers and employers had been invited to the

Washington Conference and Mr. Gompers had taken a part in the discussion of the eight-hour law.

This is the type of representation that the Director thought would meet the approval of the majority in America. The Director felt that constitutionally the Conference had the right to accept a representation of this kind. The American Federation of Labor and the Chamber of Commerce of the United States had given definite expression to the fact that they were in agreement regarding the dispatch of unofficial representation to Geneva, if it should prove possible. All agreed, however, that, in order to be productive of good, even an unofficial representation should have the at least tacit approval of the government.

In his interviews with President Harding, and Secretaries Hughes and Hoover, Mr. Thomas became convinced that they were ready to coöperate in all efforts towards solidarity and human protection. Mr. Hoover [17] gave his approval to the form of delegation to the annual Conferences described above and recommended to the United States Chamber of Commerce for consideration as to whether they could not perform a national service by acting for America on this occasion.

Meanwhile the attitude of the general public seemed to

---

[17] Mr. Hoover, in his recent book on *American Individualism* (New York, 1922, pp. 8-11) defends a philosophy quite compatible with the purpose of the International Labor Organization. As a matter of fact, that type of Individualism presupposes such national and international organization for the protection of Labor, otherwise how could these ends, for instance, be attained: "No doubt, individualism run riot, with no tempering principle, would provide a long category of inequalities, of tyrannies, dominations and injustices." Individualism "must be tempered with that firm and fixed ideal of American individualism—an equality of opportunity." . . . "We have learned that the impulse to production can only be maintained at a high pitch if there is a fair division of the products. We have also learned that fair division can only be obtained by certain restrictions on the strong and the dominant." . . . "In our Individualism we have long since abandoned the laissez-faire of the eighteenth century."

grow more favorable to the Organization. In the *New York Herald* of January 21, 1923, appeared the following:

International is a word which has acquired a sinister sense of late, especially when it is coupled with labor. It brings to the mind the numerically designated attempts of revolutionists to build a political and economic platform for themselves or it suggests the somewhat ineffectual yearnings of sentimental intellectuals toward the brotherhood of man and the uplift of humanity.

Nothing of either tendency taints the International Labor Bureau, the head of which, Albert Thomas, former French Minister of Munitions, has just returned to Europe after a successful visit to this country. The aim of the Organization he directs is to elevate Labor, not as would the intellectuals by the dissemination of idealistic propaganda; not as the Red dreamers, by stirring up blind revolt; but by close, scientific study of economic problems and of the legislation affecting labor in different parts of the world, with a view to the steady betterment of the standard of living among the workers of all countries. These activities are controlled by official delegates from forty-seven Governments and by representatives of employers and workmen.

During the first part of the year 1923, the National Economic League took a referendum on the participation of the United States in the International Labor Organization and other international problems. The result was 754 yes, 369 no, and 137 qualified votes. The Economic League is organized "to create an informed, disinterested leadership of public opinion free from partisan bias or class interest and acceptable as representing the best thought throughout the country." That vote indicated a very significant evolution of public sentiment.

After the Director's return, correspondence was resumed with the American Federation of Labor and with the Chamber of Commerce of the United States, in order to obtain the appointment of the promised delegation to the next Conference. The proposal was laid before the Board of the

United States Chamber of Commerce. The Board resolved to send, at first, not regular delegates but a group of observers. The appointment of these observers was actually made. However, at about this time, the Governing Body decided to hold the normal sessions of the Conference in June, instead of October. The fifth session of the conference, which was to take place in October, 1923, was not to be given up, but was to be limited to the discussion of one subject only, namely, the organization of an adequate system of inspection. The United States Chamber of Commerce was apprised of this change and decided that it would be more profitable for its observers to attend a normal session of the Conference which would be more representative of the work of the Organization.

In May, 1924, however, the Office learned with astonishment that the Board of the Chamber of Commerce of the United States had decided to reverse its previous decision and that no observers would be sent. The International Office was at a loss to explain this change of attitude. The Director suggested, in this report, that changes in the membership of the Board of the Chamber and the pronouncements of the new administration had perhaps prompted the decision.

The Director thinks that for the present any rapid progress toward closer relations is quite unlikely. On the other hand, he notes with pleasure that the system of what may be called limited participation has already developed to a remarkable degree.

Whatever may be the political solution of American international relations, the Office firmly hopes to maintain wide and serious scientific connections with the United States. The Organization cannot remain indifferent to the greatest industrial country in the world and cannot ignore its industrial experience, nor fail to watch with care the innumerable experiments in industrial organization and in the solution of industrial problems which are constantly being made on this side of the Atlantic.

The Office may hope to draw to an increasing degree detailed information concerning industrial conditions in America from numerous authoritative sources. On the other hand, it may hope to strengthen existing connections by supplying the United States with information regarding European conditions.

An interesting example of such coöperation may be found in the fact that the Coal Commission, set up by the United States government, after the long strikes in the coal industry, in the early winter of 1922, asked the International Labor Office to supply information on the conditions of miners and the various systems in operation in the mining industry in Europe. Likewise the important Senate Commission, appointed to study an amendment to the Constitution permitting the adoption of the Federal Child Labor Act, was anxious to learn of the work accomplished by the Office and invited the Director to lay before it, at a public meeting on January 15, 1923, all information collected on the laws affecting child labor in the various countries of the world.

In this connection, it is of particular interest to refer to a statement recently made by the American expert, Dr. Harry H. Laughlin, before the Committee of the House of Representatives on Immigration and Naturalization. Dr. Laughlin went to Europe as the representative of the Department of Labor and carried out six months' research into the migration problems in various European countries. Giving evidence before the Committee, he drew special attention to the importance of the work of the Office in that field.

For the first time in the history of the world, there is a Central Bureau which makes it its business to keep informed concerning international movement of peoples. The Office in its work, in the collection and distribution of statistical and other information performs its service of great value to both emigrant and immigrant receiving nations, and also to the cause of World Peace.

So much, then, for present and actual collaboration. As to future possibilities there are open opportunities to both the national and the state governments for the widest kind of assistance and coöperation. Such collaboration would involve no political commitments or violation of any accepted precedents.

But first of all, justice would demand that the American government make a direct and definite financial contribution to the technical research work of the International Labor Office. It will be recalled that the United States government contributed to the work of the semi-official International Labor Office at Basel, which, in respect to its information and research function, is a lineal ancestor of the International Labor Office. To the work of research and translation of labor laws, the American government contributed a thousand dollars annually until three years ago. So now likewise the United States could subsidize the publication called *Legislative Series,* containing the translation of foreign labor laws which are indispensable to our Departments of Labor, both state and national, for the efficient carrying out of their work.

Another opportunity for coöperation is offered in advisory commissions. The International Labor Office through its research activities seeks ideas and suggestions. To secure these ideas and suggestions, to mature and weigh them, it sets up advisory commissions and committees upon which American members as technical experts and advisors should be sitting. Take, for example, the International Conference of Labor Statisticians, organized under the friendly auspices of the International Labor Office. Here is a purely technical body of governmental labor statisticians assembled to bring about, if possible, a uniform classification of industries for the purpose of labor statistics, which seeks a comparable basis for international comparison of wages, standards of living, unemployment statistics, and so forth. Surely the greatest industrial country in the world has an interest in such matters.

The American Department of Labor has often wished that changes could be made in foreign labor statistics to meet the needs of users in this country. It is equally clear that we can make improvements in our statistical methods to suit the informational need of other countries as well as our own. There is indeed a mutuality of interests which calls for a sitting down together, the comparing of notes and interchange of ideas and practices. Not only the Federal government, but representatives from some of our states should find both the means and the opportunity to associate themselves in this nonpolitical, purely humanitarian, and, indeed, really tedious work of bettering our methods in labor statistics.

Another far-reaching but equally noncommittal opportunity for effective collaboration on the part of the states would be voluntarily to take upon themselves to send in annually replies to any questionnaires of the International Labor Office concerning the scope and enforcement of their respective labor laws. The states, members of the International Labor Organization, do this under an agreement contained in Section 408 of the Treaty of Peace. As each labor convention or treaty comes into force, by the adherence of a sufficient number of countries, the states are required annually to report progress in its enforcement. For this purpose, the Office prepares a very simple and brief schedule of inquiry. The first query is whether or not there exists any law in the country in question conforming to the terms of the particular draft convention; also, if so, what is the date of enactment, what is the enforcing authority, and so forth. Attention is also called to any special section in the convention and inquiry made as to measures taken or arrangements perfected for application thereof. A request for general observation or remarks is added, and the desire expressed that any statistics bearing on the subject be communicated to the Office.

It is perfectly true that any searcher after the information could discover this in the annual reports of the forty-eight different states or ascertain the substance of the state laws by consulting the statutes of each state or using the bulletins of the United States Bureau of Labor Statistics, but this is a laborious process and liable to cause misinterpretation and misunderstanding of the legislation. The advantage in doing it through a definite letter of inquiry is that each state is left free to interpret its own law and uniformity is secured by the use of an identical schedule of inquiry sent to every state. In the final analysis the International Labor Office would be merely a publishing agency for the information secured.

The reports of the member states of the Organization are now regularly published in the Annual Report of the Director of the International Labor Office. If the American states should wish to collaborate in this universal posting of the labor laws to 'the world, their reports would also be published in a special appendix to the Director's Report.

One need scarcely point out the advantages of this body of information. Comparability is the spice of labor legislation. No state whether truly sovereign or part of the federal commonwealth now ventures to revise or expand its labor laws without first inquiring what the other states have done. We must recognize this timidity in our law-making work, and provide the means whereby such seeking after knowledge may be satisfied most advantageously.

It is upon that basis of scientific and technical coöperation that the present relations between the Organization and the United States are founded. The present correspondent of the Office, at Washington, is well qualified by training and experience to extend the range and importance of that type of coöperation.

Since the presidential election in 1924, however, the advocates of the Organization have been profoundly discouraged by the declaration of Calvin Coolidge that the League of Nations controversy was to be considered settled. But to all experienced interpreters of political utterances that statement is much less significant than the declaration of President Coolidge in his address before the Chicago Commercial Club, December 4, 1924. The President spoke as follows:

We cannot suppose that we are to be benefited by great production unless the men and women who furnish it are themselves benefited by it. We cannot neglect the human element in our affairs. All the cattle and grain, all the cotton and wool, all the cloth and steel, all the shoes and automobiles will be of small advantage to us unless they contribute a more abundant life to those who produce them. Prosperity cannot be divorced from humanity.

We cannot expect, in the long course of events, to maintain our country on a permanent level of general well-being far above that of other peoples. Even if we could hope to accomplish it it would bring us little satisfaction if our prosperity must be gained and held at the cost of suffering of others. In the long course of affairs, and in a world which has become little more than a great neighborhood, our comment, our portion of good fortune, must largely depend upon the share that shall be allotted to our neighbors. At the last, those of us who are partners in the supreme service of building and bettering our civilization must go up or go down, must succeed or fail together, in our one common enterprise.

On the other hand, I am profoundly impressed with the fact that the structure of modern society is essentially a unity, destined to stand or to fail as such.

We cannot hope indefinitely to maintain our country as a specially favored community, an isle of contentment lifted above the general level of the average of the standards of humanity.

I know there was a time when many among us believed this was possible. But who, now, can continue clinging to such a faith, in view of the lesson which the War brought to us? If we could not avoid involvement in a war whose causes were foreign, and whose issues were chiefly alien to us because we had settled them for ourselves long ago, how can we hope to avoid our full share of responsibility in connection with other world problems, which, if they are ever to be solved, must be solved in an atmosphere of peace and goodwill? We must be constantly ready to help both at home and abroad where our help is desired and will be effective.

There we find, nobly set forth, a social and industrial philosophy which is bound to become that of the United States and whose implications when logically drawn and consistently followed will demand a restatement of political platforms dictated by opportunism, partisanship, or expediency.

In December, 1924, the death of Samuel Gompers came as a serious blow to the International Labor Office for it meant the loss not only of one of its founders but also of one of its loyal supporters. His successor, however, William Green, appears friendly towards the Organization. He not only knows the European situation by reason of his association with the American Labor group in Paris in 1919, but also by reason of his own personal and political predilections. Mr. Green is an ardent supporter of the League as such and is desirous of maintaining cordial relations with Labor abroad. Shortly after his election, he wrote the following to the Director:

That there were written in the Treaty of Versailles clauses outlining the fundamentals of the program for human welfare marks a distinctive effort in the constructive progress of Labor the world over. We, in America, feel a deep sense of pride that it was our leader who presided over the deliberations of the Commission on International Labor Legislation, appointed by the Peace Commissioners and who in this capacity contributed to the promotion of labor standards the world around. As we value the achievements already attained, we hope to make them the basis for further progress.

There is, however, a minority in the American Federation of Labor, which strongly opposes the International Organization of Labor. It is led by Andrew Furuseth, the head of the Seamen's Union. Mr. Furuseth had strongly urged at the Peace Conference the inclusion in the general declaration of principles of an article guaranteeing the right of seamen to leave their vessels when in harbor, a right for which he had bitterly fought in the United States and had embodied in the La Follette Act. His demand could not be granted but partial satisfaction was offered him by the addition to what is now Article 405 of the paragraph stating that, in no case, should any member of the Organization be asked or required to lessen the protection afforded to its workers by existing legislation.

In the El Paso Convention of the American Federation of Labor, 1924, Mr. Furuseth tried to have passed a resolution condemning the work of the International Labor Office in connection with the formulation of an international seamen's code. The matter was referred to the Executive Council for report and study, but nothing has come up in connection therewith since that time. Mr. Furuseth did not renew the matter before the 1925 Convention of the American Federation of Labor at Atlantic City. The attitude of Mr. Furuseth and his group is, of course, most extraordinary in view of the peculiar international character of the occupation of the seamen and the very nature of international commercial competition, but more particularly in view of the position of the American merchant marine. It should indeed be the object not only of seamen in this country, but also of shipowners, to endeavor to raise the working standards of the seamen of other countries if they would maintain impaired the very high American standards. Everything done by the International Labor Office in raising the standards of seamen has worked to the advantage of the American merchant marine, which has stood aloof and sat in the seat of the scornful. The hostility of Mr. Furuseth may subside if the eighth Conference, in June, 1926, which is to deal with the right of seamen, is able to refute his charges convincingly.

A more favorable evolution of public opinion could be accelerated by the clearing away of a number of objections still standing in the way of American participation. First, the fears of many might be allayed if it were made plain that it is quite possible to join the International Labor Organization without accepting the Covenant or ratifying the Treaty of Versailles. As some one has said, there is in participation in such technical work no more possibility of entanglements in the affairs of other continents than lurks in an international meeting of hardware merchants.

Another difficulty that stands in the way of full coöperation is the extreme diversity of legislation in our states. But there is a strong tendency in America to-day toward a clarification and coördination of our laws. Such, for example, was the object of a conference of judges, lawyers, and instructors in law held in Washington in 1923. An outcome of this conference and of others to follow may probably be the establishment of a law institute to watch over the framing of laws and their interpretation. This would considerably facilitate the task of coöperation in the formulation of international labor laws.

It cannot escape the student of economics that more and more our industrial problems are going to demand not state but national solutions. The President's Conference on Unemployment held at Washington during September and October, 1921, marked distinct progress in that direction. It was the first national conference conducted under governmental auspices for the study of unemployment. Like the annual Conferences of the International Labor Organization, it was, in a measure, of mixed composition, comprising employers and workers, although the employers were in great majority. The delegates were assisted by a large advisory committee of experts. We shall, no doubt, continue to feel the necessity of doing nationally for industrial problems what is done internationally in Geneva.

Naturally the reform most desired by the friends of the International Labor Organization is the right of the federal governments to legislate in matters referring to Labor. Jealous as the states are of all their rights, public opinion may in the course of a few years demand a change. The history of child-labor legislation seems to point in that direction. If the Federal government, conscious of what the general interest requires, endeavors to protect women and children in industry and the Supreme Court continues to declare such attempts unconstitutional, it is possible that a constitutional amendment could be passed which would definitely place labor legislation within the power of Congress.

We have amended the Constitution for the attainment of purposes which are less vital to the welfare of the American people than a proper protection of the laboring classes whence in the long run comes the strength of the nation.

The Constitution is such that, either directly or by the interpretation placed upon its provisions by the Supreme Court, interstate, national, and international coöperation in the uniform and legal protection of labor is made practically impossible. And still the founders of this nation surely desired nothing more than to have here a strong and contented people.

Whichever decision may be taken by the administration we cannot escape facing the problem of international labor legislation. The fifth Pan-American Conference held at

Santiago de Chili from March 20 to May 4, 1923, has recommended the inclusion of social problems, with special reference to conditions in American states, on the agenda of the forthcoming Pan-American conferences. The proposal refers particularly to questions such as labor agreements, protection against sickness, regulation of labor, conditions in factories, regulation of labor conditions of women and children, hygienic conditions in factories, social insurance, old age and invalidity pensions, factory inspection, labor statistical services, institution of inquiries likely to promote the conclusion of conventions between the American states providing reciprocity of treatment of workers.[18] We shall find it a delicate problem to avoid the issue and shall see ourselves carried again into the sphere of international regulation.

The present outlook reveals nothing, therefore, that should discourage the supporters of the International Labor Organization. What holds America back is not disagreement with the social ideals and moral purposes of the International Labor Organization but a puzzling mixture of political habits and economic traditions. Moreover, as soon as the American employers realize that however much the International Labor Organization may lose from the absence of the United States, the United States will in the long run lose even more, and as soon as the American people become clearly conscious that their willful isolation and their prolonged abstention have not only negative effects but are, in fact, a positive interference with general progress, with the well-being of men, and with the security of our civilization, the cause of the International Labor Organization will be definitely won.

---

[18] *Cf. Industrial and Labor Information,* Vol. VI, No. 13.
Cf. Appendix IV.

CHAPTER X

CONCLUSION

As we close this study, we feel that we have barely opened up this vast problem of the international aspects of Labor, and merely introduced to the reader the great agency devoted to it—the International Labor Organization.

Labor has entered the international field and will play in it no secondary rôle. Its interests are bound to be recognized by increasingly larger numbers, not, however, as the only interests but as a group of interests most vital to the general welfare. It must guard against excessive claims because the Bolshevistic principle that Labor is everything and therefore should possess the entire political power of the community is, in its essence, antidemocratic and in the long run self-destructive. Therefore Labor may claim a considerable influence, an influence proportioned to its importance and to its capacity for government but, in any case, its rôle must remain subordinated to the general welfare.

Whether it organizes itself into separate political parties or not, it cannot but exercise a great influence upon politics. The connection between the political program of state or national administration and the material well-being of the masses is too intimate to leave the workers indifferent towards foreign and domestic policies. More and more in national and international conventions, they will formulate resolutions of criticism or of approval and elaborate political programs of their own.

259

In the economic field we are on the eve of a remarkable growth of Labor influence. Labor is no longer simply finding fault and agitating. Labor is at work studying with great care modern economic problems. It is anxious to prove itself worthy of more direct participation in the management of industry and in the control of capital. Most of their leaders and many in the ranks have lately realized that there is no resemblance whatever between a political revolution and an economic one, the latter being infinitely more complex than the former, and they have come to see that an economic revolution, in the Russian spirit, is a stupendous delusion.

More than ever Labor is conscious of its power, but, now, duly cautioned against the use of that power in contradiction with the dictates of human experience and of sane judgment, it stands ready to coöperate. It is to be hoped that the employers and the governments will welcome this opportunity.

When Mr. Vandervelde presented to the Peace Conference the draft convention creating the International Labor Organization, he said: "There are two methods of social revolution, there is the Russian method and the British one; the Labor Commission has chosen the British one." Hence the great Labor leaders of the world, Barnes, Gompers, Jouhaux, Vandervelde, Caprini, have thrown the weight of their powerful national organization on the side of a peaceful and orderly evolution of industrial relations.

The concerted efforts of progressive governments, of far-seeing employers and of seasoned Labor leaders have given us the Organization we have analyzed in the preceding chapters.

Whatever criticism may be made of it, the opponents should not forget that there are two very distinct elements in this Organization: the idea itself and its present embodiment in the institution which functions now in Geneva.

The idea, that is, the urgent need of periodical assemblies bringing together governments, employers, workers, experts, humanitarians, to afford greater protection, fuller justice, a larger and higher life to the worker, without crippling production and hampering the employer in its legitimate efforts towards the increase of national and personal wealth—the idea of maintaining a permanent office with a competent staff and adequate resources to prepare with the utmost care the international agreements which will consecrate social progress and make its onward march safe and certain—that idea is here to stay. It is a waste of effort on the part of a few obdurate capitalists to attack the principles involved in this innovation, for they rest upon a number of well established facts.

It is a political commonplace that the interdependence of nations, primarily in the maintenance of peace, that indispensable condition of human progress, is constantly growing. Our State Department is daily gaining in importance and the Premiers of Europe are forced to give as much attention to foreign affairs as to domestic ones. Isolation, therefore, is under present conditions an outgrown and dangerous policy.

It is now an economic commonplace that the necessity for an interchange between manufactured articles and food or raw materials makes the world largely an economic unit.

It is an economic commonplace that the successful regulation of labor must, within clearly ascertainable limits, become international.

Improving communications are every day breaking down still further the differences between one country and another. Even in the United States, war conditions forced the administration to treat labor as a national question and to set up a War Labor Board to deal with it for the whole Union. Similarly world conditions now make some features at least of the labor question an international problem.

Therefore the association of governments in a political and economic undertaking, in order to bring about, in union with the interested parties, Labor and Capital, a betterment of industrial relations for the good of all, is universally considered a necessity. Hence we may say it is in vain that reactionary groups attack the idea which is the basis and inspiration of the International Labor Organization.

There may be a wide difference of opinion, however, as to the best way to bring about its concrete realization.

Various methods have been proposed and tried until now we are left in the presence of this double alternative: the creation of a superparliament of nations with the power of enacting labor legislation or the periodical calling of conferences whose decisions will be simply advisory. The first proposal, although warmly defended by able economists and jurists, longed for by Labor in general and often considered as the inevitable goal in the evolution of our political institutions, does not appear necessary nor, for the present at any rate, acceptable. The second method, exemplified by the Berne Conventions, has proved (we have had occasion to point it out in these pages) unsatisfactory.

Thereupon, the Labor Commission agreed on a compromise which, to all appearance, promises to meet our present needs without encroaching unduly upon the rights and privileges of national governments, and that compromise gave us the International Labor Organization of the League of Nations.

Whatever be the official attitude of the United States and of reactionary bodies the world over, a fact clearly stands out, namely, that there functions at Geneva an institution which is not a hasty innovation but which has been in the making for over a hundred years, which enjoys the protection of the League, is indorsed by fifty-six nations, has a budget of over one and a half million dollars a year, and is supported by the entire labor world with the exception of the revolutionary groups.

Before it finds a settled place in the new scheme of international relations it may have to undergo many modifications; such institutions are a continual creation. Moreover, a sustained effort over a period of many years will undoubtedly be necessary before the conventions, even when ratified, are safely embodied in the customs of the various nations. But a well planned and ably administered institution is now in existence.

At times it is spoken of as possessed of no influence whatever, since it cannot enforce its decisions, at other times as a dangerous organization threatening the sovereignty of the states, or again as a tool in the hands of Labor. Clearly, it is none of these things. It is a most useful institution to the maintenance of world peace. It is invested with sufficient powers to demonstrate its value; it is at the service of Capital and of the general public, as well as at the service of Labor, because economic peace is of vital concern to us all; it is not dangerous to the state because it acts within well defined limits, is organized upon a democratic and scientific basis, and is closely supervised.

It has two principal sets of enemies: those who derive profit, at times excessive and at times illegitimate, from the present economic organization and those who hope to bring about a state of things radically opposed to it to satisfy their ambition and their vanity, or, mayhap, in good faith because impervious to the light of the most recent experience.

It should be closely watched; it should be frankly criticized; it should be generously supported. The fundamental idea it embodies is sound beyond all doubt; its mechanism is logical. We may confidently, although of necessity patiently, await its results. It is not in six years that an institution, intrusted with one of the most complex tasks that have fallen to the lot of our generation, can justify its existence. But "if the temper of sincere endeavor is preserved and a due measure of patience and tact is maintained, there is no assignable end to the fruit of good works which this institution may bring forth."[1] Not only will it amply vindicate itself but it may redeem the League in the eyes of many critics, for the value of such a League is likely to grow immeasurably as it supplements its political activity with contributions of an economic and social character.

At the plenary session of the Peace Conference, on April 11, 1919, when the draft convention of the Labor Organization was formally approved by the delegates of the Allied and Associated Powers, Sir Robert Borden, of Canada, said: "It is possible that some of us would have framed the dispositions of the proposed Convention somewhat differently, but the main purpose and, after all, the great purpose, in respect of this Convention, as in respect of the League of Nations, is to secure the adhesion of the different states to an arrangement which will *tend to the welfare of humanity in the future.*"

We would fain believe that it is possible to draw from the facts as we have endeavored objectively to present them and from the lessons of history, an even more optimistic conclusion.

The International Labor Organization will not only tend to the welfare of humanity but it will give birth to a charter for the physical, moral, and intellectual well-being of the wage-earning class, and thereby strengthen and consolidate our entire democratic system in an atmosphere of world peace and coöperation.

SI VIS PACEM PARA JUSTITIAM

(Inscription on the foundation of the new building of the International Labor Office at Geneva)

---

[1] Sir Frederick Pallock, *League of Nations*, 1922, p. 186.

APPENDIX I [1]

THE CONSTITUTION OF THE INTERNATIONAL LABOR ORGANIZATION

The Convention as adopted by the Peace Conference, now Article XIII of the Treaty

The British Draft Convention, basis of the work of the Labor Commission.

SECTION I

ORGANISATION OF LABOUR

PREAMBLE

WHEREAS, The League of Nations has for its object the establishment of universal peace, and such a peace can be established only if it is based upon social justice;

WHEREAS, The League of Nations has for its object the establishment of universal peace, and such a peace can be established only if it is based upon the prosperity and contentment of all classes in all nations;

AND WHEREAS, Conditions of labour exist involving such injustice, hardship and privation to large numbers of people as to produce unrest so great that the peace and harmony of the world are imperilled; and an improvement of those conditions is urgently required; as, for example, by the regulation of the hours of work, including the establishment of a maximum working day and week,

AND WHEREAS, Conditions of labour exist which involve injustice, hardship and privation to large numbers of people, and which are productive of unrest which is a menace to the peace and harmony of the world; and an improvement of those conditions is urgently required; as, for example, by the regulation of the hours of work, the prevention of unemployment, the provision of a living

---

[1] This comparison between the British Draft Convention and the final text adopted by the Peace Conference will be found most useful to understand the work done by the Labor Commission and particularly by the American delegates, Samuel Gompers and Henry M. Robinson.

the regulation of the labour supply, the prevention of unemployment, the provision of an adequate living wage, the protection of the worker against sickness, disease and injury arising out of his employment, the protection of children, young persons and women, provision for old age and injury, protection of the interests of workers when employed in countries other than their own, recognition of the principle of freedom of association, the organisation of vocational and technical education and other measures;

WHEREAS, Also the failure of any nation to adopt humane conditions of labour is an obstacle in the way of other nations which desire to improve the conditions in their own countries:

The High Contracting Parties, moved by sentiments of justice and humanity as well as by the desire to secure the permanent peace of the world, agree to the following:

CHAPTER I

Organisation

Art. 387. A permanent organisation is hereby established for the promotion of the objects set forth in the Preamble.

The original Members of the League of Nations shall be the

wage, the protection of the worker against sickness, disease, and injury arising out of his employment, the protection of child and female labour, provision for old age and injury, protection of the interests of workers when employed in countries other than their own, recognition of the principle of freedom of association, and other measures;

WHEREAS, Also the failure of any nation to adopt humane conditions of labour is an obstacle in the way of other nations which desire to improve the conditions in their own countries;

The High Contracting Parties, moved by sentiments of justice and humanity as well as by the desire to secure the permanent peace of the world, agree to the following convention:

CHAPTER I

Organisation

1. The High Contracting Parties, being the States members of the League of Nations, agree to establish a permanent organisation for the promotion of the objects set forth in the

original Members of this organisation, and hereafter membership of the League of Nations shall carry with it membership of the said organisation.

Art. 388. The permanent organisation shall consist of:

1. A General Conference of Representatives of the Members and,

2. An International Labour Office controlled by the Governing Body described in Article 393.

Art. 389. The meetings of the General Conference of Representatives of the Members shall be held from time to time as occasion may require, and at least once in every year. It shall be composed of four representatives of each of the Members, of whom two shall be Government Delegates and the two others shall be Delegates representing respectively the employers and the workpeople of each of the Members.

Each Delegate may be accompanied by Advisers, who shall not exceed two in number for each item of the agenda of the meeting. When questions specially affecting women are to be considered by the Conference, one at least of the advisers should be a woman.

The Members undertake to nominate non-Government Delegates and advisers chosen in

Preamble, and for this purpose agree to accept the provisions contained in the following Articles.

2. The permanent organisation shall consist of (1) a General Conference of representatives of the High Contracting Parties, and (2) an International Labour Office controlled by the Governing Body described in Article 7.

3. A General Conference of representatives of the High Contracting Parties shall be held from time to time as occasion may require, and at least once in every year. It shall be composed of three representatives of each of the High Contracting Parties, of whom one shall be the Government Delegate and the others shall be Delegates representing respectively the employers and the workpeople of each of the High Contracting Parties.

The High Contracting Parties undertake to nominate non-Government delegates and advisers chosen in agreement with the industrial organisations most representative of employers or workpeople, as the case may be, in their respective countries.

Each of the delegates may be accompanied by not more than two advisers. The advisers may agreement with the industrial organisations, if such organisations exist, which are most representative of employers or workpeople, as the case may be, in their respective countries.

Advisers shall not speak except on a request made by the Delegate whom they accompany and by the special authorisation of the President of the Conference, and may not vote.

A Delegate may by notice in writing addressed to the President appoint one of his advisers to act as his deputy, and the adviser, while so acting, shall be allowed to speak and vote.

The names of the Delegates and their advisers will be communicated to the International Labour Office by the Government of each of the Members.

The credentials of Delegates and their advisers shall be subject to scrutiny by the Conference, which may, by two-thirds of the votes cast by the Delegates present, refuse to admit any Delegate or adviser whom it deems not to have been nominated in accordance with this Article.

Art. 390. Every Delegate shall be entitled to vote individually on all matters which are taken into consideration by the Conference.

If one of the Members fails to nominate one of the non-

attend the meetings of the Conference, but may not speak or vote.

A delegate may in writing, addressed to the President, appoint one of his advisers to act as his deputy, and the adviser, while so acting, shall be allowed to speak and vote.

The names of the delegates and their advisers will be communicated to the International Labour Office by the Government of each of the High Contracting Parties.

The credentials of delegates and their advisers shall be subject to scrutiny by the Conference, which may, by two-thirds of the votes cast by the delegates present, refuse to admit any delegate or adviser whom it deems not to have been nominated in accordance with the undertaking contained in this Article.

4. A Government delegate shall be entitled to two votes, and a non-Government delegate shall be entitled to one vote at any meeting of the Conference. Every delegate shall be entitled to vote inde-

Government Delegates whom it is entitled to nominate, the other non-Government Delegate shall be allowed to sit and speak at the Conference, but not to vote.

If in accordance with Article 389 the Conference refuses admission to a Delegate of one of the Members, the provisions of the present Article shall apply as if that Delegate had not been nominated.

Art. 391. The meetings of the Conference shall be held at the seat of the League of Nations, or at such other place as may be decided by the Conference at a previous meeting by two-thirds of the votes cast by the Delegates present.

Art. 392. The International Labour Office shall be established at the seat of the League of Nations as part of the organisation of the League.

Art. 393. The International Labour Office shall be under the control of a Governing Body consisting of twenty-four persons, appointed in accordance with the following provisions:

The Governing Body of the International Labour Office shall be constituted as follows:

12 persons representing the Governments;

6 persons elected by the Delegates to the Conference representing the employers;

6 persons elected by the Del-

dependently on all matters which are taken into consideration by the Conference.

If one of the High Contracting Parties fails to nominate one of the non-Government delegates whom it is entitled to nominate, the other non-Government delegate shall be allowed to sit and speak at the Conference but not to vote.

If in accordance with Article 3 the Conference refuses admission to a delegate of one of the High Contracting Parties, the provisions of the present Article shall apply as if that delegate had not been nominated.

5. The meetings of the Conference shall be held at the capital of the League of Nations.

6. The International Labour Office shall be established at the capital of the League of Nations as part of the organisation of the League.

7. The International Labour Office shall be under the control of a Governing Body consisting of 24 members, appointed in accordance with the provisions of the Protocol hereto. The Governing Body shall meet from time to time as occasion may require.

Protocol

Twelve members to be Government representatives, of

egates to the Conference representing the workers.

Of the twelve persons representing the Governments eight shall be nominated by the Members which are of the chief industrial importance, and four shall be nominated by the Members selected for the purpose by the Government Delegates to the Conference, excluding the Delegates of the eight Members mentioned above.

Any question as to which are the Members of the chief industrial importance shall be decided by the Council of the League of Nations.

The period of office of the members of the Governing Body will be three years. The method of filling vacancies and other similar questions may be determined by the Governing Body subject to the approval of the Conference.

The Governing Body shall, from time to time, elect one of its members to act as its Chairman, shall regulate its own procedure and shall fix its own times of meeting. A special meeting shall be held if a written request to that effect is made by at least ten members of the Governing Body.

Art. 394. There shall be a Director of the International Labour Office, who shall be appointed by the Governing Body and, subject to the instructions of the Governing Body, shall

whom five shall be nominated by the Governments of Great Britain, United States, France, Italy and Japan, respectively, and the rest elected from the representatives of the other States by the Conference.

Six members to be elected by the delegates to the Conference representing employers.

Six members to be elected by the delegates to the Conference representing workpeople.

All appointments to be for a term of three years. Rules might be made by the Governing Body subject to the approval of the Conference for the filling of vacancies and other matters of the same sort.

8. There shall be a Director of the International Labour Office appointed from time to time by the Governing Body, who shall, subject to the instructions of the Governing

be responsible for the efficient conduct of the International Labour Office and for such other duties as may be assigned to him.

The Director or his deputy shall attend all meetings of the Governing Body.

Art. 395. The staff of the International Labour Office shall be appointed by the Director, who shall, so far as is possible with due regard to the efficiency of the work of the Office, select persons of different nationalities. A certain number of these persons shall be women.

Art. 396. The functions of the International Labour Office shall include the collection and distribution of information on all subjects relating to the international adjustment of conditions of industrial life and labor, and particularly the examination of subjects which it is proposed to bring before the Conference with a view to the conclusion of international conventions, and the conduct of such special investigations as may be ordered by the Conference.

It will prepare the agenda for the meetings of the Conference.

It will carry out the duties required of it by the provisions of this Part of the present Treaty in connection with international disputes.

It will edit and publish in

Body, be responsible for the efficient conduct of the International Labour Office and for such other duties as may be assigned to him.

The Director or his deputy shall attend all meetings of the Governing Body.

Pending the first appointment of a Director, the functions of the Director shall be performed by the person named in the Protocol hereto.

9. The functions of the International Labour Office shall include the collection and distribution of information on all subjects relating to the international adjustment of conditions of employment, and particularly the examination of subjects which it is proposed to bring before the Conference with a view to the conclusion of international conventions, and the conduct of such special investigations as may be ordered by the Conference.

It will prepare the Agenda for the meetings of the Conference.

It will carry out the duties required of it by the provisions of this convention in connection with international disputes.

It will edit and publish a periodical paper in the French and English languages dealing

French and English, and in such other languages as the Governing Body may think desirable, a periodical paper dealing with problems of industry and employment of international interest.

Generally, in addition to the functions set out in this Article, it shall have such other powers and duties as may be assigned to it by the Conference.

Art. 397. The Government Departments of any of the Members which deal with questions of Industry and employment may communicate directly with the Director through the Representative of their Government on the Governing Body of the International Labour Office, or failing any such Representative, through such other qualified official as the Government may nominate for the purpose.

Art. 398. The International Labour Office shall be entitled to the assistance of the Secretary-General of the League of Nations in any matter in which it can be given.

Art. 399. Each of the Members will pay the travelling and subsistence expenses of its Delegates and their advisers and of its Representatives attending the meetings of the Conference or Governing Body, as the case may be.

All other expenses of the International Labour Office and

with problems of industry and employment of international interest.

10. The Government Department of any of the High Contracting Parties which deal with questions of industry and employment may communicate directly with the Director through the representative of their States on the Governing Body of the International Labour Office or failing any such representative, through such other qualified official as the Government may nominate for the purpose.

11. The International Labour Office shall be entitled to the assistance of the Chancellor of the League of Nations in any matter in which it can be given.

12. Each of the High Contracting Parties will pay the travelling and subsistence expenses of its representatives attending the meetings of the Conference or Governing Body.

All the other expenses of the International Labour Office and of the meetings of the Conference or Governing Body shall of the meetings of the Conference or Governing Body shall be paid to the Director by the Secretary-General of the League of Nations out of the general funds of the League.

The Director shall be responsible to the Secretary-General of the League for the proper expenditure of all moneys paid to him in pursuance of this Article.

be paid to the Director by the Chancellor of the League out of the general funds of the League.

The Director shall be responsible to the Chancellor of the League for the proper expenditure of all moneys paid to him in pursuance of this Article.

Chapter II

Procedure

Art. 400. The agenda for all meetings of the Conference will be settled by the Governing Body, who shall consider any suggestion as to the agenda that may be made by the Government of any of the members or by any representative organisation recognised for the purpose of Article 389.

Art. 401. The Director shall act as the Secretary of the Conference, and shall transmit the agenda so as to reach the Members four months before the meeting of the Conference, and through them, the non-Government Delegates when appointed.

Art. 402. Any of the Governments of the Members may formally object to the inclusion of any item or items in the agenda. The grounds for such objection shall be set forth in a reasoned statement addressed to the Di-

Chapter II

Procedure

13. The Agenda for all meetings of the Conference will be settled by the Governing Body, who shall consider any suggestion as to the Agenda that may be made by the Government of any of the High Contracting Parties or by any representative organisation recognised for the purpose of Article 3.

14. The Director shall act as the Secretary of the Conference, and shall circulate the Agenda to the High Contracting Parties three months before the meeting of the Conference.

15. After the circulation of the Agenda, any of the High Contracting Parties may formally object to the inclusion of any item or items in the Agenda. The grounds for such objection shall be set forth in

rector, who shall circulate it to all the Members of the Permanent Organisation.

Items to which such objection has been made shall not, however, be excluded from the agenda, if at the Conference a majority of two-thirds of the votes cast by the Delegates present is in favor of considering them.

If the Conference decides (otherwise than under the preceding paragraph) by two-thirds of the votes cast by the Delegates present that any subject shall be considered by the Conference, that subject shall be included in the agenda for the following meeting.

Art. 403. The Conference shall regulate its own procedure, shall elect its own President, and may appoint committees to consider and report on any matter.

Except as otherwise expressly provided in this Part of the present Treaty, all matters shall be decided by a simple majority of the votes cast by the Delegates present.

The voting is void unless the total number of votes cast is equal to half the number of the Delegates attending the Conference.

Art. 404. The Conference may add to any committees which it appoints technical experts, who shall be assessors without power to vote.

a reasoned statement addressed to the Director, who shall circulate it to all the High Contracting Parties. Items to which such objection has been made shall not however, be excluded from the Agenda, if at the Conference a majority of two-thirds of the votes cast is in favour of considering them.

16. The Conference shall regulate its own procedure, and may appoint Committees to consider and report on any matter.

In all matters covered by this Article, the Conference may decide by a simple majority of the votes cast.

17. The Conference may add to any Committees which they appoint technical experts, who shall be assessors without power to vote.

Art. 405. When the Conference has decided on the adoption of proposals with regard to an item in the agenda, it will rest with the Conference to determine whether these proposals should take the form: (*a*) of a recommendation to be submitted to the members for consideration with a view to effect being given to it by national legislation or otherwise, or (*b*) of a draft international convention for ratification by the Members.

In either case a majority of two-thirds of the votes cast by the Delegates present shall be necessary on the final vote for the adoption of the recommendation or draft convention, as the case may be, by the Conference.

In framing any recommendation or draft convention of general application the Conference shall have due regard to those countries in which climatic conditions, the imperfect development of industrial organisation, or other special circumstances make the industrial conditions substantially different, and shall suggest the modifications, if any, which it considers may be required to meet the case of such countries.

A copy of the recommendation or draft convention shall be authenticated by the signature of the President of the Conference and of the Director,

18. When the Conference has approved any proposals as to an item in the Agenda, these proposals shall be embodied in the form of an international convention.

This convention shall then forthwith be laid for final consideration and decision before the Conference.

If the convention receives the support of two-thirds of the votes cast, it shall be held to be adopted by the Conference, and a copy of the convention authenticated by the signatures of the President of the Conference and of the Director shall be deposited with the Chancellor of the League of Nations.

Each of the High Contracting Parties undertakes that it will within the period of one year from the end of the meeting of the Conference communicate its formal ratification of the convention to the Director, and will forthwith take all steps necessary to put the convention into operation, unless such convention is disapproved by its legislature.

and shall be deposited with the Secretary-General of the League of Nations. The Secretary-General will communicate a certified copy of the recommendation or draft convention to each of the Members.

Each of the Members undertakes that it will, within the period of one year at most from the closing of the session of the Conference, or if it is impossible owing to exceptional circumstances to do so within the period of one year, then at the earliest practicable moment and in no case later than eighteen months from the closing of the session of the Conference, bring the recommendation or draft convention before the authority or authorities within whose competence the matter lies, for the enactment of legislation or other action.

In the case of a recommendation the Member will inform the Secretary-General of the action taken.

In the case of a draft convention, the Member will, if it obtains the consent of the authority or authorities within whose competence the matter lies, communicate the formal ratification of the convention to the Secretary-General and will take such action as may be necessary to make effective the provisions of such convention.

If on a recommendation no

legislative or other action is taken to make a recommendation effective, or if the draft convention fails to obtain the consent of the authority or authorities within whose competence the matter lies, no further obligation shall rest upon the Member.

In the case of a federal State, the power of which to enter into conventions on labour matters is subject to limitations, it shall be in the discretion of that Government to treat a draft convention to which such limitations apply as a recommendation only, and the provisions of this Article with respect to recommendations shall apply in such case.

The above Article shall be interpreted in accordance with the following principle:

In no case shall any Member be asked or required, as a result of the adoption of any recommendation or draft convention by the Conference, to lessen the protection afforded by its existing legislation to the workers concerned.

Art. 406. Any convention so ratified shall be registered by the Secretary-General of the League of Nations, but shall only be binding upon the Members which ratify it.

19. Any convention so ratified shall be registered by the Director with the Chancellor of the League and shall, subject to any conditions as to ratification which may be contained in the convention itself, be binding upon all States which have ratified it or which shall subsequently adhere to it.

Art. 407. If any convention coming before the Conference for final consideration fails to secure the support of two-thirds of the votes cast by the Delegates present, it shall nevertheless be within the right of any of the Member of the Permanent Organisation to agree to such convention among themselves.

Any convention so agreed to shall be communicated by the Governments concerned to the Secretary-General of the League of Nations, who shall register it.

Art. 408. Each of the Members agrees to make an annual report to the International Labour Office on the measures which it has taken to give effect to the provisions of conventions to which it is a party. These reports shall be made in such form and shall contain such particulars as the Governing Body may request. The Director shall lay a summary of these reports before the next meeting of the Conference.

Art. 409. In the event of any representation being made to the International Labour Office by an industrial association of workers or of employers that any of the Members has failed to secure in any respect the effective observance within its jurisdiction of any convention to which it is a party, the Gov-

20. If any convention laid before the Conference for final consideration fails to secure the support of two-thirds of the votes cast, it shall nevertheless be within the right of any of the High Contracting Parties to agree to such convention among themselves.

Any convention so agreed to shall be communicated by the Governments of the States concerned to the Director, who shall register it with the Chancellor of the League of Nations.

21. The High Contracting Parties agree to make an annual report to the International Labour Office on the measures which they have taken to give effect to the provisions of conventions to which they are parties. These reports shall be made in such form and shall contain such particulars as the Governing Body may direct. The Director shall lay a summary of these reports before the next meeting of the Conference.

22. In the event of any representation being made to the International Labour Office that any of the High Contracting Parties has failed to secure in any respect the effective observance within its jurisdiction of any convention to which it is a party, the Governing Body may communicate this repre-

erning Body may communicate this representation to the Government against which it is made, and may invite that Government to make such statement on the subject as it may think fit.

Art. 410. If no statement is received within a reasonable time from the Government in question, or if the statement when received is not deemed to be satisfactory by the Governing Body, the latter shall have the right to publish the representation and the statement, if any, made in reply to it.

Art. 411. Any of the Members shall have the right to file a complaint with the International Labour Office if it is not satisfied that any other Member is securing the effective observance of any convention which both have ratified in accordance with the foregoing Articles.

The Governing Body may, if it thinks fit, before referring such a complaint to a Commission of Enquiry, as hereinafter provided for, communicate with the Government in question in the manner described in Article 409.

If the Governing Body does not think it necessary to communicate the complaint to the Government in question, or if, when they have made such communication, no statement

sentation to the State against which it is made and may invite that State to make such statement on the subject as it may think fit.

23. If no statement is received within a reasonable time from the State against which the representation is made, or if the statement when received is not deemed to be satisfactory by the Governing Body, the latter shall have the right to publish the representation and the statement, if any, made in reply to it.

24. Any of the High Contracting Parties shall have the right to file a complaint with the International Labour Office if it is not satisfied that any other of the High Contracting Parties is securing the effective observance of any convention.

The Governing Body may, if it thinks fit, before referring such complaint to a Commission of Enquiry, as hereinafter provided for, communicate with the State against which the complaint is made in the manner described in Article 22.

If the Governing Body do not think it necessary to communicate the complaint to the State against which it is made, or if, when they have made such communication, no statement in reply has been received within a reasonable time which in reply has been received within a reasonable time which the Governing Body considers to be satisfactory, the Governing Body may apply for the appointment of a Commission of Enquiry to consider the complaint and to report thereon.

The Governing Body may adopt the same procedure either of its own motion or on receipt of a complaint from a Delegate to the Conference.

When any matter arising out of Articles 410 or 411 is being considered by the Governing Body, the Government in question shall, if not already represented thereon, be entitled to send a representative to take part in the proceedings of the Governing Body while the matter is under consideration. Adequate notice of the date on which the matter will be considered shall be given to the Government in question.

Art. 412. The Commission of Enquiry shall be constituted in accordance with the following provisions:

Each of the Members agrees to nominate within six months of the date on which the present Treaty comes into force three persons of industrial experience, of whom one shall be a representative of employers, one a representative of workers, and one a person of independent standing, who shall together form a panel from

the complaining State considers to be satisfactory, the Governing Body shall apply for the appointment of a Commission of Enquiry to consider the complaints and to report thereon.

25. The Commission of Enquiry shall be constituted in accordance with the following provisions:

The High Contracting Parties agree to nominate within six months of the date on which this convention comes into force, three persons of industrial experience, of whom one shall be a representative of employers, one a representative of workpeople, and one a person of independent standing, who shall together form a panel which the members of the Commission of Enquiry shall be drawn.

The qualifications of the persons so nominated shall be subject to scrutiny by the Governing Body, which may by two-thirds of the votes cast by the representatives present refuse to accept the nomination of any person whose qualifications do not in its opinion comply with the requirements of the present Article.

Upon the application of the Governing Body, the Secretary-General of the League of Nations shall nominate three persons, one from each section of this panel, to constitute the Commission of Enquiry, and shall designate one of them as the President of the Commission. None of these three persons, shall be a person nominated to the panel by any Member directly concerned in the complaint.

Art. 413. The Members agree that, in the event of the reference of a complaint to a Commission of Enquiry under Article 411, they will each, whether directly concerned in the complaint or not, place at the disposal of the Commission all the information in their possession which bears upon the subject-matter of the complaint.

Art. 414. When the Commission of Enquiry has fully con-

from which the members of the Commission of Enquiry shall be drawn.

Upon the application of the Governing Body, the Chancellor of the League shall nominate three persons, one from each section of this panel, to constitute the Commission of Enquiry, and shall designate one of them as the President of the Commission. None of these three persons shall be a person nominated to the panel by any State directly concerned in the complaint.

26. The High Contracting Parties agree that, in the event of the reference of a complaint to a Commission of Enquiry under Article 24 they will each, whether directly concerned in the complaint or not, place at the disposal of the Commission all the information in their possession which bears upon the subject-matter of the complaint.

27. When the Commission of Enquiry has fully considered

sidered the complaint, it shall prepare a report embodying its findings on all questions of fact relevant to determining the issue between the parties and containing such recommendations as it may think proper as to the steps which should be taken to meet the complaint and the time which they should be taken.

It shall also indicate in this report the measures, if any, of an economic character against a defaulting Government which it considers to be appropriate, and which it considers other Governments would be justified in adopting.

Art. 415. The Secretary-General of the League of Nations shall communicate the report of the Commission of Enquiry to each of the Governments concerned in the complaint, and shall cause it to be published.

Each of these Governments shall within one month inform the Secretary-General of the League of Nations whether or not it accepts the recommendations contained in the report of the Commission; and if not, whether it proposes to refer the complaint to the Permanent Court of International Justice of the League of Nations.

the complaint, it shall prepare a report embodying its findings on all questions of fact relevant to determining the issue between the parties and containing such recommendations as it may think proper as to the steps which should be taken to meet the complaint and the time within which they should be taken.

It shall also indicate in this report the measures, if any, against the commerce of a defaulting State which it considers to be appropriate, and which other States would be justified in adopting.

28. The report of the Commission of Enquiry shall be communicated by the Chancellor to each of the States concerned in the complaint, and the Chancellor shall cause it to be published.

Each of these States shall within one month inform the Chancellor of the League whether or not it accepts the recommendations contained in the report of the Commission; and if not, whether it proposes to refer the complaint to an International Court.

Pending the creation of a permanent Court of International Justice, the International Court referred to in this Article shall be a tribunal of arbitration nominated by the Chancellor of the League from

Art. 416. In the event of any Member failing to take the action required by Article 405, with regard to a recommendation or draft convention, any other Member shall be entitled to refer the matter to the Permanent Court of International Justice.

Art. 417. The decision of the Permanent Court of International Justice in regard to a complaint or matter which has been referred to it in pursuance of Article 415 or Article 416 shall be final.

Art. 418. The Permanent Court of International Justice may affirm, vary or reverse any of the findings or recommendations of the Commission of Enquiry, if any, and shall in its decision indicate the measures, if any, of an economic character which it considers to be appropriate, and which other Governments would be justified in adopting against a defaulting Government.

Art. 419. In the event of any Member failing to carry out within the time specified the recommendations, if any, contained in the report of the Commission of Enquiry, or in the decision of the Permanent Court of International Justice,

among the members of the Permanent Court created by the Convention for the pacific settlement of International Disputes.

29. In the event of any of the High Contracting Parties failing to take within the specified period the action required by Article 18, any other of the High Contracting Parties shall be entitled to refer the matter to the International Court referred to above.

30. The decision of an International Court to which a complaint has been referred shall be final.

31. The International Court may affirm, vary or reverse any of the findings or recommendations of the Commission of Enquiry, if any, and shall in its decision indicate the measures, if any, against the commerce of a defaulting State which it considers to be appropriate, and which other States would be justified in adopting.

32. In the event of any State failing to carry out within the time specified the recommendations, if any, contained in the report of the Commission of Enquiry, or in the decision of the International Court, as the case may be, any other State

as the case may be, any other Member may take against that Member the measures of an economic character indicated in the report of the Commission or in the decision of the Court as appropriate to the case.

Art. 420. The defaulting Government may at any time inform the Governing Body that it has taken the steps necessary to comply with the recommendations of the Commission of Enquiry or with those in the decision of the Permanent Court of International Justice, as the case may be, and may request it to apply to the Secretary-General of the League to constitute a Commission of Enquiry to verify its contention. In this case the provisions of Articles 412, 413, 414, 415, 417 and 418 shall apply, and if the report of the Commission of Enquiry or the decision of the Permanent Court of International Justice is in favour of the defaulting Government, the other Governments shall forthwith discontinue the measures of an economic character that they have taken against the defaulting Government.

may take against the commerce of that State the measures indicated in the report of the Commission or in the decision of the Court as appropriate to the case.

33. The defaulting State may at any time inform the Governing Body that it has taken the steps necessary to comply with the recommendations of the Commission of Enquiry or in the decision of the Court, as the case may be, and may request it to apply to the Chancellor of the League to constitute a Commission of Enquiry to verify its contention. In this case the provisions of Articles 25, 26, 27, 28, 30 and 31 shall apply, and if the report of the Commission of Enquiry or decision of the International Court is in favour of the defaulting State, the other States shall forthwith discontinue the measures that they have taken against the commerce of the defaulting State.

CHAPTER III

General

Art. 421. The Members engage to apply conventions which they have ratified in ac-

CHAPTER III

General

34. The self-governing Dominions of the British Empire and India may become parties

cordance with the provisions of this Part of the present Treaty to their colonies, protectorates and possesions which are not fully self-governing:

1. Except when owing to the local conditions the convention is inapplicable, or

2. Subject to such modifications as may be necessary to adapt the convention to local conditions.

And each of the Members shall notify to the International Labour Office the action taken in respect of each of its colonies, protectorates and possessions which are not fully self-governing:

Art. 422. Amendments to this Part of the present Treaty which are adopted by the Conference by a majority of two-thirds of the votes cast by the Delegates present shall take effect when ratified by the States whose representatives compose the Council of the League of Nations and by three-fourths of the Members.

Art. 423. Any question or dispute relating to the interpretation of this Part of the present Treaty or of any subsequent convention concluded by the Members in pursuance of the provisions of this Part of the present Treaty shall be referred for decision to the Permanent Court of International Justice.

to this convention, and have the same rights and obligations thereunder as if they were independent States.

35. Any State not a party to this convention, which may hereafter become a Member of the League of Nations, shall be deemed *ipso facto* to have adhered to this convention.

36. Amendments to the Provisions of this convention may be submitted to the Conference, but shall only come into effect if they are unanimously agreed to and ratified by all the High Contracting Parties.

Chapter IV

Transitory Provisions

Art. 424. The first meeting of the Conference shall take place in October 1919. The place and agenda for this meeting shall be as specified in the Annex hereto.

Arrangements for the convening and the organisation of the first meeting of the Conference will be made by the Government designated for the purpose in the said Annex. That Government shall be assisted in the preparation of the documents for submission to the Conference by an International Committee constituted as provided in the said Annex.

The expenses of the first meeting and of all subsequent meetings held before the League of Nations has been able to establish a general fund, other than the expenses of Delegates and their advisers, will be borne by the Members in accordance with the apportionment of the expenses of the International Bureau of the Universal Postal Union.

Art. 425. Until the League of Nations has been constituted all communications which under the provisions of the foregoing Articles should be addressed to the Secretary-General of the League will be preserved by the Director of the International Labour Office, who will trans-

Chapter IV

Transitory Provisions

37. The provisions of this convention shall come into force simultaneously with the coming into force of the convention establishing the League of Nations.

38. The first meeting of the Conference shall be held as soon as possible and in any case, within six months after the provisions of this convention have come into force.

The person named in the Protocol hereto as Provisional Director shall be responsible for the summoning and organisation of the first meeting of the Conference.

mit them to the Secretary-General of the League.

Art. 426. Pending the creation of a Permanent Court of International Justice, disputes which in accordance with this Part of the present Treaty would be submitted to it for decision will be referred to a tribunal of three persons appointed by the Council of the League of Nations.

SECTION II

GENERAL PRINCIPLES

(*As inserted in the Treaty*)

Art. 427. The High Contracting Parties, recognising that the well-being, physical, moral and intellectual, of industrial wage-earners is of supreme international importance, have framed, in order to further this great end, the permanent machinery provided for in Section I, and associated with that of the League of Nations.

They recognise that differences of climate, habits and customs, of economic opportunity and industrial tradition, make strict uniformity in the conditions of labour difficult of immediate attainment. But, holding as they do that labour should not be regarded merely as an article of commerce, they think that there are methods and principles for regulating

SECTION II

GENERAL PRINCIPLES

(*As proposed by the Labour Commission*)

The High Contracting Parties declare their acceptance of the following principles and engage to take all necessary steps to secure their realization in accordance with the recommendation to be made by the International Labour Conference as to their practical application:

labour conditions which all industrial communities should endeavour to apply, so far as their special circumstances will permit.

Among these methods and principles, the following seem to the High Contracting Parties to be of special and urgent importance:

1. The guiding principle above enunciated that labour should not be regarded merely as a commodity or article of commerce.

2. The right of association for all lawful purposes by the employed as well as by the employers.

3. The payment to the employed of a wage adequate to maintain a reasonable standard of life as this is understood in their time and country.

4. The adoption of an eight-hour day or a forty-eight-hour week as the standard to be aimed at where it has not already been attained.

5. The adoption of a weekly rest of at least twenty-four hours, which should include Sunday wherever practicable.

6. The abolition of child labour and the impositions of such limitations on the labour of young persons as shall permit the continuation of their education and assure their proper physical development.

7. The principle that men and women should receive equal

1. In right and in fact the labour of a human being should not be treated as merchandise or an article of commerce.

2. Employers and workers should be allowed the right of association for all lawful purposes.

3. No child should be permitted to be employed in industry or commerce before the age of fourteen years, in order that every child may be ensured reasonable opportunities for mental and physical education.

Between the years of fourteen and eighteen, young persons of either sex may only be employed on work which is not harmful to their physical development and on condition that the continuation of their technical or general education is ensured.

4. Every worker has a right to a wage adequate to maintain a reasonable standard of life having regard to the civilisation of his time and country.

5. Equal pay should be given to women and to men for work

remuneration for work of equal value.

8. The standard set by law in each country, with respect to the conditions of labour should have due regard to the equitable economic treatment of all workers lawfully resident therein.

9. Each state should make provision for a system of inspection in which women should take part, in order to ensure the enforcement of the laws and regulations for the protection of the employed.

Without claiming that these methods and principles are either complete or final, the High Contracting Parties are of the opinion that they are well fitted to guide the policy of the League of Nations; and that, if adopted by the industrial communities who are Members of the League, and safeguarded in practice by an adequate system of such inspection, they will confer lasting benefits upon the wage earners of the world.

of equal value in quantity and quality.

6. A weekly rest, including Sunday, or its equivalent for all workers.

7. Limitation of the hours of work in industry on the basis of eight hours a day or forty-eight hours a week, subject to an exception for countries in which climatic conditions, the imperfect development of industrial organisation or other special circumstances render the industrial efficiency of the workers substantially different. The International Labour Conference will recommend a basis approximately equivalent to the above for adoption in such countries.

8. In all matters concerning their status as workers and social insurance foreign workmen lawfully admitted to any country and their families should be ensured the same treatment as the nationals of that country.

9. All States should institute a system of inspection in which women should take part, in order to ensure the enforcement of the laws and regulations for the protection of the workers.

ANNEX

The place of meeting will be Washington.

The Government of the United States of America is requested to convene the Conference.

The International Organising Committee will consist of seven members, appointed by the United States of America, Great Britain, France, Italy, Japan, Belgium and Switzerland. The Committee may, if it thinks necessary, invite other Members to appoint representatives.

Agenda:

1. Application of principle of the 8-hour day or of the 48-hour week.
2. Question of preventing or providing against unemployment.
3. Women's employment:
    (a) Before and after child-birth, including the question of maternity benefit;
    (b) During the night;
    (c) In unhealthy processes.
4. Employment of children:
    (a) Minimum age of employment;
    (b) During the night;
    (c) In unhealthy processes.
5. Extension and application of the International Conventions adopted at Berne in 1906 on the prohibition of night work for women employed in industry and the prohibition of the use of white phosphorus in the manufacture of matches.

AMENDMENT TO ARTICLE 393 OF THE TREATY OF VERSAILLES

and to the Corresponding Articles of the other Treaties of Peace adopted by the Fourth International Labor Conference, 1922

Article 393 of the Treaty of Versailles and the corresponding Articles of the other Treaties of Peace shall read as follows:

The International Labour Office shall be under the control of a Governing Body consisting of thirty-two persons:

> sixteen representing Governments,
> eight representing the Employers, and
> eight representing the Workers.

Of the sixteen persons representing Governments, eight shall be appointed by the Members of chief industrial importance, and eight shall be appointed by the Members selected for that purpose by the Government Delegates to the Conference excluding the Delegates of the eight Members mentioned above. Of the sixteen Members represented six shall be non-European States.

Any question as to which are the Members of chief industrial importance shall be decided by the Council of the League of Nations.

The persons representing the Employers and the persons representing the Workers shall be elected respectively by the Employers' Delegates and the Workers' Delegates to the Conference. Two Employers' representatives and two Workers' representatives shall belong to non-European States.

The period of office of the Governing Body shall be three years.

The method of filling vacancies and of appointing substitutes, and other similar questions, may be decided by the Governing Body subject to the approval of the Conference.

The Governing Body shall, from time to time, elect one of its number to act as its Chairman, shall regulate its own procedure, and shall fix its own times of meeting. A special meeting shall be held if a written request to that effect is made by at least twelve of the representatives on the Governing Body.

APPENDIX II

STANDING ORDERS OF THE INTERNATIONAL LABOUR OFFICE

Adopted at Washington on 21st November 1919, during the first
Session of the Conference and amended at Geneva on 3rd
November 1922, during the Fourth Session

ARTICLE 1

Composition of the Conference

1. The Conference consists of all the Delegates duly appointed
by the Members of the International Labour Organization.

2. Each Delegate may be accompanied by advisers who shall
not exceed two in number for each item on the Agenda of the
meeting.

3. Seats in the Conference room shall be assigned to the
Delegates and their advisers by the Governing Body.

ARTICLE 2

Provisional Officers of the Conference

The Conference shall be opened by the chairman of the
Governing Body of the International Labour Office, assisted by
the other Officers of the Governing Body. These provisional
officers shall continue to act until the President of the Conference
has assumed his office.

ARTICLE 3

Verification of Credentials

1. The credentials of Delegates and their advisers shall be
deposited with the International Labour Office at least fifteen
days before the date fixed for the opening of the Session of
the Conference.

2. A brief report upon these credentials, drawn up by the
Chairman of the Governing Body, shall, with the credentials,

292

be open to inspection by the Delegates on the day before the opening of the Session of the Conference. This report shall be published as an appendix to the record of the first sitting.

3. Any objections raised concerning the nomination of Delegates or advisers shall be lodged with the provisional officers of the Conference during the opening sitting and transmitted by them to the Committee charged with the verification of credentials, provided for by Article 7(c).

4. Pending final decision of the question of his admission, any Delegate or adviser to whose nomination objection has been taken shall have the same rights as other Delegates and advisers.

Article 4

Officers of the Conference

1. The Officers of the Conference shall be a President and three Vice-Presidents, who shall be of different nationalities. They shall be elected by the Conference. Women may be elected to any of these offices.

2. The Government, Employers' and Workers' Groups shall each nominate one of their number as Vice-President subject to the approval of the Conference.

3. The order in which these nominations shall be made shall vary at each Session of the Conference. The Groups shall have priority of nomination in the following rotation: Government Group, Employers' Group, Workers' Group, beginning with the Group indicated by lot at the Fifth Session of the Conference.

4. If a Group nominates a Vice-President of the same nationality as the Vice-President nominated by a Group possessing priority of nomination, such nomination shall be void.

Article 5

Secretariat

1. The secretarial work of the Conference shall be carried out by officials of the International Labour Office appointed for the purpose by the Governing Body of the said Office.

2. The Director of the International Labour Office shall be the Secretary-General of the Conference, and shall be responsible for the Secretariat. He may be assisted by one or more Assistant-Secretaries-General appointed by the Governing Body of the International Labour Office.

3. The Secretariat of the Conference shall be responsible *inter alia* for the receiving, printing, circulation and translation of documents, reports and resolutions; the translation of speeches at the sittings; the taking of shorthand notes, the printing and distribution of the reports of the proceedings; the Custody of the records of the Conference; the publication of the final records of the Sessions, and, generally, for all other work which the Conference may think fit to entrust to it.

ARTICLE 6

Procedure

The procedure of the Conference shall be as follows:

1. If an objection has been lodged against any item on the Agenda by the Government of any of the Members, the Conference, after hearing the report presented by the Governing Body thereon, shall, in accordance with Article 402 of the Treaty of Versailles, decide whether such item is to be retained on the Agenda or not.

2. The Conference shall elect a Committee of Selection as provided in Article 7(b).

3. During the Session and on the date fixed by the Committee of Selection, the Conference shall discuss the report submitted by the Director of the International Labour Office on the steps taken to give effect to the decisions of previous Sessions and the results achieved.

4. The Conference shall decide whether it will take as the basis of its discussion on any item of the Agenda the suggested draft conventions or recommendations prepared by the International Labour Office, and shall decide whether such draft conventions or recommendations shall be considered in full Conference or referred to a Committee for report. These decisions may be preceded by a debate in full Conference on the general principles of the suggested draft convention or recommendation.

5. If the draft convention or recommendation is considered in full Conference each clause shall be placed before the Conference for adoption. During the debate and until all the clauses have been disposed of, no motion other than a motion to amend a clause of such draft convention or recommendation, or a motion as to procedure, shall be considered by the Conference.

6. If the draft convention or recommendation be referred to a Committee, the Conference shall, after receiving the report of the Committee, proceed to discuss the draft convention or recommendation in accordance with the rules laid down in paragraph 5. This discussion shall not take place before the day following that on which copies of the report have been circulated to the Delegates.

7. During the discussion of the articles of a draft convention or recommendation, the Conference may refer one or more articles to a Committee.

8. If a draft convention contained in the report of a Committee is rejected by the Conference, any Delegate may ask the Conference to decide forthwith whether the draft convention shall be referred back to the Committee to consider the transformation of the draft convention into a recommendation. If the Conference decides to refer the matter back, the report of the Committee shall be submitted to the approval of the Conference before the end of the Session.

9. The provisions of a draft convention or recommendation as adopted by the Conference shall be referred to the Drafting Committee provided for in Article 7, for the preparation of a final text. This text shall be circulated to the Delegates.

10. No amendment shall be allowed to this text, but notwithstanding this provision the President, after consultation with the three Vice-Presidents, may submit to the Conference amendments which have been handed to the Secretariat the day after the circulation of the text as revised by the Drafting Committee.

11. On receipt of the text prepared by the Drafting Committee and after discussion of the amendments, if any, submitted in accordance with the preceding paragraph, the Conference shall proceed to take a final vote on the adoption of the draft convention or recommendation in accordance with Article 405 of the Treaty of Versailles.

12. If a draft convention on a final vote fails to obtain the necessary two-thirds majority, but obtains a simple majority, the Conference shall decide forthwith whether the draft convention shall be referred to the Drafting Committee to be drafted in the form of a recommendation. If the Conference approves the reference to the Drafting Committee, the proposals contained in the draft convention shall be submitted for the approval of the Conference in the form of a recommendation before the end of the Session.

ARTICLE 7

Committees

(a) PROVISIONS APPLICABLE TO ALL COMMITTEES

1. In accordance with Article 403 of the Treaty of Versailles, the Conference may set up Committees for any purpose which it considers desirable.

2. Every Committee shall appoint a Chairman, and one or more reporters to present the result of its deliberations to the Conference. Advisers may be appointed as reporters.

3. Subject to the approval of their Group, Delegates may appoint substitutes to represent them on Committees. In cases where the Group has appointed the States and not the persons by name to represent it on a Committee, a Delegate may at any time appoint as his substitute one of his advisers.

4. An official of the Secretariat of the Conference shall be appointed to act as Secretary to each Committee. He will be required to undertake such duties as may be decided upon by the Committee or the Chairman.

5. As a general rule the sittings of the Committees shall not take place at the same time as a plenary sitting of the Conference.

(b) COMMITTEE OF SELECTION

1. As provided in Article 6, the Conference shall, as soon as constituted, appoint a Committee of Selection nominated by the Groups and consisting of twelve members of the Government Group, six members of the Employers' Group, and six members of the Workers' Group. In none of these categories shall a country have more than one member.

2. The principal task of this Committee shall be to determine the order of work of the Conference, having regard to its decisions; it shall fix the date of the plenary sittings and the Agenda of each sitting, and shall decide what resolutions are to be discussed by the Conference at each sitting.

3. It shall also determine, as hereinafter provided in this Article, the constitution of the other Committees.

(c) CREDENTIALS COMMITTEE

1. The Conference shall elect a Committee to verify the credentials of Delegates and advisers. This Committee shall consist

of a Government Delegate, an Employers' Delegate and a Workers' Delegate, whose names shall be proposed to the Conference by the Committee of Selection.

2. This Committee shall examine such cases as may be mentioned in the report of the Chairman of the Governing Body provided for in Article 3, or in individual protests, and shall forthwith present a report.

(*d*) DRAFTING COMMITTEE

1. The Committee of Selection shall appoint a Drafting Committee consisting of at least three persons, who need not be either Delegates or advisers.

2. This Committee shall draw up in the form of draft conventions or recommendations the decisions adopted by the Conference. It shall ensure agreement between the French and English texts of any draft conventions or recommendations, the translation of which is undertaken by the Secretariat.

(*e*) OTHER COMMITTEES

1. When it has been decided to set up any Committee other than those specified in (*c*) and (*d*) the Committee of Selection, having fixed in the number of persons of which such Committee shall be composed, shall ask each group to furnish a list setting out in order of preference a larger number of names than there are places allotted to the group on the Committee in question.

2. The Committee of Selection shall examine the lists furnished by the three Groups and, if it appears desirable that any adjustment should be made in the composition of the Committee so as to secure representation more adequate for the subject with which the Committee will deal or more satisfactory as regards the allocation of seats to the various nationalities, shall endeavour to secure such adjustment, subject to the approval of the representatives of the groups who are present.

ARTICLE 8

Right of Admission to Sittings of the Conference

1. The sittings of the Conference shall be public except in cases where it has been expressly decided to the contrary.

2. At public sittings arrangements shall be made by the Sec-

retariat of the Conference for the accommodation of distinguished strangers and the press.

3. Apart from delegates and advisers the only persons permitted to enter the body of the hall shall be:

(a) One secretary or interpreter for each Delegation;
(b) Representatives on the Governing Body who are not delegates or advisers at the Conference;
(c) The Director of the International Labour Office and the officials of the Secretariat of the Conference.

ARTICLE 9

Duties of the President

1. The President shall declare the opening and close of the sittings. Before proceeding to the Agenda, he shall bring before the Conference any communications which may concern it.

2. He shall direct the debates, maintain order, ensure the observance of the Standing Orders by such means as circumstances may demand, accord or withdraw the right to address the Conference, put questions to the vote and announce the result of the vote.

3. The President shall not take part in the debates and shall not vote. If he is himself a Delegate he may appoint a substitute in accordance with the provisions of Article 18.

4. In the absence of the President during a sitting or any part thereof one of the Vice-Presidents, taken in rotation, shall preside.

5. A Vice-President acting as President shall have the same rights and duties as the President.

ARTICLE 10

Right to Address the Conference

1. No Delegate shall address the Conference without having asked and obtained permission of the President.

2. Speakers shall be called upon in the order in which they have signified their desire to speak.

3. No Delegate shall speak more than once upon the same motion, resolution or amendment, without the special permission of the Conference, provided that the mover of a motion, resolution or amendment shall have the right to speak twice unless the closure has been adopted in accordance with Article 14.

4. The President may require a speaker to resume his seat if his remarks are not relevant to the subject under discussion.

5. A Delegate may at any time rise to a point of order, which shall be decided forthwith by the President.

6. Except with the special consent of the Conference no speech shall exceed fifteen minutes exclusive of the time for translation.

7. Interruptions and audible conversations are not permitted.

8. Members of the Governing Body who are not Delegates or advisers at the Conference, and the Director of the International Labour Office or his representative may address the Conference if invited to do so by the President.

ARTICLE 11
Languages

1. The French and English languages shall be the official languages of the Conference.

2. Speeches in French shall be summarized in English and vice versa by an interpreter belonging to the Secretariat of the Conference.

3. A Delegate may speak in his own language, but his Delegation must provide for a summarized translation of his speech into one of the two official languages by an interpreter attached to the Delegation. This summarized translation shall then be rendered in the other official language by an interpreter belonging to the Secretariat.

4. The translation and circulation of documents shall be in the hands of the Secretariat, and the practice adopted at the Washington Conference as regards translation and distribution of documents in the Spanish language shall be continued.

ARTICLE 12
Motions, Resolutions and Amendments

1. Any Delegate may move motions, resolutions or amendments, in accordance with the following rules.

2. No resolution relating to an item on the Agenda shall be moved at any sitting of the Conference unless a copy has been handed in to the Secretariat of the Conference at least two days previously. Any resolution thus handed in shall be

circulated by the Secretariat not later than the day following that on which it was received.

3. Amendments to a resolution may be moved without previous notice provided always that a copy of the text of any amendment shall be handed in to the Secretariat of the Conference before such amendment is moved. If an amendment to a resolution has been moved no amendment other than an amendment to the original amendment shall be moved until the original amendment has been disposed of. Amendments shall be voted on before the resolution to which they refer.

4. A Delegate may withdraw an amendment which he has moved unless an amendment to it is under discussion or has been adopted.

5. In the case of motions as to procedure, no previous notice need be given, nor need a copy be handed in to the Secretariat of the Conference. Motions as to procedure include the following: a motion to refer the matter back; a motion to postpone consideration of the question; a motion to adjourn the sitting; a motion to adjourn a debate on a particular question; a motion that the Conference proceed with the next item on the Agenda for the sitting.

6. No motion, resolution or amendment shall be discussed unless and until it has been seconded.

7. Except as hereinafter provided, no resolution other than those relating to items on the Agenda shall be moved at any sitting of the Conference unless a copy has been deposited with the Director of the International Labour Office at least seven days before the date fixed for the opening of the Session of the Conference. Any resolution so deposited shall be distributed to the Delegates by the International Labour Office not later than the date fixed for the opening of the Session of the Conference.

8. Notwithstanding the above provisions, the President may, with the approval of the other officers of the Conference and after twenty-four hours' notice has been given of his intention, submit to the Conference any resolution relating either to urgent matters or to matters of an entirely formal nature.

Article 13

Proposals Involving Expenditure

Any motion or resolution involving expenditure shall in the first instance be referred to the Governing Body, which, after consultation of its Finance Committee, shall communicate its opinion to the Conference. This communication shall be circulated to the Delegates at least twenty-four hours before the motion or resolution is discussed by the Conference.

ARTICLE 14

Closure

1. Any Delegate may move the closure of the discussion either on a particular resolution or amendment or on the general question.

2. The President shall put a motion for the closure of the discussion if it is supported by at least thirty Delegates. Before putting it to the vote, however, he shall read out the names of those Delegates who had signified their wish to speak before the closure had been moved.

3. The President shall grant any Group which has not yet taken part in the discussion an opportunity if it so desires to have its opinion on the subject under discussion expressed by a speaker appointed by it.

4. If application is made for permission to speak against the closure, it shall be accorded subject to the condition that no speaker shall be allowed to speak for more than five minutes.

ARTICLE 15

Voting

1. The Conference shall vote by a show of hands or by a record vote.

2. Voting shall be a show of hands except as hereinafter provided.

3. Votes by a show of hands shall be counted by the Secretariat and the result announced by the President.

4. In case of doubt as to the result, the President may cause a record vote to be taken.

5. A record vote shall be taken in all cases in which a majority of two-thirds of the votes is required by Part XIII of the Treaty of Versailles.

6. A record vote may also be taken on any question if a request to that effect has been made in writing by not less than twenty Delegates and handed in to the President.

7. Record votes shall be taken by calling upon each individual

Delegate, each Delegation voting in turn in the French alphabetical order of the names of the Members of the International Labour Organization.

8. The vote shall be recorded by the Secretariat and announced by the President.

9. The names of the Delegates voting in a record vote shall be inserted in the verbatim report of the sitting.

10. Except as provided in paragraph 4 of this Article, it shall not be within the competence of the President to cause a record vote to be taken.

ARTICLE 16

Quorum

In accordance with Article 403 of the Treaty of Versailles a vote is not valid if the number of votes cast for and against is less than half the number of Delegates officially inscribed for the Session of the Conference and having the right to vote (Article 390, paragraph 2). This number shall be determined after the presentation of the brief report referred to in paragraph 2 of Article 3. If any Delegate is not finally admitted the number constituting the quorum shall be modified accordingly for the subsequent sitting.

ARTICLE 17

Majority

In order to determine the majorities by record vote all votes cast, for and against, shall be counted, so that in order to be adopted, it is necessary that the proposal submitted to the Conference obtain, as the case may be, more than half, or two-thirds of the votes cast.

ARTICLE 18

Substitutes

1. In accordance with Article 389 of the Treaty of Versailles a Delegate may by notice in writing addressed to the President appoint one of his advisers to act as his substitute. Such notice must be addressed to the President before the sitting, unless a new question comes up for discussion in the course of the sitting.

The notice shall specify the sitting or sittings at which the substitute will act.

2. Substitutes may take part in the debates and may vote under the same conditions as Delegates.

ARTICLE 19
Verbatim Reports

1. A verbatim report shall be printed at the conclusion of each sitting by the Secretariat. There shall be included in the report the list of Delegates present at the sitting, together with any texts adopted and the results of any votes taken.

2. Before the report is printed in its final form, any Delegate may demand the right to revise any part of the report containing a speech which he has made. Speeches or parts of speeches that have not been delivered during the sitting shall not be published in the report.

3. In order that any proposed corrections may be inserted, they should be handed in to the Secretariat during the evening following the sitting.

4. The verbatim reports shall be signed by the President of the Conference and the Secretary-General.

ARTICLE 20
Election of the Governing Body of the International Labour Office

1. The Conference shall proceed every three years in the course of its Session to elect the Governing Body of the International Labour Office in accordance with Article 393 of the Treaty of Versailles.

2. For this purpose, the Government Delegates of all the Members, excepting those of the eight Members of chief industrial importance within the meaning of the said Article, shall meet in order to select the four Members whose Governments shall nominate representatives to the Governing Body.

3. The Delegates of the Employers and of the Workers shall meet separately in order to elect their six representatives to the Governing Body. These representatives shall be elected by name.

4. If a vacancy in the Governing Body occurs among the Employers' or Workers' representatives, and if the Governing

Body has not, in accordance with Article 393 of the Treaty of Versailles, provided for the method of filling such vacancies, the Delegates at the Conference belonging to the category concerned shall assemble during the course of the ensuing Session in order to fill the vacancy.

5. If the Governing Body has, in accordance with Article 393 of the Treaty of Versailles, provided for the filling of vacancies, the decisions taken by the Governing Body in this respect shall be submitted to the Conference for its approval or otherwise.

6. If the decisions of the Governing Body are not approved by the Conference, a new election shall be held in accordance with the provisions of paragraphs 2 and 3 hereof.

ARTICLE 21

Standing Orders for the Groups

1. Each Group shall hold official meetings in order to transact the following business:

(a) The nomination of a Vice-President (Article 4).
(b) The nomination of Members for the Committee of Selection (Article 7b).
(c) The nomination of Members for other Committees (Article 7e).
(d) Elections for the Governing Body (Article 20).
(e) Any other matters referred to Groups by the Committee of Selection or by the Conference.

2. The first of these official meetings shall be held as soon as possible after the Conference meets. At this first meeting a representative of the Secretariat shall be present, if the Group so desires, to inform the Group as to procedure, and the Group shall elect a Chairman, a Vice-Chairman and a Secretary.

3. The Secretary of each Group shall report forthwith to the officers of the Conference the results of all official meetings.

4. The Group may at any time hold non-official meetings for discussion or for the transaction of non-official business.

5. At official meetings only Delegates shall vote, provided always that a Delegate may, by notice in writing to the President, appoint one of his advisers to act as his substitute, if he himself is unable to be present, in accordance with the provisions of Article 18 for the meetings of the Conference.

ARTICLE 22

Procedure of Voting at Elections

1. The President of the Conference or a person nominated by him shall direct the actual procedure of voting in elections required for the appointment of Committees, of the Governing Body or of the Vice-Presidents of the Conference; he shall convoke in due time the Delegates who have a right to vote, shall see that the votes are regularly counted and shall communicate to the Conference the results of the election.

2. At least twenty-four hours' notice shall be given of meetings for the election of representatives to the Governing Body.

APPENDIX III

ANALYSIS OF THE VOTES OF ONE OF THE INTERNATIONAL LABOR
CONFERENCES (GENEVA, 1921)* AS AN ILLUSTRATION OF
THE DISTRIBUTION OF THE VOTES

SUBJECTS VOTED	FOR				AGAINST			
	Government Delegates	Employer Delegates	Worker Delegates	Total	Government Delegates	Employer Delegates	Worker Delegates	Total
Agenda								
Retention on agenda of Item II†	32	7	24	63	26	13	....	39
Retention on agenda of Item III‡	52	14	24	90	10	7	....	17
Retention on agenda of Item IV§	55	14	24	93	7	6	....	13
Conventions Adopted								
1. Combination of agricultural workers	52	16	24	92	1	4	....	5
2. Compensation in agriculture	47	11	23	81	6	7	....	13
3. Age of children in agriculture	44	17	24	85	....	1	....	1
4. White lead	47	18	25	90	....	....	....	....
5. Age of trimmers or stokers	58	18	24	100	....	....	....	....
6. Medical examination of children at sea	55	17	24	96	....	....	....	....
7. Weekly rest in industry	46	2	25	73	4	20	....	24

* Total number of delegates: government delegates, 69; employer, 24; worker, 25.
† Adaptation to agricultural labor of the Washington decisions concerning the regulation of the hours of work. This item failed by five votes to get the necessary two-thirds majority, and was abandoned.
‡ Adaptation to agricultural labor of the Washington decisions concerning:
    (a) Measures for the prevention of or providing against unemployment;
    (b) Protection of women and children. This item was retained.
§ Special measures for the protection of agricultural workers: (a) Technical agricultural education; (b) Living-in conditions of agricultural workers; (c) Guaranty of the rights of association and combination; (d) Protection against accident, sickness, invalidity, and old age. This item was retained.

ANALYSIS OF THE VOTES OF ONE OF THE INTERNATIONAL LABOR
CONFERENCES (GENEVA, 1921) AS AN ILLUSTRATION OF
THE DISTRIBUTION OF THE VOTES—*Continued*

SUBJECTS VOTED	FOR				AGAINST			
	Government Delegates	Employer Delegates	Worker Delegates	Total	Government Delegates	Employer Delegates	Worker Delegates	Total
Recommendations Adopted								
1. Technical agricultural instruction..........	55	19	23	97	....	....	....	....
2. Unemployment in agriculture.............	49	2	24	75	1	18	....	19
3. Insurance in agriculture.	47	13	24	84	....	2	....	2
4. Night work of children in agriculture........	45	13	24	82	3	2	....	5
5. Night work of women in agriculture...........	47	19	24	90	4	....	....	4
6. Protection of women in childbirth...........	33	8	24	65	8	6	....	14
7. Living-in conditions of agricultural workers...	40	10	24	74	6	6	....	12
8. Weekly rest in commerce..............	50	18	24	92	....	....	....	....

APPENDIX IV

CONVENTIONS AND STATE ACTION [*]

A. First Session (Washington, October 29-November 29, 1919)

I. *Hours of Work*

Ratifications Registered with League	Decisions Taken by "Competent Authority"	Submitted to "Competent Authority"	States Which Have Taken Other Measures	States Which Have Sent No Information
Austria	*Approval*	Argentina	Australia	Albania
Bulgaria	....	Belgium	China	Bolivia
Czechoslo-		Brazil	Guatemala	Colombia
vakia	*Rejection*	Chili	Luxemburg	Ccsta Rica
Greece	Switzerland	Cuba	Nicaragua	Ecuador
India		Denmark	Panama	Ethiopia
Italy	*Other deci-*	Esthonia	Salvador	Haiti
Roumania	*sions (ad-*	France	Kingdom of	Hedjaz
France	*journment,*	Germany	the Serbs,	Honduras
	etc.)	Japan	Croats,	Irish Free
	Canada	Latvia	and Slo-	State
	Finland	Lithuania	venes	Liberia
	Gr. Britain	Netherlands	Uruguay	Paraguay
	Hungary	New Zealand	So. Africa	Persia
		Norway	Spain	Peru
		Poland	Sweden	Portugal
		Siam	Venezuela	

II. *Unemployment*

Ratifications Registered with League	Decisions Taken by "Competent Authority"	Submitted to "Competent Authority"	States Which Have Taken Other Measures	States Which Have Sent No Information
Austria	*Approval*	Argentina	Australia	Albania
Bulgaria	Hungary	Belgium	Guatemala	Bolivia
Denmark		Brazil	Luxemburg	China
Esthonia	*Rejection*	Canada	Nicaragua	Colombia
Finland	Siam	Chili	Panama	Costa Rica
Gr. Britain		Cuba	Salvador	Ecuador
Greece	*Other deci-*	Czechoslo-	Kingdom of	Ethiopia
India	*sions (ad-*	vakia	the Serbs,	Haiti
Italy	*journment,*	France	Croats,	Hedjaz
Japan	*etc.)*	Germany	and Slo-	Honduras
Norway	....	Latvia	venes	Irish Free
Poland		Lithuania	Uruguay	State
Roumania		Netherlands		Liberia
So. Africa	Sweden	New Zealand		Paraguay
Spain	Switzerland	Venezuela		Persia
				Peru
				Portugal

[*] This table is based upon the Official Report of the Director to the 1925 Conference. For further progress in ratifications of conventions see p. 316.

A. First Session (Washington, October 29-November 29, 1919)—
Continued

III. *Childbirth*

Ratifications Registered with League	Decisions Taken by "Competent Authority"	Submitted to "Competent Authority"	States Which Have Taken Other Measures	States Which Have Sent No Information
Bulgaria Greece Roumania Spain	*Approval* Hungary Italy *Rejection* Gr. Britain Siam Switzerland *Other decisions (adjournment, etc.)* Finland	Argentina Austria Belgium Brazil Canada Chili Cuba Czechoslovakia Denmark France Germany Japan Latvia Lithuania Netherlands New Zealand Norway Poland So. Africa Sweden Venezuela	Australia China Esthonia Guatemala India Luxemburg Nicaragua Panama Portugal Salvador Kingdom of the Serbs, Croats, and Slovenes Uruguay	Albania Bolivia Colombia Costa Rica Ecuador Ethiopia Haiti Hedjaz Honduras Irish Free State Liberia Paraguay Persia Peru

IV. *Night Work of Women*

Austria Belgium Bulgaria Czechoslovakia Esthonia Gr. Britain Greece India Italy Netherlands Roumania So. Africa Switzerland	*Approval* France Hungary *Rejection* Siam *Other decisions (adjournment, etc.)* Finland	Argentina Brazil Canada Chili Cuba Denmark Germany Japan Latvia Lithuania New Zealand Norway Poland Spain Sweden Venezuela	Australia Guatemala Luxemburg Nicaragua Panama Portugal Salvador Kingdom of the Serbs, Croats, and Slovenes Uruguay	Albania Bolivia China Colombia Costa Rica Ecuador Ethiopia Haiti Hedjaz Honduras Irish Free State Liberia Paraguay Persia Peru

A. First Session (Washington, October 29-November 29, 1919) — *Continued*

V. *Minimum Age*

Ratifications Registered with League	Decisions Taken by "Competent Authority"	Submitted to "Competent Authority"	States Which Have Taken Other Measures	States Which Have Sent No Information
Belgium	*Approval*	Argentina	Australia	Albania
Bulgaria	Finland	Austria	China	Bolivia
Czechoslo-	Japan	Brazil	Guatemala	Colombia
vakia	Netherlands	Canada	Luxemburg	Costa Rica
Denmark		Chili	Nicaragua	Ecuador
Esthonia	*Rejection*	Cuba	Panama	Ethiopia
Gr. Britain	Siam	France	Portugal	Haiti
Greece		Germany	Salvador	Hedjaz
Poland	*Other deci-*	Italy	Kingdom of	Honduras
Roumania	*sions (ad-*	Latvia	the Serbs,	Irish Free
Switzerland	*journment,*	Lithuania	Croats,	State
	etc.)	New Zealand	and Slo-	Liberia
	Hungary	Norway	venes	Paraguay
	India	So. Africa	Uruguay	Persia
		Spain		Peru
		Sweden		
		Venezuela		

VI. *Night Work of Young Persons*

Austria	*Approval*	Argentina	Australia	Albania
Belgium	Finland	Brazil	China	Bolivia
Bulgaria	Hungary	Canada	Guatemala	Colombia
Denmark		Chili	Luxemburg	Costa Rica
Esthonia	*Rejection*	Cuba	Nicaragua	Ecuador
Gr. Britain	Siam	Czechoslo-	Panama	Ethiopia
Greece		vakia	Portugal	Haiti
India	*Other deci-*	France	Salvador	Hedjaz
Italy	*sions (ad-*	Germany	Kingdom of	Honduras
Netherlands	*journment,*	Japan	the Serbs,	Irish Free
Poland	*etc.)*	Latvia	Croats,	State
Roumania	....	Lithuania	and Slo-	Liberia
Switzerland		New Zealand	venes	Paraguay
		Norway	Uruguay	Persia
		So. Africa		Peru
		Spain		
		Sweden		
		Venezuela		

B. Second Session (Genoa, June 15-July 10, 1920)

I. *Minimum Age (Sea)*

Ratifications Registered with League	Decisions Taken by "Competent Authority"	Submitted to "Competent Authority"	States Which Have Taken Other Measures	States Which Have Sent No Information
Belgium	*Approval*	Argentina	Australia	Albania
Bulgaria	Finland	Austria	Czechoslo-	Bolivia
Denmark	Hungary	Canada	vakia	Brazil
Esthonia		Chili	France	China
Gr. Britain	*Rejection*	Cuba	Greece	Colombia
Japan	Siam	Germany	Haiti	Costa Rica
Netherlands	Switzerland	Italy	Luxemburg ⟩	Ecuador
Poland		Latvia	Kingdom of	Ethiopia
Roumania	*Other deci-*	Lithuania	the Serbs,	Guatemala
Spain	*sions (ad-*	New Zealand	C r o a t s,	Hedjaz
Sweden	*journment,*	Norway	and S l o -	Honduras
	etc.)	Venezuela	venes	Irish Free
	India		So. Africa	State
				Liberia
			Portugal	Nicaragua
			Salvador	Panama
			Uruguay	Paraguay
				Persia
				Peru

II. *Unemployment Indemnity*

Belgium	*Approval*	Argentina	Australia	Albania
Bulgaria	Netherlands	Austria	Czechoslo-	Bolivia
Esthonia		Canada	vakia	Brazil
Italy	*Rejection*	Chili	Greece	China
Poland	India	Cuba	Haiti	Ecuador
Spain	Siam	Denmark	Luxemburg	Costa Rica
	Switzerland	France	Kingdom of	Ethiopia
		Germany	the Serbs,	Guatemala
	Other deci-	Japan	C r o a t s,	Hedjaz
	sions (ad-	Latvia	and S l o -	Honduras
	journment,	Lithuania	venes	Hungary
	etc.)	New Zealand	So. Africa	Irish Free
	Gr. Britain	Norway		State
	Roumania	Venezuela	Portugal	Liberia
	Sweden		Salvador	Nicaragua
			Uruguay	Panama
				Paraguay
				Persia
				Peru

B. Second Session (Genoa, June 15-July 10, 1920)—*Continued*

III. *Employment for Seamen*

Ratifications Registered with League	Decisions Taken by "Competent Authority"	Submitted to "Competent Authority"	States Which Have Taken Other Measures	States Which Have Sent No Information
Belgium	*Approval*	Argentina	Australia	Albania
Bulgaria	Netherlands	Austria	Czechoslovakia	Bolivia
Esthonia		Canada		Brazil
Finland	*Rejection*	Chili	Greece	China
Italy	India	Cuba	Haiti	Colombia
Japan	Siam	Denmark	Luxemburg	Costa Rica
Norway	Switzerland	France	Kingdom of	Ecuador
Poland		Germany	the Serbs,	Ethiopia
Sweden	*Other decisions (adjournment, etc.)*	Latvia	Croats, and Slovenes	Guatemala
		Lithuania		Hedjaz
		New Zealand		Honduras
		Spain	So. Africa	Hungary
	Gr. Britain	Venezuela		Irish Free
	Roumania		Persia	State
			Peru	Liberia
			Portugal	Nicaragua
			Salvador.	Panama
			Uruguay	Paraguay

C. Third Session (Geneva, October 25-November 19, 1921)

I. *Minimum Age (Agriculture)*

Ratifications Registered with League	Decisions Taken by "Competent Authority"	Submitted to "Competent Authority"	States Which Have Taken Other Measures	States Which Have Sent No Information
Austria	*Approval*	Brazil	Albania	Argentina
Czechoslovakia	Bulgaria	Canada	Australia	Belgium
	Hungary	Chili	Lithuania	Bolivia
Esthonia	Latvia	China	Kingdom of	Colombia
Italy		Cuba	the Serbs,	Costa Rica
Japan	*Rejection*	Denmark	Croats,	Ecuador
Poland	Gr. Britain	Germany	and Slovenes	Ethiopia
Sweden	India	Netherlands		France
	Norway	New Zealand		Greece
	Siam	So. Africa	Nicaragua	Guatemala
		Spain	Panama	Haiti
	Other decisions (adjournment, etc.)	Switzerland	Paraguay	Hedjaz
		Venezuela	Persia	Honduras
			Peru	Irish Free
	Finland		Portugal	State
	Roumania		Salvador	Liberia
			Uruguay	Luxemburg

C. Third Session (Geneva, October 25-November 19, 1921)—
Continued

II. *Rights of Association (Agriculture)*

Ratifications Registered with League	Decisions Taken by "Competent Authority"	Submitted to "Competent Authority"	States Which Have Taken Other Measures	States Which Have Sent No Information
Austria	*Approval*	Brazil	Albania	Argentina
Czechoslovakia	Bulgaria	Canada	Australia	Belgium
		Chili	Lithuania	Bolivia
Esthonia	*Rejection*	China	Kingdom of	Colombia
Finland	Japan	Cuba	the Serbs,	Costa Rica
Gr. Britain	Norway	Denmark	C r o a t s,	Ecuador
India	Siam	Germany	and S l o -	Ethiopia
Irish Free		Netherlands	venes	France
State	*Other decisions (adjournment, etc.)*	New Zealand		Greece
Italy		So. Africa	Peru	Guatemala
Latvia		Spain	Portugal	Haiti
Poland		Switzerland	Salvador	Hedjaz
Sweden	Hungary	Venezuela	Uruguay	Honduras
	Roumania			Liberia
				Luxemburg
				Nicaragua
				Panama
				Paraguay
				Persia

III. *Workmen's Compensation (Agriculture)*

Denmark	*Approval*	Austria	Albania	Argentina
Esthonia	Bulgaria	Brazil	Australia	Belgium
Gr. Britain	Hungary	Canada	Czechoslovakia	Bolivia
Irish Free		Chili	vakia	Colombia
State	*Rejection*	China	Latvia	Costa Rica
Poland	India	Cuba	Lithuania	Ecuador
Sweden	Japan	Germany	Kingdom of	Ethiopia
	Norway	Italy	the Serbs,	France
	Siam	Netherlands	C r o a t s,	Greece
		New Zealand	and S l o -	Guatemala
	Other decisions (adjournment, etc.)	So. Africa	venes	Haiti
		Spain		Hedjaz
		Switzerland	Peru	Honduras
	Finland	Venezuela	Portugal	Liberia
	Roumania		Salvador	Luxemburg
			Uruguay	Nicaragua
				Panama
				Paraguay
				Persia

C. Third Session (Geneva, October 25-November 19, 1921)—
Continued

IV. *White Lead*

Ratifications Registered with League	Decisions Taken by "Competent Authority"	Submitted to "Competent Authority"	States Which Have Taken Other Measures	States Which Have Sent No Information
Austria Czechoslovakia Esthonia Latvia Poland Spain Sweden	*Approval* Bulgaria Greece Hungary Roumania *Rejection* India Japan Norway Siam *Other decisions (adjournment, etc.)* Finland	Brazil Canada China Chili Cuba Denmark France Germany Gr. Britain Italy Netherlands New Zealand So. Africa Switzerland Venezuela	Albania Australia Belgium Lithuania Kingdom of the Serbs, Croats, and Slovenes	Argentina Bolivia Colombia Costa Rica Ecuador Ethiopia Guatemala Haiti Hedjaz Honduras Irish Free State Liberia Luxemburg Nicaragua Panama Paraguay Persia Peru Portugal Salvador Uruguay

V. *Weekly Rest (Industry)*

Czechoslovakia Esthonia Finland India Italy Latvia Poland Roumania Spain	*Approval* Bulgaria Greece Hungary *Rejection* Gr. Britain Japan Norway Siam Sweden *Other decisions (adjournment, etc.)* Germany	Austria Belgium Brazil Canada Chili China Cuba Denmark Netherlands New Zealand So. Africa Switzerland Venezuela	Albania Australia France Lithuania Kingdom of the Serbs, Croats, and Slovenes Persia Peru Portugal Salvador Uruguay	Argentina Bolivia Colombia Costa Rica Ecuador Ethiopia Guatemala Haiti Hedjaz Honduras Irish Free State Liberia Luxemburg Nicaragua Panama Paraguay

C. THIRD SESSION (GENEVA, OCTOBER 25-NOVEMBER 19, 1921)—
Continued

VI. *Minimum Age for Trimmers and Stokers*

Ratifications Registered with League	Decisions Taken by "Competent Authority"	Submitted to "Competent Authority"	States Which Have Taken Other Measures	States Which Have Sent No Information
Denmark	*Approval*	Austria	Albania	Argentina
Esthonia	Bulgaria	Brazil	Australia	Belgium
India	Hungary	Canada	Czechoslo-	Bolivia
Italy	Sweden	Chili	vakia	Colombia
Latvia		China	Lithuania	Costa Rica
Poland	*Rejection*	Cuba	Kingdom of	Ecuador
Roumania	Japan	France	the Serbs,	Ethiopia
Spain	Norway	Germany	C r o a t s,	Greece
	Siam	Gr. Britain	and S l o-	Guatemala
		Netherlands	venes	Haiti
	Other decisions (adjournment, etc.)	New Zealand		Hedjaz
		So. Africa		Honduras
		Switzerland		Irish Free
		Venezuela		State
	Finland			Liberia
				Luxemburg

VII. *Medical Examination of Young Persons (Sea)*

Esthonia	*Approval*	Austria	Albania	Argentina
India	Bulgaria	Brazil	Australia	Belgium
Italy	Hungary	Canada	Czechoslo-	Bolivia
Japan	Sweden	Chili	vakia	Colombia
Latvia		China	Lithuania	Costa Rica
Poland	*Rejection*	Cuba	Kingdom of	Ecuador
Roumania	Norway	Denmark	the Serbs,	Ethiopia
Spain	Siam	France	C r o a t s,	Greece
		Germany	and S l o-	Guatemala
	Other decisions (adjournment, etc.)	Gr. Britain	venes	Haiti
		Netherlands		Hedjaz
		New Zealand	Peru	Honduras
		So. Africa	Portugal	Irish Free
	Finland	Switzerland	Salvador	State
		Venezuela	Uruguay	Liberia
				Luxemburg
				Nicaragua
				Panama
				Paraguay
				Persia

RECOMMENDATIONS AND STATE ACTION *
A. First Session (Washington, October 29-November 29, 1919)

I. *Unemployment*

States Which Have Acted upon the Recommendation	States Which Have Officially Submitted the Recommendation to Competent Authority	States Which Have Supplied Other Official Information	States Which Have Supplied No Official Information
Belgium	Argentina	Australia	Albania
Bulgaria	Austria	Czechoslovakia	Bolivia
Denmark	Brazil	Greece	China
Finland	Canada	Latvia	Colombia
France	Chili	Luxemburg	Costa Rica
Great Britain	Cuba	Panama	Esthonia
India	Germany	Kingdom of the	Ecuador
Italy	Hungary	Serbs, Croats,	Ethiopia
Norway	Japan	and Slovenes	Guatemala
Netherlands	Lithuania		Haiti
New Zealand	South Africa	Peru	Hedjaz
Poland	Venezuela	Portugal	Honduras
Roumania		Salvador	Irish Free State
Siam		Uruguay	Liberia
Spain			Nicaragua
Sweden			Paraguay
Switzerland			Persia

II. *Reciprocity of Treatment*

Belgium	Argentina	Australia	Albania
Bulgaria	Austria	Czechoslovakia	Bolivia
Denmark	Brazil	Esthonia	China
Finland	Canada	Greece	Colombia
France	Chili	Latvia	Costa Rica
India	Cuba	Luxemburg	Ecuador
Italy	Germany	Panama	Ethiopia
Netherlands	Hungary	Kingdom of the	Great Britain
New Zealand	Japan	Serbs, Croats,	Guatemala
Norway	Lithuania	and Slovenes	Haiti
Poland	South Africa		Hedjaz
Roumania	Venezuela	Persia	Honduras
Siam		Peru	Irish Free State
Spain		Portugal	Liberia
Sweden		Salvador	Nicaragua
Switzerland		Uruguay	Paraguay

* This table is based upon the Official Report of the Director to the 1925 Conference. For progress in ratification of conventions see p. 308.

A. First Session (Washington, October 29-November 29, 1919) — *Continued*

III. *Anthrax*

States Which Have Acted upon the Recommendation	States Which Have Officially Submitted the Recommendation to Competent Authority	States Which Have Supplied Other Official Information	States Which Have Supplied No Official Information
Belgium	Argentina	Australia	Albania
Bulgaria	Austria	Czechoslovakia	Bolivia
Denmark	Brazil	Greece	China
Finland	Canada	Latvia	Colombia
France	Chili	Luxemburg	Costa Rica
Great Britain	Cuba	Panama	Ecuador
India	Germany	Kingdom of the	Esthonia
Italy	Hungary	Serbs, Croats,	Ethiopia
Netherlands	Japan	and Slovenes	Guatemala
New Zealand	Lithuania		Haiti
Norway	South Africa	Peru	Hedjaz
Poland	Venezuela	Portugal	Honduras
Roumania		Salvador	Irish Free State
Siam		Uruguay	Liberia
Spain			Nicaragua
Sweden			Paraguay
Switzerland			Persia

IV. *Lead Poisoning*

Belgium	Argentina	Australia	Albania
Bulgaria	Austria	Czechoslovakia	Bolivia
Denmark	Brazil	Greece	China
France	Canada	Latvia	Colombia
Great Britain	Chili	Luxemburg	Costa Rica
India	Cuba	Panama	Ecuador
Italy	Finland	Portugal	Esthonia
Netherlands	Germany	Kingdom of the	Ethiopia
New Zealand	Hungary	Serbs, Croats,	Guatemala
Norway	Japan	and Slovenes	Haiti
Poland	Lithuania		Hedjaz
Roumania	South Africa	Persia	Honduras
Siam	Venezuela	Peru	Irish Free State
Spain		Salvador	Liberia
Sweden		Paraguay	Nicaragua
Switzerland			Paraguay

A. First Session (Washington, October 29-November 29, 1919) — *Continued*

V. *Government Health Service*

States Which Have Acted upon the Recommendation	States Which Have Officially Submitted the Recommendation to Competent Authority	States Which Have Supplied Other Official Information	States Which Have Supplied No Official Information
Belgium	Argentina	Australia	Albania
Bulgaria	Austria	Czechoslovakia	Bolivia
Denmark	Brazil	Greece	China
Finland	Canada	Latvia	Colombia
France	Chili	Luxemburg	Costa Rica
Great Britain	Cuba	Panama	Ecuador
India	Germany	Kingdom of the	Esthonia
Italy	Hungary	Serbs, Croats,	Ethiopia
Netherlands	Japan	and Slovenes	Guatemala
New Zealand	Lithuania		Haiti
Norway	South Africa	Peru	Hedjaz
Poland	Venezuela	Portugal	Honduras
Roumania		Salvador	Irish Free State
Siam		Uruguay	Liberia
Spain			Nicaragua
Sweden			Paraguay
Switzerland			Persia

VI. *White Phosphorus*

Adherence to the Berne Convention before the Washington Convention	Adherence to Berne Convention in Application of Washington Recommendation	States Which Have Officially Submitted Recommendation to Competent Authority	States Which Have Supplied Other Official Information	States Which Have Supplied No Official Information
Canada	Australia	Argentina	Guatemala	Albania
Denmark	Austria	Brazil	Latvia	Bolivia
France	Belgium	Chili	Panama	Colombia
Germany	China	Cuba	Kingdom of	Costa Rica
Gr. Britain	Czechoslovakia	Hungary	the Serbs,	Ecuador
Italy		Lithuania	Croats,	Ethiopia
Luxemburg	Free City of	Venezuela	and Slovenes	Haiti
Netherlands	Danzig			Hedjaz
New Zealand	Esthonia	*Other Actions*	Peru	Honduras
Norway	Finland	Bulgaria	Portugal	Irish Free State
So. Africa	India	Greece	Salvador	Liberia
Spain	Japan	Siam	Uruguay	Nicaragua
Switzerland	Poland			Paraguay
	Roumania			Persia
	Sweden			

B. Second Session (Genoa, June 15-July 10, 1920)

I. *Hours of Work* (*Fishing*)

States Which Have Acted upon the Recommendation	States Which Have Officially Submitted the Recommendation to Competent Authority	States Which Have Supplied Other Official Information	States Which Have Supplied No Official Information
Bulgaria	Argentina	Australia	Albania
Canada	Austria	Belgium	Bolivia
Chili	Cuba	Czechoslo-	Brazil
France	Denmark	vakia	China
India	Finland	Esthonia	Colombia
Italy	Germany	Greece	Costa Rica
Sweden	Great Britain	Haiti	Ecuador
Switzerland	Lithuania	Japan	Ethiopia
	Netherlands	Latvia	Guatemala
	New Zealand	Luxemburg	Hedjaz
	Norway	Poland	Honduras
	Roumania	Kingdom of the	Hungary
	Siam	Serbs, Croats,	Irish Free State
	Venezuela	and Slovenes	Liberia
		South Africa	Nicaragua
		Spain	Panama
		Portugal	Paraguay
		Salvador	Persia
		Uruguay	Peru

II. *Hours of Work* (*Inland Navigation*)

Bulgaria	Argentina	Australia	Albania
Canada	Austria	Belgium	Bolivia
Chili	Cuba	Czechoslovakia	Brazil
France	Denmark	Esthonia	China
India	Finland	Haiti	Colombia
Italy	Germany	Japan	Costa Rica
Sweden	Great Britain	Latvia	Ecuador
Switzerland	Lithuania	Luxemburg	Ethiopia
	Netherlands	Poland	Greece
	New Zealand	Kingdom of the	Guatemala
	Norway	Serbs, Croats,	Hedjaz
	Roumania	and Slovenes	Honduras
	Siam	South Africa	Hungary
	Venezuela	Spain	Irish Free State
			Liberia
		Portugal	Nicaragua
		Salvador	Panama
		Uruguay	Paraguay
			Persia
			Peru

B. Second Session (Genoa, June 15-July 10, 1920)—*Continued*

III. *National Seamen's Codes*

States Which Have Acted upon the Recommendation	States Which Have Officially Submitted the Recommendation to Competent Authority	States Which Have Supplied Other Official Information	States Which Have Supplied No Official Information
Bulgaria	Argentina	Australia	Albania
Canada	Austria	Belgium	Bolivia
Chili	Cuba	Czechoslovakia	Brazil
France	Finland	Denmark	China
India	Germany	Esthonia	Colombia
Italy	Great Britain	Haiti	Costa Rica
Sweden	Lithuania	Japan	Ecuador
Switzerland	Netherlands	Latvia	Ethiopia
	New Zealand	Luxemburg	Greece
	Norway	Poland	Guatemala
	Roumania	Kingdom of the	Hedjaz
	Siam	Serbs, Croats,	Honduras
	Venezuela	and Slovenes	Hungary
		South Africa	Irish Free State
		Spain	Liberia
		Peru	Nicaragua
		Portugal	Panama
		Salvador	Paraguay
		Uruguay	Persia

IV. *Unemployment Insurance (Seamen)*

Bulgaria	Argentina	Australia	Albania
Canada	Austria	Belgium	Bolivia
Chili	Cuba	Czechoslovakia	Brazil
France	Finland	Denmark	China
India	Germany	Esthonia	Colombia
Italy	Great Britain	Haiti	Costa Rica
Sweden	Lithuania	Japan	Ecuador
Switzerland	Netherlands	Latvia	Ethiopia
	New Zealand	Luxemburg	Greece
	Norway	Poland	Guatemala
	Roumania	Kingdom of the	Hedjaz
	Siam	Serbs, Croats,	Honduras
	Venezuela	and Slovenes	Hungary
		South Africa	Irish Free State
		Spain	Liberia
		Peru	Nicaragua
		Portugal	Panama
		Salvador	Paraguay
		Uruguay	Persia

C. Third Session (Geneva, October 25-November 19, 1921)

I. *Unemployment (Agriculture)*

States Which Have Acted upon the Recommendation	States Which Have Officially Submitted the Recommendation to Competent Authority	States Which Have Supplied Other Official Information	States Which Have Supplied No Official Information
Finland	Austria	Albania	Argentina
France	Brazil	Australia	Belgium
Poland	Bulgaria	Czechoslovakia	Bolivia
Siam	Canada	Denmark	Colombia
Switzerland	Chili	India	Costa Rica
	China	Japan	Cuba
	Germany	Latvia	Ecuador
	Great Britain	Lithuania	Esthonia
	Hungary	Roumania	Ethiopia
	Netherlands	Kingdom of the	Greece
	New Zealand	Serbs, Croats,	Guatemala
	Norway	and Slovenes	Haiti
	South Africa	Spain	Hedjaz
	Sweden		Honduras
	Venezuela	Paraguay	Irish Free State
		Persia	Italy
		Peru	Liberia
		Portugal	Luxemburg
		Salvador	Nicaragua
		Uruguay	Panama

II. *Childbirth (Agriculture)*

France	Austria	Albania	Argentina
Poland	Brazil	Australia	Belgium
Siam	Bulgaria	Czechoslovakia	Bolivia
Switzerland	Canada	Denmark	Colombia
	Chili	Japan	Costa Rica
	China	Latvia	Cuba
	Finland	Lithuania	Ecuador
	Germany	Roumania	Esthonia
	Great Britain	Kingdom of the	Ethiopia
	Hungary	Serbs, Croats,	Greece
	India	and Slovenes	Guatemala
	Netherlands	Spain	Haiti
	New Zealand	Panama	Hedjaz
	Norway	Paraguay	Honduras
	South Africa	Persia	Irish Free State
	Sweden	Peru	Italy
	Venezuela	Portugal	Liberia
		Salvador	Luxemburg
		Uruguay	Nicaragua

C. Third Session (Geneva, October 25-November 19, 1921)—
Continued

III. *Night Work of Women (Agriculture)*

States Which Have Acted upon the Recommendation	States Which Have Officially Submitted the Recommendation to Competent Authority	States Which Have Supplied Other Official Information	States Which Have Supplied No Official Information
Czechoslovakia	Austria	Albania	Argentina
France	Brazil	Australia	Belgium
Great Britain	Bulgaria	Denmark	Bolivia
Poland	Canada	Japan	Colombia
Siam	Chili	Latvia	Costa Rica
Switzerland	China	Lithuania	Cuba
	Finland	Roumania	Ecuador
	Germany	Kingdom of the	Esthonia
	Hungary	Serbs, Croats,	Ethiopia
	India	and Slovenes	Greece
	Netherlands	Spain	Guatemala
	New Zealand		Haiti
	Norway	Panama	Hedjaz
	South Africa	Paraguay	Honduras
	Sweden	Persia	Irish Free State
	Venezuela	Peru	Italy
		Portugal	Liberia
		Salvador	Luxemburg
		Uruguay	Nicaragua

IV. *Night Work of Young Persons (Agriculture)*

Czechoslovakia	Austria	Albania	Argentina
France	Brazil	Australia	Belgium
Poland	Bulgaria	Denmark	Bolivia
Siam	Canada	Japan	Colombia
Switzerland	Chili	Latvia	Costa Rica
	China	Lithuania	Cuba
	Finland	Roumania	Ecuador
	Germany	Kingdom of the	Esthonia
	Great Britain	Serbs, Croats,	Ethiopia
	Hungary	and Slovenes	Greece
	India	Spain	Guatemala
	Netherlands		Haiti
	New Zealand	Panama	Hedjaz
	Norway	Paraguay	Honduras
	South Africa	Persia	Irish Free State
	Sweden	Peru	Italy
	Venezuela	Portugal	Liberia
		Salvador	Luxemburg
		Uruguay	Nicaragua

C. Third Session (Geneva, October 25-November 19, 1921)—
Continued

V. *Technical Agricultural Education*

States Which Have Acted upon the Recommendation	States Which Have Officially Submitted the Recommendation to Competent Authority	States Which Have Supplied Other Official Information	States Which Have Supplied No Official Information
Czechoslovakia	Austria	Albania	Argentina
Finland	Brazil	Australia	Belgium
France	Bulgaria	Denmark	Bolivia
Poland	Canada	India	Colombia
Roumania	Chili	Japan	Costa Rica
Siam	China	Latvia	Cuba
Switzerland	Germany	Lithuania	Ecuador
	Great Britain	Kingdom of the	Esthonia
	Hungary	Serbs, Croats,	Ethiopia
	Netherlands	and Slovenes	Greece
	New Zealand	Spain	Guatemala
	Norway		Haiti
	South Africa	Panama	Hedjaz
	Sweden	Paraguay	Honduras
	Venezuela	Persia	Irish Free State
		Peru	Italy
		Portugal	Liberia
		Salvador	Luxemburg
		Uruguay	Nicaragua

VI. *Living-in Conditions (Agriculture)*

France	Austria	Albania	Argentina
Poland	Brazil	Australia	Belgium
Siam	Bulgaria	Czechoslovakia	Bolivia
Sweden	Canada	Denmark	Colombia
Switzerland	Chili	Japan	Costa Rica
	China	Latvia	Cuba
	Finland	Lithuania	Ecuador
	Germany	Roumania	Esthonia
	Great Britain	Kingdom of the	Ethiopia
	Hungary	Serbs, Croats,	Greece
	India	and Slovenes	Guatemala
	Netherlands	Spain	Haiti
	New Zealand	Panama	Hedjaz
	Norway	Paraguay	Honduras
	South Africa	Persia	Irish Free State
	Venezuela	Peru	Italy
		Portugal	Liberia
		Salvador	Luxemburg
		Uruguay	Nicaragua

C. Third Session (Geneva, October 25-November 19, 1921)—
Continued

VII. *Social Insurance* (*Agriculture*)

States Which Have Acted upon the Recommendation	States Which Have Officially Submitted the Recommendation to Competent Authority	States Which Have Supplied Other Official Information	States Which Have Supplied No Official Information
Czechoslovakia	Austria	Albania	Argentina
France	Brazil	Australia	Belgium
Poland	Bulgaria	Denmark	Bolivia
Siam	Canada	Japan	Colombia
Switzerland	Chili	Latvia	Costa Rica
	China	Lithuania	Cuba
	Finland	Roumania	Ecuador
	Germany	Kingdom of the	Esthonia
	Great Britain	Serbs, Croats,	Ethiopia
	Hungary	and Slovenes	Greece
	India	Spain	Guatemala
	Netherlands		Haiti
	New Zealand	Panama	Hedjaz
	Norway	Paraguay	Honduras
	South Africa	Persia	Irish Free State
	Sweden	Peru	Italy
	Venezuela	Portugal	Liberia
		Salvador	Luxemburg
		Uruguay	Nicaragua

VIII. *Weekly Rest in Commerce*

States Which Have Acted upon the Recommendation	States Which Have Officially Submitted the Recommendation to Competent Authority	States Which Have Supplied Other Official Information	States Which Have Supplied No Official Information
Czechoslovakia	Austria	Albania	Argentina
Finland	Brazil	Australia	Belgium
France	Bulgaria	Denmark	Bolivia
India	Canada	Japan	Colombia
Poland	Chili	Latvia	Costa Rica
Roumania	China	Lithuania	Cuba
Siam	Czechoslovakia	Kingdom of the	Ecuador
Switzerland	Germany	Serbs, Croats,	Esthonia
	Great Britain	and Slovenes	Ethiopia
	Hungary	Spain	Greece
	Netherlands	Nicaragua	Guatemala
	New Zealand	Panama	Haiti
	Norway	Paraguay	Hedjaz
	South Africa	Persia	Honduras
	Sweden	Peru	Irish Free State
	Venezuela	Portugal	Italy
		Salvador	Liberia
		Uruguay	Luxemburg

D. Fourth Session (Geneva, October 18-November 3, 1922)

Emigration Statistics

States Which Have Acted upon the Recommendation	States Which Have Officially Submitted the Recommendation to Competent Authority	States Which Have Supplied Other Official Information	States Which Have Supplied No Official Information
Canada	Austria	Australia	Albania
Czechoslovakia	Bulgaria	Brazil	Argentina
Finland	Chili	Cuba	Belgium
France	Great Britain	Denmark	Bolivia
India	Latvia	Esthonia	China
Japan	Netherlands	Luxemburg	Colombia
Poland	Norway	New Zealand	Costa Rica
Roumania	Switzerland	Kingdom of the Serbs, Croats, and Slovenes	Ecuador
Siam	Venezuela	Spain	Ethiopia
South Africa		Sweden	Germany
			Greece
			Guatemala
			Haiti
			Hedjaz
			Honduras
			Hungary
			Irish Free State
			Italy
			Liberia
			Lithuania
			Nicaragua
			Panama
			Paraguay
			Persia
			Peru
			Portugal
			Salvador
			Uruguay

E. Fifth Session (Geneva, October 22-29, 1923)

Organization of Systems of Inspection

States Which Have Acted upon the Recommendation	States Which Have Officially Submitted the Recommendation to Competent Authority	States Which Have Supplied Other Official Information	States Which Have Supplied No Official Information
Belgium France Great Britain India Roumania Siam South Africa Switzerland	Australia Austria Bulgaria Canada Chili Cuba Czechoslovakia Finland Germany Netherlands Hungary New Zealand Norway Venezuela	Albania Denmark Kingdom of the Serbs, Croats, and Slovenes Spain Persia Peru Poland Portugal Salvador Sweden Uruguay	Argentina Bolivia Brazil China Colombia Costa Rica Ecuador Esthonia Ethiopia Greece Guatemala Haiti Hedjaz Honduras Irish Free State Italy Japan Latvia Liberia Lithuania Luxemburg Nicaragua Panama Paraguay

F. Sixth Session (Geneva, June 16-July 5, 1924)

Workers' Spare Time

States Which Have Acted upon the Recommendation	States Which Have Officially Submitted the Recommendation to Competent Authority	States Which Have Supplied Other Official Information	States Which Have Supplied No Official Information
India	Finland	Austria Esthonia	All the states members except Austria, Esthonia, Finland, and India